WITHD
WRIGHT STATE UNIVERSITY LIBRARIES

COLS   WRIGHT STATE UNIVERSITY
        UNIVERSITY LIBRARY

0 0013 0080088 3

Women, Work, and School

Women, Work, and School

Occupational Segregation and the Role of Education

EDITED BY

Leslie R. Wolfe

Westview Press

BOULDER • SAN FRANCISCO • OXFORD

LC
1752
.W53
1991

All rights reserved. No part of this publication may be reproduced or transmitted in any form or by any means, electronic or mechanical, including photocopy, recording, or any information storage and retrieval system, without permission in writing from the publisher.

Copyright © 1991 by the Center for Women Policy Studies

Published in 1991 in the United States of America by Westview Press, Inc., 5500 Central Avenue, Boulder, Colorado 80301, and in the United Kingdom by Westview Press, 36 Lonsdale Road, Summertown, Oxford OX2 7EW

Library of Congress Cataloging-in-Publication Data
Women, work, and school : occupational segregation and the role of
  education / edited by Leslie R. Wolfe.
    p. cm.
  Based on presentations at a seminar convened by the Center for
    Women Policy Studies in May, 1988.
  Includes index.
  ISBN 0-8133-8000-6
  1. Women—Education—United States—Congresses. 2. Afro-American
women—Education—Congresses. 3. Occupational training for women—
United States—Congresses. 4. Labor supply—United States—Effect
of education on—Congresses. 5. Sex discrimination in employment—
United States—Congresses. 6. Sex discrimination in education—
United States—Congresses. I. Wolfe, Leslie R. II. Center for
Women Policy Studies.
LC1752.W53 1991
376'.973—dc20   90-20997
                                                                            CIP

Printed and bound in the United States of America

The paper used in this publication meets the requirements
of the American National Standard for Permanence of Paper
for Printed Library Materials Z39.48-1984.

10   9   8   7   6   5   4   3   2   1

Contents

Figures and Tables

Preface

During the remainder of this century and into the next, policy change will focus on restructuring the economy and the schools for increased productivity and competitiveness. Specific policy recommendations for local, state, and federal action to improve the educational and employment status of women must be part of this larger policy environment. However, most policy recommendations relating to occupational segregation are vague and focus on improved enforcement of federal antidiscrimination laws and improved efforts (usually through federally funded programs under the Vocational Education Act, for example) to encourage girls and young women to take math and science courses in school and to enter vocational training for "men's jobs."

An informed, sophisticated assessment of the relationship of occupational segregation and low income to education is essential to developing concrete proposals for change. For example, it is still true that young women will adapt to the inferior labor market opportunities they find open to them, thereby "choosing" what they believe is available. While the opening of opportunities is critical, educating these young women (and their parents and teachers) to believe that other opportunities will exist is equally as important.

The papers in this volume present an initial blueprint for further research and policy development—for economists and educators alike—into the relationship between the supply side (education) and the demand side (workplace) of the employment equation. The contributors specifically address the educational, training, and employment needs of women of color, which are central to efforts to address structural problems of both race and sex discrimination. Although solutions to the problems of women of color will not per se solve the problems of white women or men of color, this focus will clarify the most recalcitrant barriers to equity for women and persons of color in our schools and workplaces and may lead to the development of innovative strategies to address these barriers.

To meet these goals, the Center for Women Policy Studies convened a policy seminar on occupational segregation and its roots in education in May 1988. The seminar brought together key leaders in these fields for two days of debate and discussion. This volume is the result; we hope it will contribute to the continuing debate and to implementation of new strategies to improve the educational and employment experiences of women in the United States.

Leslie R. Wolfe
Center for Women Policy Studies

Acknowledgments

The Center for Women Policy Studies gratefully acknowledges the support and encouragement of many friends and colleagues whose expertise and commitment have made this work possible. We are most grateful to June Zeitlin and Alison Bernstein, our program officers at the Ford Foundation; in addition to providing funding for the seminar, they gave us their knowledge and moral support, which have been invaluable and deeply appreciated. To Susan Berresford, vice-president of the Ford Foundation and the first funder of the Center in the early 1970s—our gratitude for her continuing support. Brigid O'Farrell and Julianne Malveaux, who served as consultants to the project, contributed their time, energy, and expertise to the planning of both the seminar and this volume; Aileen Hernandez offered the benefit of her many years as both policymaker and advocate for women. Finally, the staff of the Center worked long hours to complete this volume; we are especially grateful to CWPS administrator Nancy Natsuko Yamaguchi and to our former CWPS intern Mimi Mei Shen Ka.

L.R.W.

PART ONE

Defining the Context

1

Introduction

LESLIE R. WOLFE

HISTORICAL OVERVIEW

In 1976, *SIGNS* published a special edition, edited by Martha Blaxall and Barbara Reagan, on *Women and the Workplace: The Implications of Occupational Segregation,* based on a conference on occupational segregation held earlier that year. The papers presented looked at the social institutions, historical roots, and economic dimensions of occupational segregation—covering a range of issues, including, for example, analyses of conflicts in women's work and family roles, portrayal of the structural barriers to full integration of women into the work force, assessments of legal remedies, and analyses of the relationship of sex segregation and capitalism. The volume included an article by the codirector of the Center for Women Policy Studies, Margaret Gates, on "Occupational Segregation and the Law" and another by Center board member Jessie Bernard on "Historical and Structural Barriers to Occupational Desegregation."

In the years since, sociologists, economists, legislators, educators, feminist theorists, activists, and legal scholars have continued to address issues relating to the employment of women, as women continue to enter and remain in the work force in ever-increasing numbers. Research by the Center since 1973, for example, has examined the feminization of poverty, vocational training for women offenders, occupational segregation in "nontraditional" jobs (including corrections, police, and the law), and sexual harassment of women in employment.

Most of the research, analysis, and advocacy during the past twenty years has focused on three broad areas. First, research on the status of women in the workplace has addressed several key issues, including occupational segregation, pay equity, and low-wage employment. In addition, substantial attention has been focused on increases in female participation in the paid labor force, especially in the professions—law, business, and medicine—and in previously male-dominated occupations that have been nontraditional for women. These are efforts to answer the question: Where are we now?

In addition, analyses have addressed the economic, social, and political forces that maintain occupational segregation, the wage gap, and unequal treatment of women, especially women of color, as students and workers. In the professions, the recent emphasis has been on the "glass ceiling" that apparently restricts women's access to upper management and leadership positions. These are efforts to answer the question: What is keeping us where we are?

Finally, policy alternatives and intervention strategies have been proposed to ensure full integration of women into the workplace, the achievement of wage equity, and the transformation of the workplace to accommodate women's (and families') needs. These are efforts to answer the question: How do we achieve our ultimate goals, in both the short and long term?

During the same period, there has been an explosion of research on sex-role stereotyping in education and its impact on girls' aspirations and achievements. A variety of educational equity programs and policies have been developed and implemented, with support from federal programs such as the Women's Educational Equity Act and the Vocational Education Act and from private foundations. Many of these efforts to transform girls' and women's educational experiences have focused on moving girls into math and science courses and into nontraditional vocational education programs.

However, despite some success, recent data indicate that, although more young women are taking advanced mathematics in high schools, fewer of them major in the sciences at the undergraduate level and an even smaller number pursue graduate degrees in science-related fields, and there is evidence of continuing decline. For example, the number of women with bachelor's degrees in engineering increased from 744 in 1974 to 10,761 in 1984. But, after a decade of growth in the number of women in the engineering profession, the percentage of women first-year college engineering students has fallen from 17.1 percent in the fall of 1983 to 16.5 percent in 1984. African American enrollments in engineering peaked in 1982 and then declined by more than 12 percent in the succeeding three years; Hispanic enrollments increased slightly in 1984.[1]

The pattern of sex segregation remains particularly clear in vocational education programs, which are the only educational programs designed specifically to prepare students for the world of work. Despite both Title IX's prohibition of sex discrimination in education and sex equity requirements in the Vocational Education Amendments of 1976, our nation's vocational education system remains largely sex segregated.

Although gains have been made, women still are overwhelmingly concentrated in programs preparing students for clerical and service jobs; in 1984, for instance, women still were only a fraction of the students in the traditionally male courses of study, remaining almost invisible, therefore, in these higher-paying trades. According to the Vocational Education Data System of the U.S. Department of Education, women in 1984 were 87 percent of students in community health, 92 percent in cosmetology, and 92 percent in clerical/secretarial and only 5 percent of students in electrical technology, 10 percent in electronics, 6 percent in appliance repair, 4 percent in tool and die making, and 4 percent in small engine repair.

In recent years, occupational segregation and women's work force participation have become the central issues around which others—such as educational equity, changing family structures, and alleviation of women's poverty—have revolved. Several important reports (see references)—most based on research conferences on occupational segregation, pay equity, women's work and family roles, women in poverty, and the relationship of women's work to new technologies—have been published. Taken together, these volumes (particularly the National Academy of Sciences' *Women's Work, Men's Work*) provide a comprehensive overview of our current knowledge about occupational segregation.

Further, reports such as the U.S. Commission on Civil Rights' *Disadvantaged Women and Their Children* suggest that discrimination by race and sex in the job market is largely a result of the sex and race stereotyping and discrimination in education and training programs, which restrict women's occupational options and are based on outmoded notions of women's proper roles in the home and workplace.

Finally, current concern for U.S. competitiveness in the world economy and the desire of both political and industry leaders to ensure an educated, technologically skilled work force for the twenty-first century have led to a focus on the "new demographics" and the "retooling" of the education system to serve the economic needs of industry. Yet women's needs as students, workers, and parents are rarely addressed from feminist perspectives, despite demographic projections that suggest that 80 percent of new entrants into tomorrow's work force will be women, people of color, and/or new immigrants.[2]

THE ROLE OF EDUCATION IN REDUCING OCCUPATIONAL SEGREGATION

Most of the reports and conferences on occupational segregation mention the role of education; many include thoughtful articles reviewing some of the research literature on sex stereotyping in curriculum, classroom interaction, and counseling; sex segregation in vocational education and training programs; and sex-role socialization of girls and boys from preschool onward. And most agree that the schools play a critical role in shaping young women's career choices and options. But the analysis generally does not focus more deeply on these issues.

Feminist educators and education researchers know a great deal, based on twenty years of research and intervention, about girls' and women's lack of access to math, science, and technology education in both academic and vocational-training settings and about the nature and impact of sex-role socialization. But a sophisticated assessment of this knowledge rarely informs the essential discussions of occupational segregation. For example, although *Women's Work, Men's Work* suggests that educational practices may perpetuate sex-role stereotypes, the authors of that book believe that the evidence for such a claim is scanty; a comprehensive analysis of both research findings and practitioners' experience is not pursued.

A 1983 Center for Women Policy Studies report on women and poverty, "Poverty Viewed as a Woman's Problem—The U.S. Case," noted that during the past two decades, women have increased their participation more than men at all levels of education and training. Although women's labor force participation increased substantially during this period, *so did their poverty.* Clearly, occupational segregation and educational inequities are linked, but the nature of this complex relationship has not been adequately explored.

Most employment-oriented research addresses its policy recommendations to high school vocational education, despite the proven importance of entering the "supply side" much earlier. Educators and equity advocates know that girls' early preparation (at the elementary and middle school levels) is essential to prepare them to enter both nontraditional vocational education programs and academic programs in the sciences at the high school level and beyond. In addition, the significant role being played by community colleges and some women's colleges in providing both higher education and vocational training to young women and to "reentry" and low-income women is rarely noted. Yet community colleges, with their dual function to provide both academic preparation for students who will move on to four-year institutions and vocational training for students who are entering the trades, have led other institutions in providing an accessible educational setting for low-income women, reentry women, women with work and family responsibilities who require flexible schedules and support services, and others.

Community colleges in many states also have been in the forefront of creative efforts to provide both academic and vocational opportunities to adult women. For instance, in the early 1970s, Middlesex County College in New Jersey established a comprehensive women's resource center that has developed programs to recruit women into the college's Engineering Technologies and Science Division, to prepare them for "high-tech" occupations; LaGuardia Community College in New York City developed an experiential education program for adult working-class women that provided work experience, academic preparation, and intensive campus-based support services to enable women students to enter technological occupations; and the San Jose (California) Community College District developed a model technology education and career counseling program for women.

OCCUPATIONAL SEGREGATION, EDUCATIONAL EQUITY, AND WOMEN OF COLOR

Only passing attention usually is given to the educational and employment status and needs of women of color. It generally is focused primarily on African American women[3] and involves analyses of employment data by race and sex. Thus, policy recommendations often do not take into account the differential status and needs of women from different racial/ethnic groups. For example, higher levels of education tend to benefit white women more than women of color in the job market; and women of color still work primarily in the lowest wage, least secure jobs in every industry from service to high-tech.

Finally, discussions of traditional versus nontraditional employment often overlook the fact that occupations considered traditional for white women may represent new frontiers for some women of color and vice versa. Systematic attention to the issues of combined race and sex segregation both in schools and in the workplace may provide some new perspectives and strategies to benefit not only women of color but also white women and men of color. This perspective can be infused into considerations of all issues affecting women, to ensure that the diverse needs of African American, Latina, Native American, and Asian American and Pacific Islander women are addressed.

NOTES

1. These data were reported by the Scientific Manpower Commission, *Manpower Comments,* October 1985, p. 13, cited in T. Cusick, P. Johnson, and L. R. Wolfe (1986), *Beyond the Star Trek Syndrome to an Egalitarian Future: 'Where No One Has Gone Before.'* Washington, DC: PEER, p. 7.

2. See Harold L. Hodgkinson, *All One System: Demographics of Education, Kindergarten Through Graduate School* (Washington, DC: Institute for Educational Leadership, 1985).

3. See Julianne Malveaux, "Recent Trends in Occupational Segregation by Race and Sex," Committee on Women, Employment and Related Social Issues, National Academy of Sciences, 1982; and Julianne Malveaux, "The Economic Interests of Black and White Women: Are They Similar?" *Review of Black Political Economy,* (Summer 1985), pp. 5–27.

REFERENCES

Hartmann, H., Kraut, R. E., and Tilly, L. A. (eds.) (1986). *Computer chips and paper clips: Technology and women's employment.* Washington, DC: National Academy Press.

National Commission for Employment Policy (1981). *Increasing the earnings of disadvantaged women.* Washington, DC: NCEP.

———— (1980). *Education, sex equity and occupational stereotyping: Conference report.* Washington, DC: NCEP.

Reskin, B. F., and Hartmann, H. (eds.) (1986). *Women's work, men's work: Sex segregation on the job.* Washington, DC: National Academy Press.

Selden, C., Mutari, E., Rubin, M., and Sacks, K. (1982). *Equal pay for work of comparable worth: An annotated bibliography.* Chicago, IL: ALA.

Simms, M. C., and Malveaux, J. (eds.) (1986). *Slipping through the cracks: The status of black women.* New Brunswick, NJ: Transaction Books.

Treiman, D. J., and Hartmann, H. (eds.) (1981). *Women, work and wages: Equal pay for jobs of equal value.* Washington, DC: National Academy Press.

Waite, L. J., and Berryman, S. E. (1985) *Women in nontraditional occupations.* Santa Monica, CA: The Rand Corporation.

2

The New Demographics and Its Impact on Policy Development for Women of Color

JUANITA TAMAYO LOTT

The policy debate today centers on the productivity of the U.S. population and the ability of the United States to maintain current living standards while competing with a global population that seeks to fulfill its own rising expectations. Demographics has become a frame of reference for understanding this debate specifically in terms of consumer and labor markets. The topic of demographics encompasses an enormous body of data. The visible and long-term effects of demography on public policies is only beginning to be acknowledged and understood. Given these two realities, the purpose of this paper is modest. It is limited to an examination of what is meant by the *new demographics,* particularly in relation to women of color. Specifically, it examines and evaluates the accuracy of four popular assumptions about who this population is in view of historical and current data. From this clarification, the challenge of developing public policies to diminish or eliminate sex segregation in education and in the workplace on behalf of women of color is investigated.

The term *new demographics* is used to describe the changing U.S. population of producers and consumers. What is the new demographics? It is a catchy phrase—another buzzword used to describe whole populations—not unlike the terms *underclass* or *immigrants*. The most popular connotation of the new demographics is a population that is aging, more colored, poorer, not necessarily native born, and not necessarily English-speaking. When the new demographics is addressed in terms of race and gender, it refers to women, particularly women in the labor force, women on welfare, and women of color.

As consumers, white women and people of color, both native and immigrant, are commonly viewed as recipients of benefits without payment or work. As producers, they are viewed as unwelcome competition for U.S. citizens and/or native white males, as groups that depress wages and take jobs traditionally held by male citizens. Their proportion of the U.S. population is increasing while resources become scarcer, space becomes more densely populated, and marketable skills become more competitive.

FOUR ASSUMPTIONS ABOUT
THE NEW DEMOGRAPHICS

Assumption One: The new demographics reflects populations, newly arrived in this country, who do not fit the traditional definition of "American."

It is assumed that these populations are different from the long-held profile of an American. That profile was defined by the founding fathers in 1776 and was of a white, free, male property owner. The first census of the United States conducted in 1790 affirmed this definition.[1] As recently as the 1970 census, the predominant stereotype of an American was a white, middle-class, English-speaking, native-born, young-to-middle-aged male who was the head of household and the primary, and oftentimes sole, income earner. At the same time, white women and people of color, the groups associated with the new demographics, have always existed in the United States. For example, census data from 1910 included separate counts for "White, Negro, Mexican, American Indian, Chinese, Japanese and Filipino populations" (U.S. Department of Commerce, 1933). Historically, people of color, including American Indians, Hispanics, and Asians settled in the Americas long before a United States existed.[2] Blacks have been settled in the United States at least as long as Whites, and Native Americans were present in the continent many centuries before white settlement.

More strikingly, by the 1970s, documentation existed to describe the demographic, social, and economic status of white women and people of color in comparison to white men. In August 1978, the U.S. Commission on Civil Rights released *Social Indicators of Equality for Minorities and Women*. This report was historic and unique for two reasons. First, it provided analyses by gender and detailed race using white males as the measure for comparison over a period of time: 1960, 1970, and 1976. Second, it focused not on traditional measures of production, consumption, and satisfaction but on the degree of inequality in the distribution of resources. Consistently, women and populations of color ranked below white men on detailed social indicators of education, employment, income, and housing. *Social Indicators* documented the following concerns of people of color and white women:

> Underdevelopment of human skills through delayed enrollment, nonenrollment in secondary education and nonparticipation in higher education; lack of equivalent returns for educational achievement in terms of occupational opportunities and earnings; discrepancies in access to jobs, particularly those having greater-than-average stability, prestige, and monetary returns; inequality of income, relatively lower earnings for equal work, and diminished chances for salary and wage increases; a higher likelihood of being in poverty; and proportionately higher expenditures for housing, less desirable housing conditions, restricted freedom of choice in selecting locations in which to live, and greater difficulty in attaining homeownership (United States Commission on Civil Rights, 1978:3).

In conclusion, the report stated:

> These indicators have demonstrated many forms of inequality. . . . Some general tendencies . . . stand out. In the area of education, minorities and women are more likely to be behind in school, not enrolled in high school, without a high school or college education, educationally overqualified for the work they do, and earning less than comparably educated majority males.
>
> In addition, women and minority males are more likely to be underemployed (especially if they are teenagers), to have less prestigious occupations and to be concentrated in different occupations than majority males. With regard to income, minorities and women have less per capita household income, lower earnings even after such determinants of earnings as education, weeks of work, age, and occupational prestige have been adjusted to equality among groups; smaller annual increases in earnings with age; and a greater likelihood of being in poverty.
>
> Finally, minority- and female-headed households are more likely to live in central cities than the suburbs where majority-headed households live, less likely to be homeowners, more likely to live in overcrowded conditions, and more likely to spend more than a quarter of their family income on rent.
>
> Although these indicators are useful, they do not fulfill the general need for social indicators for women and minorities. They are but an initial attempt with limited data sources. A more adequate system of social indicators for women and minority men is needed so that our progress toward equality can be monitored in a wide range of areas (such as health, quality of housing and neighborhoods, and criminal victimization) in which the effects of discrimination and disadvantage continue to prevent some groups of people from enjoying the opportunities and benefits available to most of their fellow citizens" (U.S. Commission on Civil Rights, 1978:86).

In August 1985 a similar report by the U.S. Department of Health and Human Services on the health status of African Americans and other populations of color indicated continuing disparities in mortality, morbidity, and life expectancy between people of color and the overall American health profile:

> Despite the unprecedented explosion in scientific knowledge and the phenomenal capacity of medicine to diagnose, treat, and cure disease, Blacks, Hispanics, Native Americans and those of Asian/Pacific Islander heritage have not benefitted fully or equitably from the fruits of science or from those systems responsible for translating and using health science technology. . . .
>
> Although tremendous strides have been made in improving the health and longevity of the American people, statistical trends show a persistent, distressing disparity in key health indicators among certain subgroups of the population. In 1983, life expectancy reached a new high of 75.2 years for whites and 69.6 for Blacks, a gap of 5.6 years. Nevertheless, Blacks today have a life expectancy already reached by Whites in the early 1950s, a lag of about thirty years. Infant mortality rates have fallen steadily for several decades for both Blacks and Whites. In 1960, Blacks suffered 44.3 infant deaths for every 1,000 live births, roughly twice the rate for Whites, 22.9. Moreover, in 1981, Blacks suffered 20 infant deaths per 1,000 live births, still twice the White level of 10.5, but similar to the White rate of 1960 (U.S. Department of Health and Human Services, 1985:1–2).

Given the above, the first assumption about the new demographics is subject to correction and clarification. Far from being "new" populations, white women and people of color have been in the United States at least as long as white males and in significant numbers. Together, they constitute a numerical majority of the U.S. population today and for the foreseeable future.[3] However, by social, economic, and health indicators, women and men of color, especially black and American Indian men, have not fared and continue not to fare as well as white men. Their status historically has been secondary and ignored. Recent, targeted attention has been directed to men of color because of their growing consumer and labor force participation. It has become obvious that their participation is mandatory to maintain U.S. productivity. This attention is related to a second assumption about the new demographics—that these lesser-known labor force participants are less productive and competitive than white men.

Assumption Two: Populations composing the new demographics, white women and peoples of color, both immigrant and native born, have been and will continue to be secondary labor force participants to white men.

The status of women in the labor force as noteworthy in itself was captured in 1979 as "the subtle revolution" (Smith, 1979). That women might become more than secondary workers was becoming a distinct possibility:

> The movement of women into the paid labor market is a revolution in the sense that it is bringing about a fundamental change in social and economic conditions. The division of labor between the sexes in which men and women work outside the home for pay while women engage in unpaid housework is breaking down. . . .
>
> But the revolution associated with the women's movement into the paid labor force is, in many ways, a subtle revolution. It is subtle in that it has been gradual, not traceable to any abrupt change. Decade after decade the percentage of the female population in the labor force (that is, women's participation rate) has been increasing. Since 1947, when statistics began to be collected on a regular basis, the participation rate of women has increased in all but four years. . . .
>
> The revolution is subtle in that its origins are difficult to understand. Many economists point to the increasing attractiveness of the paid labor market to women, as real wages have risen and work opportunities (particularly in white collar jobs) have expanded. Many sociologists point to changes in sex-role attitudes, rising divorce rates, and falling birthrates. Other explanations offered at one time or another include the invention of labor-saving devices for the home, rising education levels, inflation, unemployment, and movement away from rural areas. Probably all have been important in various periods. (Smith, 1979:1–2)

The increasing labor force participation of women has been confirmed in many studies since then. The findings are summarized in a recent Census Bureau report:

> Striking changes in the economic pursuits and status of women have marked the last two decades: more women are in the labor force than ever before; they are more likely to have continuous lifetime work experience; they are better educated; and the law mandates greater opportunity for equal employment. And yet, as a group, most women continue to work in traditionally female, low-paying occupations. Women have not achieved significant average gains relative to men, and they still constitute a majority of the poverty population. Some observers interpret differences in the economic situation of men and women to be the result of labor market and societal discrimination, others emphasize the substantial responsibilities and commitment of women to the care of the family, while other observers point to the voluntary choices of some women. The sources of the substantial difference in the economic activities and rewards of men and women, however, are not known, and, as dramatic as some of the changes have been, most historical patterns persist (Taeuber and Valdisera, 1986:vi).

Attention to the expanded role of people of color, both native and immigrant, in the labor force has come more recently. Like white women, people of color are increasing their proportion of the labor force. Unlike white women, however, they have not greatly increased their rates of higher education, except for Asian American women. In 1987, the U.S. Department of Labor commissioned a report from the Hudson Institute, *Workforce 2000: Work and Workers for the 21st Century,* which stated:

> The cumulative impact of the changing ethnic and racial composition of the labor force will be dramatic. The small net growth of workers will be dominated by women, blacks and immigrants. White males, thought of only a generation ago as the mainstays of the economy will comprise only 15 percent of the net additions to the labor force between 1985 and 2000" (Hudson Institute, 1987:95).
>
> For black men and Hispanics, the job market will be particularly difficult. . . . In contrast to their rising share of the new entrants into the labor force, black men will hold a declining fraction of all jobs if they simply retain existing shares of various occupations. Black women, on the other hand, will hold a rising fraction of all jobs if they retain their current shares of each occupation, but this increase will be less than needed to offset their growing share of the workforce (Hudson Institute, 1987:101).

In 1954, the composition of the labor force was two-thirds white men, 29 percent white women, 7 percent black and other male, and 4 percent black and other female (U.S. Department of Labor, 1982). Since then, the white male portion has continued to decrease, the black male portion has been steady at 6 percent, plus or minus 1 percent, and the other groups have increased. For example, in 1972, white males declined to just over half of the labor force, at 55 percent. White females increased to one-third while African American males were 6 percent and African American females 4 percent. In 1986, white males had declined to less than half, at 49 percent, and black males decreased to 5 percent. Black females increased to 5 percent while white females increased by 5 percent to 38 percent of the labor force (Fullerton, 1987:Table 5). The Bureau of Labor Statistics (BLS) projects that for the year 2000, white males will continue to decline to 45 percent of the labor force as other groups increase their composition of the labor force (Fullerton, 1987). White females will increase to 40 percent; African American males will increase to 6 percent, as will African American females. Asians will increase to 4 percent (up from 3 percent in 1986) and Hispanics will increase to 10 percent (up from 7 percent in 1986).[4]

Men of color and women have worked throughout their history in the United States. As recently as 1960, men of color and white men had similar labor force participation rates, between 83 and 86 percent

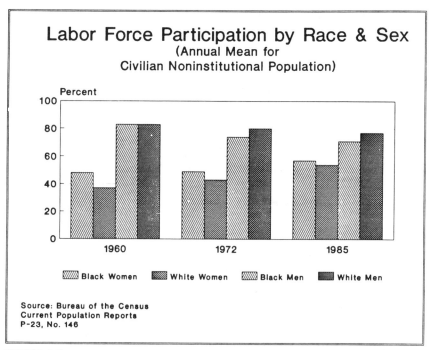

FIGURE 2.1

(U.S. Department of Labor, 1982). In subsequent years both have decreased their participation. By 1985 the labor force participation rate for white men was 77 percent and for African American men 71 percent (Scc Figure 2.1.) Women of color have had higher overall labor force participation rates than white women, even when married. For example, in 1954 African American and other women of color had a labor force participation rate approaching one-half (46 percent) compared to one-third (33 percent) for white women (U.S. Department of Labor, 1982). By 1985, this gap had decreased with African American women holding a slight edge at 56.5 percent, compared to 54.1 percent for white women (Fullerton, 1987:23).

Historically, men and women of color were continuous and active participants in the labor force. They are currently joined by white women, who are increasing their participation. While the composition of men and women of color in the labor force has historically stayed the same, reflecting their percentage of the population, their labor force participation rates have been similar to or higher than those of their white counterparts. This suggests a greater need for more workers to offset the disproportionately lower incomes of people of color. That is, for families of color, more than one worker was and continues to be needed to approximate

**Median Income of Year-Round,
Full-Time Workers, by Race and Sex**
(1984 constant dollars)

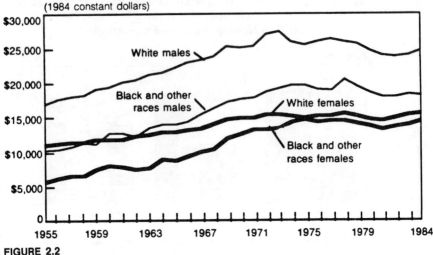

FIGURE 2.2

Source: Bureau of the Census, *Current Population Reports* p-23, No. 146

the income of one worker in white families. From 1955 through 1984,
white males consistently had the highest median weekly earnings of year
round, full-time workers; nonwhite males had the second highest earnings;
white women were third, and women of color earned the least (see Figure
2.2). At the same time, the number of white families with more than
one worker has been growing, so that the earnings gap between white
families and families of color widens. The rise in single, female-headed
households exacerbates this situation; while such households have increased
in recent decades across all races, the greatest increases have been in
families of color (see Figure 2.3).

In recent years, the lower-class position of people of color has been
reinforced by job losses in manufacturing, retail, and other industries
that do not require a college education. Such positions were located in
generally urban areas where people of color are heavily concentrated.
Higher-level positions, on the other hand, have been created in industries
such as electronics and biotechnology that require higher education. Such
industries have relatively few minority workers and are located in the
suburbs, which are settled primarily by white persons (Wilson, 1987:160).

What distinguishes men of color and women from white male labor
force participants in general is that the overall historical and current
occupations of men of color and women have paid less, are accorded
lower prestige, and lack upward mobility. In addition, the educational
preparation and employment training of people of color have been below

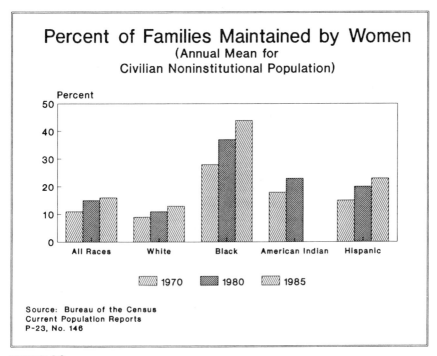

FIGURE 2.3

that of white men and women. Furthermore, as labor needs in the post–World War II era shifted to high school, college, and graduate education and nonphysical skills, allowing expanded mobility for white natives and immigrants, people of color remained primarily in pre–World War II occupations requiring less education and more manual skills. These differences continued even in a period of affluence (see the following discussion of cohorts). Without societal understanding and innovative creative public policies for the near future, the differences between occupations that are primarily labor intensive and sentient and those that are primarily intellectual and electronic will widen (Zuboff, 1988).

In short, unless there is a redistribution of workers so that people of color and women are allowed into higher segments of the labor force and offered the education, training, and other benefits to facilitate this mobility, they will continue to occupy lower status positions. The result overall is fewer primary workers, with declining white male labor force participation. While white females and a few people of color may assume some of the traditional white male occupations, these occupations may lose prestige, in part because of the increased proportion of women and people of color in these new occupations or positions. As Kanter observed (1977), at first the lone token person of color or white woman encounters instances of "status leveling" and is treated in terms of traditional, stereotypical roles. For example, women managers are treated as secretaries and men of color in professional positions are viewed as laborers.

In the opposite trend, research on pay equity indicates that as people of color and white women increase their numbers in traditionally white male occupations, there is a real fear that such positions will lose status and may be resegregated and/or downgraded, resulting in limited opportunities for advancement within the occupation (see O'Farrell and Harlan, 1984). At the same time, the greater presence of men of color and women in a labor force that is expanding primarily in occupations at lower levels of skill, status, and pay, will result in increasing numbers of secondary status workers.

Assumption Three: The new demographics is associated with a lower standard of living, including a poorer and older population.

The demographic trends for the current and future U.S. population are similar to the U.S. population historically and to the global population today. In other words, what is traditional is poverty, not affluence. The prevailing stereotype of the American Dream was true for only a segment of the U.S. population for a finite, and relatively brief, period of time. It is quickly being replaced by lowered expectations for all segments of society except the wealthiest. The higher living standard of the United States is a relatively new phenomenon, coming primarily at the end of World War II. The period from World War II through the early 1970s was a period of unprecedented affluence (Teitelbaum and Winter, 1985). It was a unique period that may be viewed as an aberration; this period saw the development of a middle class composed primarily of white families, particularly in suburban communities. Previously, most Americans, white and of color, were working-class people who worked more than forty hours a week and whose material worth was modest. Being poor was not deviant but the norm; being poor continues to be the norm for most of the world today.

The affluence of the post–World War II era is not indicative of the history of the United States, especially the history of its people of color. The people who benefitted from this wealth are the cohorts primarily of white males born in two periods: 1914–1929, the period from World War I to the Great Depression of 1929, and those born between 1930 and 1945, roughly the period of the Depression through World War II. These populations came of age when opportunities were expanding (Easterlin, 1980), and they became the major beneficiaries of government-supported income security policies and programs that previously did not exist, such as the Social Security programs, the G.I. education bill, and later, Medicare and the Employment Retirement Income Security Act (ERISA).

For example, those born in 1914 entered the labor force in the 1930s and were in their mid-twenties at the dawn of World War II. After the war, the United States was in an excellent position to advance with little, if any, competition from other First and Second World nations, who were busy rebuilding war-torn economies and communities. Third World nations, the countries of origin for most people of color, and Native American lands within the United States, were in the midst of liberation movements from colonial and U.S. rule, respectively.

After the war, the World War I/Depression babies—predominantly the white men who were the primary labor force participants in more prestigious occupations—were recipients of preferential veteran status in federal employment, mortgage financing (particularly for suburban housing), and financial aid for higher education. Additionally this cohort was in its prime labor-force participation period during the post-Sputnik era and the accompanying expansion of federal programs in the 1960s. As icing on the cake, these World War I/Depression babies were induced into early retirement, with pensions supplemented by Social Security and cost-of-living adjustments (COLAs) during the 1970s to make room for the larger cohort of baby boomers (Hayward, Grady, and McLaughlin, 1988). Again, these beneficiaries were predominantly white males who worked in stable, year-round occupations that included retirement and other benefits. In contrast, the bulk of occupations for females and nonwhite males in this cohort included migratory, manual skilled, less-than-full-time, and/or lower-paying positions without Social Security and similar benefits. In general, white females were either not in the paid labor force or participated as less than full-time workers, making them ineligible for benefits.

Similarly advantaged, the cohort born between 1930 and 1945 had the good fortune to be a small population, both absolutely and relative to the baby boomers who followed them. The Depression/World War II babies entered the labor force in the 1960s and were able to work their way into management positions during the 1970s. This mobility was due in large part to the efforts of various social movements, notably the Civil Rights Movement of the 1950s and 1960s and the Great Society's War on Poverty, which produced federal policies and programs creating socioeconomic opportunities, including employment opportunities for educated middle- and upper-class employees at least equal to or greater than those for working-class and poor people. This cohort was also able to achieve highly because of the early retirements of their predecessors.

They, in turn, are eligible for early retirement beginning now through the end of the twentieth century.

The Depression/World War II cohort will be the new elderly, living beyond current average life expectancies. The life expectancies for this cohort will expand to be between 85 and 100 years (Adler, Kitchen, and Irion, 1987). Again, the beneficiaries of this cohort are primarily white males. To a smaller extent, white females are also beneficiaries in two ways: Many more white females have entered the labor force than in previous cohorts and are entitled to benefits in their own rights;[5] additionally, as spouses of white male earners, who generally work full time, year round in covered positions, they are oftentimes entitled to survivor benefits.

Although the U.S. population is commonly thought to be aging, this trend is primarily true of the white population and of females. White females have the highest life expectancy of all population groups. Estimates for 1984 by the National Center for Health Statistics show life expectancy at birth for white females to be 78.8 years, followed by African American females at 75.2 years, white males at 71.8 years, with the lowest life expectancy for African American males at 66.3 years (Adler, Kitchen, Irion, 1987:41). The median age of the white population as of 1983 was 31.3 years old compared to 28.7 years for Asian and Pacific Islanders, 24.9 for African Americans, 23 for Hispanics and 22.4 for Native Americans (U.S. Department of Health and Human Services, 1985:51–58). People of color are primarily younger populations; many are in their prime childbearing years. Assuming that women of color overall continue to have higher fertility rates and higher average numbers of children compared to white women, who are more likely to delay childbearing to later years and have a fertility rate less than or equal to replacement rate (O'Connell and Bachu, 1987), people of color will continue to be younger and increasing while the white population will be older and decreasing.

The American assumption that future generations will have higher living standards than previous ones is questionable even without consideration of the new demographics. For example, consumer costs, most notably in housing and higher education, have increased greatly in the last ten years. Demand for higher education and single-family housing are demands of white, middle-class and upper-class families more than of lower-class families and people of color; the former are disproportionately represented in higher education and homeownership.

Furthermore, there are simply more people living longer with greater demands competing for scarce resources. Population increases due to fertility and immigration are accompanied by decreased mortality and advances in medical technology that have stretched life expectancy from babies delivered prematurely to elderly people living to be centenarians. Individuals are also living in more households because of the rise in single-person households and the high divorce rates that result in families maintaining more than one household.

In sum, while a lower standard of living is associated with the new demographics, it is simplistic and erroneous to conclude that their relationship is causal. Rather, such a standard is accurate historically for the United States and globally today. This alternate view suggests that the post–World War II affluence of the United States through the early 1970s may be a unique, one-time phenomenon. The period of this affluence is declining, and current and future living standards will be more consistent with prior periods and with the rest of the world.

Assumption Four: The U.S. population can be described in binary terms: white males and others or, more specifically, white males and the populations defined by the term new demographics.

For decades, data on the U.S. population were presented and analyzed in terms of "white" and "other." Studies relating to income, employment, and education have focused primarily on white males. Historically, attention to white females and people of color has either been peripheral, footnoted, or nonexistent. In recent years, studies such as *Social Indicators of Equality for Minorities and Women,* mentioned above, have emerged; they represent new and pioneering efforts to balance this attention. But these studies continue to use white males as the basis for comparison. The effect, intentional or not, is to view white males (and other populations) as homogeneous. Further, white men implicitly are viewed as an inherent or absolute standard. For example, in pay-equity studies, the measure of comparable worth commonly assumes that jobs held by white males have greater value than jobs held by other groups precisely *because* they are held by white males. The question this type of reasoning leads to is the more limited one of, What would a job pay if performed by white males? rather than the more general question, What would a job pay regardless of race or gender (or age, class, and so on) if it were inherently valued? The difficulty in raising the latter question is that much of our knowledge, at least of employment issues, interrelates personal specific traits such as gender and race with job-specific traits (Lott, 1986:44–45). In fact, white males and other populations are quite heterogeneous across and within groups; standards for evaluating their status are subject to change.

This binary mentality also extends to much feminist analysis, which fails to distinguish between the predominant focus of such work—white, urban, educated, middle-class women—and other women. On the issue of pay equity, for example, a feminist explanation for women's lower wages is not just in terms of occupational segregation but includes late entry into the labor force, historically low labor-force participation rates and family responsibilities. Such an explanation is incorrect for women of color—who earn even lower wages than white women, despite historically higher and longer labor-force participation rates, with larger average numbers of children and higher rates of being sole heads of households. Similarly, in terms of housing, many white feminists speak positively of intergenerational, planned communities for women and their children. For women of color, such a concept is a reality, but a negative one, in the form of public housing that segregates and isolates them and their children, breaking down traditional neighborhoods and the various family (and extended family) structures of people of color. On the issue of child care, day care that allows parents to pursue paid employment is assumed as a positive, unquestionable objective by feminists. Yet, many women, particularly women of color, assess the long-term benefits of day care in the context of their view that parental care and work outside of the paid labor force are equally valuable, especially in the transmission of specific cultural values and traditions. With the emerging focus on women of color, sensitivity to differences among these groups must be recognized and articulated along with commonalities with each other, with men, and with white women.

In understanding the many and varied populations that compose the total U.S. population, the demographic variables of race/ethnicity, gender, age, nativity, marital status, and household composition have been reframed and even redefined. They are subject to continuing modification as understanding of the differences and similarities among groups increases. The old binary classification scheme for examining population data in terms of white/nonwhite, American born/not American born, married/ not married, or head of household/not head of household has been outdated since the 1980 census.

For example, with respect to race, five categories are currently used for federal statistical reporting programs. These are American Indian/ Alaskan Native, Asian/Pacific Islander, Black, White, and Other. These categories may change.[6] Additionally, because of the need to capture the Hispanic population, this ethnic group can be extracted from the five racial categories and regrouped as Hispanic-specific data. The racial groups themselves can be broken down into finer sub-groups; for example, detailed socioeconomic data are available from the 1980 census for twelve Asian American groups and five Pacific Islander groups (U.S. Department of Commerce, Bureau of the Census, 1988a). Each American Indian tribe is an autonomous entity. With respect to household, when there is more than one adult in a household, there is no longer a "head" of household. Indeed, marital status and family composition now are viewed as dynamic rather than static entities.

Similarly, related socioeconomic data including educational attainment, occupational categories, income by wealth and poverty, income by wage and nonwage sources, housing status and its related data on family composition, and living arrangements over the life cycle have been refined with expanded definitions that may vary over time. Within a population, distinctions are made, such as highly skilled versus lowly skilled new immigrants, and upper-class and low-income African Americans. Similarly, standard definitions of "the poor" and "the homeless" are being refined. Contrary to traditional patterns, "the poor" are not limited to unemployed adults but increasingly include employed persons and children; they are differentiated by categories such as "working poor" and "persistently poor." "The homeless" are not only single, unemployed adult males but also growing numbers of employed persons and their families. Policy-related data must reflect this new reality.

The existence of voluminous, if not readily accessible, statistical information—coupled with advances in statistical methods and electronic processing in the last decade—has facilitated the use of demographic and other population-related data in the policymaking arena. Profiles and projections are developed about the characteristics and behaviors of various segments of the population. While such use should be encouraged, support should be accompanied by caution about the limits of statistical information.

The danger resides in not recognizing the limits of quantitative data. Statistics reflect only the population that is enumerated. Census counts and labor force participation rates reflect only the people who are counted. For example, every decade the Census Bureau must evaluate the decennial count of the U.S. population in view of complementary data, including vital statistics and emigration/immigration data and postenumeration surveys. The difference is commonly known as the *undercount,* which varies from population to population and is more sensitive to error for smaller groups such as individual ethnic groups of people of color.[7]

Similarly, labor force statistics assume that persons are either gainfully employed or looking for work. They do not include individuals who have given up looking for employment. They also reflect the civilian noninstitutional segment of the population. A plausible assumption of equal importance is that people of color are disproportionately represented in the military and other institutional populations, such as prisons. Furthermore, they are more likely to no longer be actively seeking employment, given their low return on investment in the labor force. These persons, like the homeless and other vulnerable populations, are not accounted for in baseline statistics, let alone projections.

Another limitation is that the process of collecting, analyzing, and releasing data is long and arduous. Readily available data do not describe current conditions but the point in time at which the data were collected. For example, detailed decennial census data are not available for years after the actual census. The utility of such data in describing rapidly growing and mobile populations, such as people of color with high immigration and fertility rates or the increasing number of homeless families, is limited.[8]

Moreover, clarification and examination of many new groups, or of familiar groups delineated by various categories, is a relatively new exercise. Researchers and developers of policy by and large have been white males. Their questions regarding the new demographics have been asked from their particular historical and privileged status. As women and people of color assume these roles, their questions about demography will similarly complement their status as workers and consumers.

In short, while the U.S. population continues to be discussed in binary terms, such discussion is outdated, limited, and ineffective, not only in describing the U.S. population but also in developing public policies that impact these diverse groups differently.

IMPLICATION OF THE NEW DEMOGRAPHICS FOR THE DEVELOPMENT OF PUBLIC POLICIES ON BEHALF OF WOMEN OF COLOR

The four assumptions about the new demographics that have been examined here are questionable assumptions that provide incomplete understanding of the changing U.S. population. They must be corrected to ensure the development of accurate and effective public policies.

While the first assumption, that the new populations do not fit the traditional definition of who is an American, appears true at face value, it is also true that people of color and white women have existed in the United States since and before its inception. But citizenship was specifically denied to them; people of color have always had restricted entry to the United States as residents and citizens. Native peoples continue to struggle for lands taken by American settlers. What is new is that white women and people of color are growing in numbers, are visible within and beyond their stereotypical roles, and compose a critical mass as consumers and producers.

The second assumption, that people of color and white women will continue to be secondary labor force participants, may or may not be true. If they are not encouraged or allowed to obtain higher-level education and training skills and promoted to professional and managerial occupations, they will remain secondary workers—assuming that they remain in the labor force. Moreover, the United States then would have a greater proportion of secondary workers than previously, as white males continue to decrease their proportion of the labor force and as the nature of work becomes increasingly electronic and global. Those most likely to attain higher-status occupations are those who are well educated for a rapidly changing technological world, regardless of race, gender, and nativity.

Examination of the third assumption, that the new demographics is associated with a lower standard of living, suggests that such a standard is more consistent with the United States historically and the rest of the world today. In the development of public policies during an era of trade and budget deficits, it may be more useful to view the previous period of affluence after World War II as a unique, temporary occurrence.

The last assumption, that the American population can be viewed in dualistic terms of white males and "others," is outdated. Any profile of the U.S. population must be cognizant of its diverse peoples not only by race, ethnicity, and gender but also by nativity, region, and social, health, and economic factors.

This reality complicates the ability to develop policies on behalf of any group but particularly women of color as a group because they must be seen not by themselves but in relation to each other, to white women, to men, and to other women of color abroad. Furthermore, the unit of analysis for women of color often is not themselves as individuals but as members of families and communities. This view is shared by women of color themselves as a strength and asset; a more complete analysis of white women *and* women of color should portray them both as individuals and as members of families. For example, several issues identified primarily with women of color, such as Aid to Families with Dependent Children (AFDC) and mail-order brides, include familial relations as a central factor. In contrast, issues identified primarily with white women such as pay equity, access to equal credit, higher education, and promotional opportunities are related to their identity as individuals, separate from family-related identities. Even a common issue such as child care is perceived differentially in the policy arena with women of color believed to require child care to participate in the paid labor force to support their families and white women seen as requiring child care to pursue personal and professional goals.

The families and communities of today's people of color are more diverse in terms of structure, composition, and geographical location. They may no longer share a common sense of history, particularly as younger, educated members enter the mainstream and as established communities are joined by new immigrants. This complexity and diversity is further complicated by the fact that the conditions for developing policies are not optimistic or affluent as in the post–World War II era.

Thus, the task of setting policies that would benefit women, particularly women of color, is not an easy one. Traditional policy development has assumed a homogeneous population (white males) or a binary population consisting of those affected by specific policies (the poor, the elderly, the military, business owners, for instance) and the rest of the population. As peoples who have been invisible and second-class citizens in the development of public policies, people of color and women, particularly women of color, have a unique role and responsibility in the development of policies toward the twenty-first century. Their view is from every point of the socioeconomic continuum, from the bottom up, including views from the middle and the top in token but useful positions.

Women of color have learned effective lessons from active roles in the development of policies in the areas of civil rights, poverty programs, welfare reform, and pay equity, among others. They are aware of the importance of coalition building across many different populations and interest groups; of providing a national goal, vision, and policy while respecting and encouraging local, autonomous solutions; of balancing monied resources with voluntary and in-kind contributions that promote self reliance; and of understanding the differential impact of policies on various segments of the population across and within racial and ethnic groups by place of residence, place of origin, family composition, education, and economic status.

With respect to educational and employment policies, women of color have experienced first hand the importance of education and training that are directly relevant to daily living, provide survival skills in mainstream society, and ensure employment that pays living wages and provides on-the-job training for continuous learning and advancement. Education and employment policies on behalf of women and people of color can no longer be limited to affirmative action and compensatory programs and results.

Women of color form a critical mass of U.S. society as producers and consumers in civilian and military life. In a world that is predominantly composed of people of color, the leadership of the United States, in order to be functional and relevant, must include citizens and residents who have ties of culture, language, and kinship with the peoples of Latin America, the Caribbean, Africa, Asia, and the Pacific. In addition to their relationships with people of color globally, women of color bring to the policy arena their experience with a diversity of family structures and household compositions.

While policies affecting U.S. families have been based on the New Deal model of a nuclear family with a male breadwinner, a full-time homemaker, and children, American families have always assumed many forms. The families of people of color historically have not reflected the family of the New Deal largely because of slavery and restrictive internment, immigration, employment, and economic policies. Moreover, families of people of color traditionally have been inclusive, extended structures varying in size in order to meet the needs of family members and the demands of society (Billingsley, 1968). In the United States, men and women of color have assumed flexible work and family roles to ensure the survival and advancement of their families (Lott, 1978). A growing proportion of single-headed households with children are headed by women who are their families' sole support. This reality affects policy development with vast implications for the care of children and for the educational and employment opportunities of women. The challenge is no longer simply to make women of color equal in education, employment, and income to white men but also to bridge the gap between the women of color who are single heads of household and the highly educated, highly paid, childless white couples who are joint heads of household. Similarly, the extended family structure, which has reemerged as households of people of color absorb additional relatives due to immigration and refugee policies, is ripe for investigation and development of public policies that would benefit communities and families in addition to individuals. Employment and education policies should take these various family structures into consideration and utilize them as vehicles for promoting opportunities rather than rejecting them as barriers or irrelevant units of analysis.

Women of color can set the stage for new ways to develop effective public policies that: (1) acknowledge and build upon their history and life experiences; (2) include their familial and community relationships as well as their status as individuals; (3) are sensitive to the many diversities of the U.S. population; and (4) encompass the global dimension of education, employment, and economic policies.

NOTES

1. The items in the first census were limited to six: name of the head of family and number of persons in a household by the categories of free white males, 16 years and older; free white males under 16; free white females; all other free persons (i.e., free Blacks); and slaves. (U.S. Department of Commerce, 1984)

2. See, for example, Marina Espina, "Filipinos in New Orleans," *Proceedings of the Louisiana Academy of Sciences,* XXXVII (December 1975), pp.117–121.

3. This distribution has occurred despite a history of excluding peoples from the United States who were other than white, Anglo Saxon Protestants. Specific examples include the Chinese Exclusion Act of 1882 and the Gentleman's Agreement of 1907, which barred Japanese immigration. Similarly, although Blacks had been brought to the United States from Africa as slaves for centuries,

the proposed immigration bill of 1915 included an amendment to exclude all members of the African or black race from immigrating to the United States. This bill passed the Senate but was defeated in the House after intensive lobbying by the National Association for the Advancement of Colored People (NAACP). For a review of historical discrimination in U.S. immigration laws, see *The Tarnished Golden Door: Civil Rights Issues in Immigration* (Washington, DC: U.S. Commission on Civil Rights, September 1980).

4. The figures do not total to 100 percent since Hispanics are not a mutually exclusive group but may be of any race.

5. This cohort was able to take advantage of a series of employment and educational opportunities directed towards women in the 1960s and 1970s, beginning with the passage of Title VII of the Civil Rights Act. During this period the women's movement generated scores of organizations and support groups for women entering higher education and the paid labor force.

6. In recent years, there has been discussion among academics and Census Bureau staff regarding a separate category for people of Middle Eastern and Arabic ancestry.

7. In 1990, the challenge to count the U.S. population was greater because of the rising number of homeless people. The assumption of the decennial census is that each person has a physical home with an address and that respondents can read and write English. Due to the rising number of homeless people and of native and foreign-born residents with inadequate English literacy skills to fill out a census form, a complete and accurate count of the U.S. population in the 1990 census is questionable.

8. On the other hand, more timely research such as case studies, including recent work to compare Mexican immigrant employees with black native employees in Los Angeles, suffers from limited findings that may not apply to other workers or other places. Even a series of case studies may or may not discern general trends.

REFERENCES

Adler, M., Kitchen, S., and Irion, A. (1987). *Databook on the elderly: A statistical portrait*. Washington, DC: Office of the Assistant Secretary for Planning and Evaluation, U.S. Department of Health and Human Services.

Billingsley, A. (1968). *Black families in white America*. Englewood Cliffs, NJ: Prentice-Hall, Inc.

Easterlin, R. (1980). *Birth and fortune*. New York, NY: Basic Books, Inc.

Espina, M. (1975). "Filipinos in New Orleans." *Proceedings of the Louisiana Academy of Sciences*, 37:117–121.

Fullerton, H. (1987). "Labor force projections: 1986 to 2000." *Monthly Labor Review*, 110 (9):19–29.

Hayward, M. D., Grady, W. R. and McLaughlin, S. D. (1988). "Changes in the retirement process among older men in the United States: 1972–1980." *Demography*, 25:371–386.

Hudson Institute (1987). *Workforce 2000: Work and workers for the 21st century.* Indianapolis, IN: Hudson Institute.

Kanter, R. M. (1977). *Men and women of the corporation.* New York, NY: Basic Books, Inc.

Lott, J. T. (1986). *A review of comparable worth literature and its relevance for the National Institutes of Health.* Report prepared for the National Institutes of Health. Silver Spring, MD: Tamayo Lott Associates.

———— (1978). "Institutional and social factors shaping the growth of Asian American families." *Conference on Pacific and Asian American families and HEW-related issues.* Washington, DC: U.S. Department of Health, Education and Welfare.

McLaughlin, S. D., Melber, B. D., Billy, J.O.G., Zimmerle, D. M., Winges, L. D., and Johnson, T. R. (1988). *The changing lives of American women.* Chapel Hill, NC: The University of North Carolina Press.

O'Connell, M., and Bachu, A. (1987). *Fertility of American women: June 1986.* (Current Population Reports, Population Characteristics, Series P–20, No. 421). Washington, DC: U.S. Bureau of the Census.

O'Farrell, B., and Harlan, S. L. (1984). "Job integration strategies: Today's programs and tomorrow's needs." In Reskin, B. (ed.) *Sex segregation in the workplace: Trends, explanations, remedies.* Washington, DC: National Academy Press.

Smith, R. E. (ed.) (1979). *The subtle revolution: Women at work.* Washington, DC: The Urban Institute.

Taeuber, C., and Valdisera, V. (1986). *Women in the American economy.* (Current Population Reports, Special Studies, Series P–23, No. 146) Washington, DC: U.S. Bureau of the Census.

Teitelbaum, M. S., and Winter, J. M. (1985). *The fear of population decline.* Orlando, FL: Academic Press, Inc.

U.S. Commission on Civil Rights (1980). *The tarnished golden door: Civil rights issues in immigration.* Washington, DC: U.S. Government Printing Office.

U.S. Commission on Civil Rights (1978). *Social indicators of equality for minorities and women.* Washington, DC: U.S. Government Printing Office.

U.S. Department of Commerce, Bureau of the Census (1984). L. Cho and R. L. Hearn (eds.). *Census of Asia and the Pacific: 1980 round.* Honolulu, HI: East-West Population Center.

U.S. Department of Commerce, Bureau of the Census (1933). *Fifteenth census of the United States: 1930 population, II.* Table 4. Washington, DC: U.S. Government Printing Office.

U.S. Department of Commerce, Bureau of the Census (1988a). *Asian and Pacific Islander population in the United States: 1980.* (PC80–2–1E). Washington, DC: U.S. Government Printing Office.

———— (1988b). *Statistical abstract of the United States, 1988.* Washington, DC: U.S. Government Printing Office.

U.S. Department of Health and Human Services (1985). *Report of the secretary's task force on Black and minority health, I.* Executive Summary. Washington, DC: U.S. Government Printing Office.

U.S. Department of Labor, Bureau of Labor Statistics (1982). Bulletin No. 2096, September 1982. Washington, DC: U.S. Government Printing Office.
_____ (1988). *Employment and earnings,* 35 (1). Washington, DC: U.S. Government Printing Office.
Wilson, W. J. (1987). *The truly disadvantaged: The inner city, the underclass and public policy.* Chicago, IL: The University of Chicago Press.
Zuboff, S. (1988). *In the age of the smart machine: The future of work and power.* New York, NY: Basic Books, Inc.

3

Education in a Democratic Society: From the 1960s to the 1980s

MARILYN GITTELL

Public education policy in the United States reflects society's struggle to balance the values of individualism and equality. The translation of these values into educational goals has led, some analysts suggest, to a conflict in the society's effort to achieve educational excellence and its commitment to pursue equality through universal education. Equality, they posit, requires everyone in the society to have equal access to equal education regardless of their background, thus lowering the quality of education. In fact, one can make a strong case for the opposite conclusion, that improved quality has resulted from the struggle for equality.

Organized efforts to reform and expand education in different eras of U.S. history have encouraged the development of innovative curriculum, promoted more imaginative teaching, and led to creation of more stimulating educational environments. Major education reforms followed the expansion of public education responding to the need to reach new students in the system. Progressive education in the 1920s and the open classroom in the 1960s, for example, were tied to efforts to improve the quality of public education and to reach a broader cross section of new students. Head Start, one of the major educational reforms of the 1960s, expanded preschool experiences for poor children, providing them with higher quality, enriching educational experiences earlier in their lives. The Head Start program exemplifies the direct relationship between the quality of the education provided and its equity goal—increasing the number of low-income students and students of color in preschool. Indeed, striving to reach wider populations forces educators to rethink the content of the curriculum, teaching methods, and the education process.

An historical challenge to the U.S. political system has been to remove or minimize the barriers to education for large segments of the population who have been denied equal access to schooling. Excluded populations include new immigrants, people of color, working-class people, and women. Their deprivation or exclusion takes place in several ways: overt and subtle denial of access to secondary and higher education institutions; inferior resources allocated to schools they are forced to attend; lower quality and insensitivity of teaching in these schools; curricula and school policies that discourage these students from attending classes; and disciplinary actions that push them out of school early.

Large segments of the population were virtually excluded from secondary and postsecondary education in the United States until after World War II. One of the most dramatic changes in American education after World War II was the adoption of the G.I. Bill of Rights, which gave all returning veterans financial support for college. Large numbers of men from working-class families who otherwise could not have gone to college were given access to the system as a result of the funding provided by the G.I. Bill. Another benefit was that returning veterans were kept off the unemployment rolls, reflecting society's frequent use of education as an economic policy, serving the needs of the marketplace.

In 1954, when the Supreme Court decision in the *Brown* v. *Board of Education* case established that "separate was not equal," African Americans began to demand access to equal educational programs. A major battle was waged in the 1960s and 1970s to bring the level of schooling to an equal standard for African Americans, Hispanics, and women. Demands for school reform in cities throughout the country led to the elimination of tracking, reallocation of resources, affirmative action, compensatory programs, and curriculum reform. In the decade from 1954 to 1964 efforts to establish federal compensatory education programs failed. The federal effort in the late 1960s and early 1970s sought to achieve equality for large numbers of students of color by providing them with access to the educational system.

Compensatory education, established as a function of federal educational policy under the several education laws adopted since 1964, provided federal grants-in-aid to local school districts to make up for the historic deficit that resulted from "separate" or segregated schools. After a decade of federal aid, at its peak in the late 1970s, federal support amounted to only 8 percent of all expenditures for education. States continued to pay 50 percent of the costs of education.

It was not surprising, therefore, that the country was soon to face a major retreat from its stated commitment to universal, quality secondary and postsecondary education. In the Reagan era, a series of reports bemoaned the "decline" in educational standards, and the apparent return to "mediocrity" was subtly attributed to the decade of compensatory programs. The solution to the problem was seen as a return to the past, to a traditional curriculum of knowledge. This return to what had been rejected as inferior education content in the 1950s and 1960s was somehow to produce "educational excellence." It is not surprising that only a few years later, in the mid-1980s, test results suggested that this emphasis on basic skills was producing poorly educated graduates who did not think critically. But this stress on "excellence" produced the desired end; the system again could tolerate exclusion or underservice to large segments of minority and lower-income populations. In the 1980s, the dropout rate for African American and Hispanic high school students increased and the number of African American and Hispanic students in college decreased.

The thrust of the national rhetoric of educational reform in the 1980s has been "excellence"; in practice, the states that are cited as among the most prominent reformers—South Carolina, Mississippi, Texas, and Arkansas—have adopted educational programs that strengthen minimum standards of performance, have allocated additional resources to schools, and asserted state supervision by increasing certification and testing requirements. But most of these states had lagged far behind in measures of educational quality up until then. The governors of those states that were fostering education reform were arguing for a skilled workforce to attract industry and jobs; they were not focusing on educational excellence! Ironically, therefore, what is credited to the Reagan administration as reform through excellence could more accurately be labeled achieving equality among states, by bringing states with limited educational access and opportunities up to the level of the more advanced states. This demonstrates that quality and equality are interdependent concepts and are more appropriately thought of as common rather than conflicting goals.

When quality and equality are perceived as conflicting efforts, the populations with low status in the system invariably suffer. Thus, in the 1980s the abandonment of the major elements of the 1960s' educational reforms—to be more inclusive, to guarantee universal postsecondary education, and to compensate for past deprivation—had a considerable impact on lower-income women seeking to improve their access to schooling and jobs. The change in commitment since the 1960s has meant that affirmative-action efforts, elimination of sex stereotyping in curricula and textbooks, allocation of additional resources to make up for deficits imposed on lower-income girls and women in their early education, and provision of counseling and support groups for women, no longer have priority in most educational institutions. Those institutions need no longer pretend to worry about inequities.

By the late 1970s, however, the reaction to the federal compensatory effort was a rekindling of the argument that educational excellence had been sacrificed to the pursuit of equality. The critics of federal programs never defined educational excellence except to suggest that it was what existed in schools sometime in the past, nor did they define decline. And none of the commentators espousing these homilies presented any evidence of a connection between the "decline" in quality and the opening up of the system to women and people of color. Certainly African Americans, Hispanics, and women did not want to see the "excellence" of the past—which had deprived them of an education—reinstated.

Prior to the 1960s, there were faults with schooling in America; however, middle-class students were not dependent on the schools for their education and subsequent employment and were therefore able to survive the deficiencies in the system. In addition, U.S. educational institutions generally *were* successful in educating the middle class and the elite. It was the broadening of the base of the student population that presented a new challenge to school systems in the 1960s and 1970s. That required a major social investment and commitment; it required extensive additional resources and time to create new educational programs to reach new, previously ignored populations. A limited federal investment for one decade was not adequate to fulfill the demands of a bold new experiment in universal education. If either quality or universality could be abandoned, the struggle would be more manageable.

The 1980s educational agenda has taken the professionals off the hook on confronting the particular needs and concerns of lower-income women of color. This is in an era when credentialing, and a college education in particular, have become more necessary to employment. One in every four workers in the United States is now a college graduate, as against one in five ten years ago. An additional 20 percent have completed one to three years of college. Among white workers, 26 percent are college graduates, 15 percent of black workers and 13 percent of Hispanic workers are college graduates. According to the U.S. Department of Labor, the jobless rate for college graduates in 1987 was 1.7 percent compared with 3.7 percent for workers with one to three years of college, 5.4 percent for high school graduates, and 9.4 percent for non-high school graduates. A college education is becoming ever more essential to employment and, although an education does not guarantee a job, without it chances are slim that one can retain employment in the primary labor market.

The one continuing pressure that lower-income women can exert on the system is a reminder that they represent a potential new constituency in higher education. No expansion of the education system can take place without strong response to their needs. Like other new constituencies that preceded them, however, women must press for reforms that guarantee them access to high-quality educations. Without affirmative action, extensive revision of curricula, and elimination of sex stereotyping, low-income women will still be educated to prepare them for the most unstable jobs in the lowest-paying fields.

Public education has two major purposes in U.S. society: to prepare people for citizenship and to prepare them for employment. The reform movement of the 1960s appreciated that fact, especially with regard to the previously excluded populations that were to be served. In the 1990s, one cannot be sure that there is any interest in achieving either goal for large segments of the U.S. population. Indeed, the pretense of conflict between excellence and equality is being used to justify a return to more exclusionary policies.

Public education is essential to maintaining the myths of the U.S. political system. It also is the means provided for upward mobility in the society and to prepare citizens for participation in the democratic process as citizens of the community and the nation. Historically, access to the education system has been an attraction for immigrant populations and a reward for workers. A dysfunctional education system disrupts the market system and challenges political stability. For these reasons efforts to open the system must continue, as in the 1960s and 1970s, to be the hallmark of American education; the cyclical efforts to close the system, as in the 1980s, must be viewed as short-term aberrations and must be rejected by policymakers and educators as counterproductive.

4

Gender Practices and Employment: The *Sears* Case and the Issue of Choice

PHYLLIS PALMER
AND ROBERTA SPALTER-ROTH

This chapter is about a basic conceptual, legal, and moral concept—free choice—that was used successfully by Sears, Roebuck and Company to defend itself against discrimination charges brought by the Equal Employment Opportunity Commission (EEOC). The ideal of free choice seems, in this instance, to be hostile to the improvement of women's economic status in the United States; it requires a closer analysis.

First, we describe some salient points of the judge's reasoning in the *Sears* case, noting especially his emphasis on the legal protection of "free choice" and his implicit definition of nondiscrimination in employment as equal respect for men's and women's job choices. Second, we reexamine the origins of the 1964 Civil Rights Act to see how the protection of "choice" came to seem an essential (though perhaps unspecified) element of nondiscrimination policy, a value supported inferentially by much social science thinking. Third, we offer some different ways to rethink the meaning of choice and implications for public policies to end sex discrimination. Fourth, we indicate implications for policymaking of a revised conception of choice. And finally, we make some brief comments on the importance of integrating statistical with more experiential methodologies in order to understand this revised conception of choice.

THE LEGAL CASE

In 1986, an Illinois federal district court judge, John Nordberg, ruled that the Equal Employment Opportunity Commission (EEOC) failed to prove its complaint that Sears, Roebuck and Company historically discriminated against female employees (*EEOC v. Sears*, 1986). The facts of the case on which the EEOC based its challenge were that at Sears, commission sales jobs were held primarily by men, and that these jobs paid higher wages than the noncommission sales jobs that were primarily staffed by women. In defense, Sears offered several explanations for how the company could end up with a gender-differentiated sales force without having engaged in intentional *or* unintentional discriminatory hiring.

In his decision, Judge Nordberg noted numerous erroneous assumptions made by the EEOC's statistical expert in designing his proofs of disparate treatment of women and men. An underlying theme was criticism of the expert's assumption that women had the same aspirations as men; assuming such an essential fact, the judge noted, was unwarranted in light of other testimony about how women's life and work goals diverged from men's. Moreover, historical and psychological evidence was borne out by Sears's own difficulties in persuading women to apply for traditionally male-dominated jobs.

The judge cited in a footnote the "reasonable, well-supported opinions" of historian Dr. Rosalind Rosenberg and an interview study conducted with women workers at Sears by employment consultant Juliet Brudney as demonstrating that the "overall tendencies of many women" were toward jobs different from those preferred by many men (U.S. District Court, 1986: note 43). The judge relied on historical and interview evidence to dismiss the first assumption of the EEOC statistical data: that female and male applicants had similar job aspirations.

Rosenberg's testimony argued that "the assumption that women and men have identical interests and aspirations regarding work is incorrect." Throughout the history of the United States and in all documented societies, work has been divided by gender, presumably entailing different attitudes towards performance and rewards for work. Moreover, women's relatively greater responsibility for children and domestic space, a commitment reinforced by marriage laws requiring male financial support, meant that most women were loath to accept the same employment burdens as men—who were expected to spend less time on household work. Even when women needed to enter the labor force for economic reasons, or were encouraged to do so by national defense needs (as in World War II), according to Rosenberg, they had aspirations and attitudes different from men's. Women's psychology, their socialization, and the experiences consequent on these (such as not playing competitive sports as often as men do), according to Rosenberg, lead women to make different choices about education, work, and career demands (Rosenberg, 1986).[1]

In contrast, Alice Kessler-Harris, professor of history at Hofstra University, testified for the EEOC that "history does not sustain the notion that women have, in the past, chosen not to take non-traditional jobs."

Women have always sought good jobs and fought for and eagerly entered any well-paying jobs that employers made available to them. Moreover, Kessler-Harris pointed out that whenever the society decided it needed women's labor, it was willing (and able) to convince women that taking on jobs previously held by men did not conflict with women's female identity. Kessler-Harris concluded that women, like men in this society, seek jobs that they think they have a good chance of getting: Job aspiration results from opportunities perceived and not from internalized and unchanging goals (Kessler-Harris, 1986).

The Sears lawyers (who were first into the fray with Rosenberg's expert opinion) adroitly emphasized the notion of choice. The EEOC and its expert witness responded in kind, and Judge Nordberg, presented with a case in which the issue of culpability seemingly centered on the factual question of whether or not women employees at Sears had chosen lower-paying jobs than jobs chosen by men, ruled that the EEOC had not proved that women had not made such choices (U.S. District Court, 1986).[2] The judge ruled that Sears had not discriminated and was not liable to pay damages to women employees because the women had chosen the jobs they held at Sears.

HISTORICAL ORIGINS OF NONDISCRIMINATION LAW

What does a non–sex discriminatory workplace look like, both in terms of how employees are treated and of labor force composition? How did choice become a criterion to determine whether or not an employer discriminated against women? When race discrimination was taken as a model for sex discrimination, the answers seemed clear. Assuming that all people have similar aspirations and abilities regardless of race, then a racially integrated labor force would be the outcome of equitable treatment of individual workers; statistical measures of equal outcomes in placement could logically be taken to represent equal (nondiscriminatory) treatment of workers.

The historical development of nondiscrimination thinking in the context of racial exclusion helps explain why the issue could be construed this way in the *Sears* case. Affirmative action programs were designed in the context of laws prohibiting discrimination against racial and ethnic minorities. Drawn up in the crisis atmosphere of World War II and the subsequent euphoria of the Civil Rights Movement, presidentially issued regulations and federal laws prohibited employers from automatically excluding potential employees solely on the basis of race or ethnicity (or religion, often a category equivalent to racial or ethnic difference).

The problem of discrimination was seen as the exclusion of workers from consideration for jobs. People of color who had trained for particular jobs and then applied, only to be turned away because the employer did not think a black person should earn such high wages or thought his white employees would refuse to work with "coloreds,"[3] asked initially only for government protection of their freedom to choose. The government did not protect free choices of those who did not want to work with people of color since these were considered antithetical to the interests of a nation mobilizing its entire population for a war effort and holding up a model of human freedom to challenge Nazi Germany and the Soviet Union. Demonstrating that the United States cared about justice for all, including the ability to compete fairly for a job, was deemed a more significant national interest than protecting white workers' racial comfort. Such justice arguably increased the national ability to fight wars and to produce goods and offered a working model of the liberal principle that freedom and power are synonymous.

With employment discrimination outlawed, however, it soon became apparent that the historical legacy of racial and ethnic exclusions could be corrected only by affirmative actions: in education and training programs, in job testing, and in promotions. Modes of recruitment and channels of family and community knowledge about job availability had to be opened up. Job tests and promotion criteria designed according to the experiences of white workers had to be rethought to include the experiences of African American workers (Freeman, 1978).[4] All these criteria were reviewed to protect job aspirants from unreasonable, and now illegal, exclusion.

It is not surprising that, in a context of formal exclusionary policies, feminist theorists and political advocates initially analyzed sex discrimination as parallel to race discrimination, assuming that women, given the chance, would have work aspirations and abilities similar to men's, would get jobs for which they had not previously been considered, and that the labor force would thus be integrated by gender. Since major feminist statements began to be made in the 1960s—in the report of the Kennedy Presidential Commission on the Status of Women (1963), Betty Friedan's *The Feminine Mystique* (1963), and the charter of the National Organization for Women (NOW) (1966), for example—such writings have presumed that women's employment is beneficial and that women should and would, given the opportunity, participate in the labor market on the same footing as men. In the wake of the Kennedy Commission's report, Congressional passage of the Equal Pay Act (1963) and inclusion of "sex" as a prohibited category for job discrimination in the 1964 Civil Rights Act, the governmental machinery for enforcement was presumed to work the same way to alleviate both sex and race discrimination.

As long as actions were clearly needed to break down overt channelling of men and women into different training and jobs and to open up paths for women to choose professional training, jobs, and career paths that had previously been limited to men, few questions were raised. Obviously discriminatory past practices—employment advertisements specifying "male wanted" and "female wanted" corporate job categories absolutely excluding either women or men from consideration, pay scales in which women were systematically paid less—were not easy targets, but they were relatively noncontroversial ones. The government was simply dismantling barriers to women's free choices.[5]

The Supreme Court's decision in *Johnson* v. *Transportation Agency, Santa Clara County* (1987) underscores the law's tendency to protect a worker's right to be considered fairly for a job for which she has prepared herself and which she has chosen (Santa Clara County, 1987). Diane Joyce trained for the job of road dispatcher, applied for the position, and scored well on the relevant tests. As the first woman to apply for a traditionally male job, Joyce was given *some* special consideration by a county government voluntarily working to integrate previously sex-segregated jobs and was hired for the job. Paul Johnson, a competing applicant who received a slightly higher score than Joyce on the interview segment of the hiring process, sued the county alleging "reverse" sex discrimination. The Supreme Court upheld the principle that nondiscrimination consists of giving those previously excluded from particular jobs an opportunity to demonstrate their competence and to get a slight edge in being evaluated for jobs they choose to pursue. Statistical evidence was used in this case to counter Paul Johnson's claim that Santa Clara County had no reason to prefer Diane Joyce. Santa Clara County demonstrated the severity of past gender segregation through quantitative methods. This evidence was not taken to prove that employers had "intentionally" and unlawfully discriminated but simply as facts to demonstrate that the county acted reasonably to rectify gender segregation. The *Santa Clara County* decision bolsters the implicit notion, prevalent since 1964, that a nondiscriminatory employment situation is achieved when women have a pattern of hires, promotions, training chances, income, and benefits similar to men's (within limitations of the legally allowed variables of education, seniority, and merit).[6]

Defining equality as nonexclusion leads logically to evaluating the effectiveness of measures against discrimination by the standard of how similar women's position in the labor force is to men's; the goal becomes a world in which women and men are indistinguishable in the labor market, either in jobs held or wages earned.[7] Among large labor forces, where treatment of hundreds of thousands of individuals is difficult to monitor (as is true in the practices reviewed in the *Sears* case), using statistical measures to show unwarranted differences between women and men has become the primary way to prove employer discrimination. Sears battled the statistical evidence with its own statisticians, but it also backed up one step to raise the fundamental question: Did women want the same jobs as men? Had Sears excluded women from jobs they were qualified for and wanted? If women did not choose the same jobs as men, then Sears could not be held culpable for unfair exclusion.

Numerous cases during the 1970s and 1980s have shown that discrimination against women has been substantially different from racial discrimination; that women have not been so often excluded by individual employer or government action as they have been by society-wide beliefs and behavior. Society, and not just particular employers, discriminated against women. Women also accepted society-wide norms about appropriate female and male roles and behavior, and in this sense they chose the jobs and career paths deemed appropriate for women. Using choice in this way, to stand for acquiescence or effective socialization, is not the way choice is typically used in social science or legal theory, where it is taken to mean the freedom to act on one's rational calculation of personal benefit.

Since choice is a central issue in the *Sears* case, the decision provides an opportunity to rethink the appropriateness of choice as a concept in doing research on and making policy about sex discrimination. If race and sex discrimination are so different in form, what did the 1964 Civil Rights Act expect to change? What acts were being made illegal, and what arrangements would, in future, constitute nondiscrimination? The *Sears* decision provides an opportunity to ask the questions: What is the social good we seek to advance with a policy on women's employment? and, How shall we think about the balance between individual choice and socialization?

THE "CHOICE" PROBLEM

What does the word "choice" mean anyway? It is used in various ways within different intellectual systems: as a description of a particular political system; a logic premise; an ethical goal; an experiential state; and a descriptive psychology, to mention the most obvious. Let us look at how the term "choice" is used in public policy and related social science writings in order to disentangle some of the moral values and social realities being asserted and described.

Political Theory

Some public policy theorists represent choice as one half of a dichotomy: freedom from governmental regulation or constraint by the government. In these terms, one has choice or one does not; there are no in-between states. For example, in *Gender Justice* (1986) Kirp, Yudof, and Franks juxtapose the liberal goal of enhancing individual freedom to the radical goal of equalizing women's and men's employment status and incomes. The liberal goal requires the protection of women's "right to choose" whatever jobs they want, even if these are less well-paying and secure than the jobs men choose. To use government authority to push for a society in which women and men hold the same sorts of jobs, with similar career patterns, incomes, and family responsibilities is depicted by Kirp and his colleagues as radical action that sacrifices individual liberty to authoritarian zeal.

The *Gender Justice* argument is in accord with the notion of affirmative action as a protection from exclusion. The authors assert that if women want the same jobs in the labor market as men, then their ability to choose such jobs should be protected. But they assume that women are unlikely to choose the same jobs as men[8] and that job integration is the goal of authoritarian ideologues. This use of "choice" implies that women's socialization to aspire to jobs that pay less than men's and to organize their adult lives around marriage and child care is *not* a result of government actions and, therefore, does not diminish women's liberty; women's choice to take jobs that leave them less economically and socially powerful than men is an exercise of freedom because it is not enforced by government. If women choose to behave in traditionally female ways and not to be marked as social deviants, then it is not the responsibility of government (and of public policy) to interfere.

The message that women make economically diminishing, albeit socially correct, decisions and that their freedom to do so must be protected by the government is one that may be taken from Kirp, Yudof, and Frank's work and from the *Sears* decision. The argument conveniently ignores the government's support for female (and male) socialization; publicly funded school courses and publicly licensed media, for instance, purvey traditional notions of appropriate female and male behavior and social roles.

The argument that conforming to social norms is the same as choosing certain behavior makes some sense in the context of the *Sears* case. The only alternatives, given the dichotomy of freedom or coercion, were deciding that women had chosen the jobs they were in *or* that Sears, Roebuck and Company had acted to exclude women from other jobs that they wanted. Since Sears had acted no differently from other social institutions and with values no different from dominant sex-role norms, the company felt it should not be financially liable because it had not anticipated changing gender norms. The only option to finding Sears at fault was to decide that women employees had wanted typically female jobs, even though they were lower-paying than typically male jobs. The adversarial system allowed only a "yes, they discriminated," or "no, they didn't."[9] Saying that women "choose" economic dependence and possible impoverishment over economic independence, however, sounds suspiciously like adding the insult of stupidity to the injury of low wages.

Underlying the ideal that government should not intervene in people's choices about where to work and what to work at is the feeling that private decisions should not be liable to public interference.[10] Feminist analysts have pointed out that "public" and "private" are not bounded spaces, but social concepts, as are choice and government intervention. The "private" family as a scene of child abuse and wife-beating is open to regulation in its "public" capacity as child-rearing agency and marital institution. Husbands cannot choose to beat their wives, and wives cannot choose to be beaten.[11] A powerful husband's choice to beat his wife is a different mental process made in a different context than the "choice" of a powerless wife to be beaten without protest.

Economics

Another version of the "free choice" versus "state planning" dichotomy is offered by economists.[12] Much economic theory works on a carefully defined, often mathematical notion of decision making—rational individuals with maximum information making uncoerced decisions. The model is a logical one and not necessarily descriptive of reality; that is, it provides a quantitative formula for determining how to get the most things a group wants for the least expense but does not describe how people behave.

The logical model fits well, of course, with the dominant political values of the United States: Choice is equated with freedom from governmental regulation and coercion. In brief, some economists have argued that a person chooses a job (whether paid employment, housework, or a combination) freely and for the greatest well-being for herself and the economy at large when state authorities do not intervene. The implicit assertion is that women making rational decisions in their daily existences are making logical calculations of benefits.

Other forms of familial compulsion and coercion, such as a husband saying he does not want his wife to work at a full-time job or young children's afternoon care requiring the mother to work part-time hours, are assumed to be factors that the wife evaluates according to her personal desires and goals: The individual woman assesses the costs of preparing for higher-paying jobs and balances this against the costs of damage to her marriage partnership and the health of her children and then acts on her preference among these alternatives. She may decide, by rational calculation, to work at a less high-paying and time-demanding job in order to maximize her overall family well-being.[13] When women make decisions to take jobs that require less personal investment so that they can expend attention and energy on other tasks such as child care and housework, then government is unwise to interfere in these decisions, even though the woman may find herself impoverished at some point as a result of the decision.[14]

The logic of free choice, useful in modelling alternatives for decision making, does not adequately account for the decision of such a wife, who is sensible but not rational in the sense of economic calculation. This may be because the wife has a different objective from her husband or her employer. As one economic theorist, Thomas C. Schelling, has pointed out, the economic method was not intended to make judgments among objectives but among alternative methods of reaching objectives (Schelling, 1984). The economist's use of choice to indicate that it is logically useful to assume free and rational decisions in making policy decisions can easily be misunderstood to mean that this social science defends the ethical superiority of traditional divisions of labor by sex.

Sociology

Mainstream sociologists have assumed that people make choices about the organization of their lives using the values and behaviors internalized through the socialization process and responding to social sanctions of approval and disapproval.[15] Throughout their lives, in different social settings, individuals learn norms, possibilities, appropriate roles and behaviors. Within society-wide and contradictory rules, they find a tolerable path for their individual needs. As norms and rules change, individuals adapt and change; indeed, they may attempt to change the rules.

Individual occupational aspirations are usually sex typed, and sex stereotypes are learned at the earlier grade levels in school (see Sadker and Sadker, Chapter 5). Young women are more likely to aspire to female occupations and young men are more likely to aspire to typically male occupations (Marini and Brinton, 1984). While women may aspire to or choose occupations on the basis of their socialized sex-identification, a variety of studies have shown a less than .50 correlation between young women's occupational aspirations and subsequent occupational attainments. Any particular individual changes her mind about the relative attractiveness of jobs, presumably as she learns more about herself, about occupations available, and as social norms change.

Sociologists have described the intense pressures in the United States and other societies for women and men to take sex stereotyped jobs and work roles. Indeed, some mainstream sociologists have assumed that these pressures are so great that women come to think about and to assess jobs differently from the ways men do: Women weigh family service higher than income, to which men presumably give more weight. Roslyn Feldberg and Evelyn Nakano Glenn point out this untested assumption within sociological writings and challenge the notion that women separate income earning from their overall calculations of family well-being (Feldberg and Glenn, 1982).[16]

Likewise, what individuals choose has changed historically as opportunities have changed; for example, women took heavy industrial jobs during the male labor shortage of World War II. For sociologists, sex segregation, the sex-typing of particular occupations, and changes over time are the consequences of individual preferences exercised within particular labor markets and job possibilities.

Along with sex stereotypic socialization, sociologists also investigate the institutional processes by which individuals are recruited, hired, allocated to jobs, trained, and promoted, and which are both formal and informal. In a review of the literature, Patricia Roos and Barbara Reskin (1984) describe how firms' formal procedures or rules, such as veterans' preferences, seniority systems, nepotism, and recommendation requirements, have negative effects on women's occupational participation. Much has also been written on the effects of informal procedures such as sexual harassment at construction sites, in firehouses, and in squad cars in constraining women's occupational choices (Carothers and Crull, 1984).

One insight from sociological and historical work is that government itself has been one agent of socialization. In the United States, the government has supported education and training programs that track students by gender and race to meet changing political, social, and economic needs. Individuals have made decisions about jobs appropriate for them under governmental influence since at least the beginning of the twentieth century.[17]

In short, the term choice is used to indicate: freedom from government regulation (political theory); uncoerced rational calculation (economic theory); acting in conformity to or deviance from social norms (sociology); selecting from many alternatives available for one's life (history); and, preferring one thing to another (popular discourse). These meanings overlap in particular debates and in individual minds. They change in nature depending on context.

In the *Sears* case, the company used the term to mean that Sears, Roebuck and Company had conformed to socialized expectations about women's work and was not liable for unfairly denying women's preferences.

The EEOC countered with the argument that women had chosen among alternatives they perceived to be available and that Sears's setting job criteria in conformity with gender norms discouraged women from aspiring to jobs previously held by men.

Let us consider briefly two new ways of thinking about "choice" that are more operational and less theoretical than those discussed above. First, choice may be understood as a subjective state—individuals *feel* desire for something or to do something; choice can be seen as a contingent mental state open to influence, rather than an unyielding moral stance or a psychological essence.[18] Second, choice is what people do as they select among alternatives for action. Neither idea of choice interferes with an ethical defense of individual liberty. Each, conceived in this more contingent fashion—providing people with information to change their feelings and reorganizing institutions to increase alternatives—opens up terrain for policymakers to rethink the issue of nonsex discrimination.

PUBLIC INTEREST IN
INFLUENCING WOMEN'S CHOICES

Why does the public have an interest in pursuing nonsex discrimination, at least in employment? Women's economic well-being has become a significantly more urgent social concern during the past twenty years. Rising rates of divorce mean that more women will be self-supporting than in earlier decades; and many of these divorced women have children, so the financial care of future citizens and workers will increasingly devolve on women. These facts intensify in significance with the rising numbers of never-married women with and without children. Instead of images of an army of Amazons taking on the world, as the "New Woman" was often pictured in the 1910s and 1920s, contemporary images are of poor women, poor households, and poor children who also are women of color, as the proportions of African American, Puerto Rican, Native American, and Mexican American women facing self-reliance grow faster than the proportions among white women.

Influencing Aspirations

In light of this growing social problem, social commentators have begun to rethink the goals intended in antidiscrimination efforts. In brief, goals are for women, as much as for men, to hold jobs that pay them living wages. While some believe such equalization of income requires gender integration of jobs, others view such integration as a secondary goal to improving women's income position. Many nonintegrationists support policies of "pay equity" or "comparable worth" as a means of raising women's pay in "traditional" women's jobs, without achieving gender integration of the labor force.

Education and occupational socialization are areas in which society has accepted government intervention as legitimate on some grounds. We are deciding as a society that we are unwilling to let adolescents ridicule "brainiacs" and pressure peers not to study. Local governments are willing to pay for educational programs—and to suffer political hardships—in order to coerce students to tackle their books if they want to play football or be leaders in student government.[19] Faced with intense competition to bring in industries to replace lost oil business, Texas politicians will nowadays take flak to keep students in math classes.

Moreover, experiments in changing girls' job aspirations and women's job selections that have been undertaken since the early 1970s indicate that such change is welcomed, even in a society that retains strong sex-role training. Many companies have been successful in recruiting and placing women in jobs previously considered inappropriate for women through the following innovative techniques: going beyond high school shop classes, trade schools, and military services to CETA referrals, women's physical education classes, and women in blue collar community organizations as recruits for nontraditional jobs; preparing for women workers by sending supervisors to sexual harassment workshops; sending women to pretraining programs to familiarize them with tools and terms that men learn in shop courses, the military, or "just tinkering around with their fathers"; recruiting women for developmental activities from which they were traditionally excluded on the grounds that it did not pay to train women since they would leave the job to bear and to care for children (O'Farrell and Harlan, 1984).

Changing Institutional Alternatives

Assisting parents in the care of children in some fashion (child care facilities, tax breaks, regulation of work leave, referrals) is the most obvious way public policy can change the alternatives women see as available when they seek employment. The lack of adequate, affordable child care is a constraint that has affected women's access to and retention of jobs more than men's.

Important in itself, child care is a good example of how women's and men's perceptions (subjective desires) and rational calculation of alternatives (institutional options) have been shaped by a society that promotes sex differentiation. When women are said to make a choice about going to work, seeking particular kinds of jobs, and managing their child bearing or child care accordingly, the implicit assumption is that they make these decisions with the same feelings and perceptions as men do.[20] This proposition has not been tested, however, by probing people's perceptions. We do recognize that when men, in the past, made the decision to concentrate on work, they did so with a perception that their children were well cared for and that their domestic labor was tended to by a wife working in the home full-time or part-time. When women make the decision to concentrate on paid employment, they make that choice without such a vision of life. What men experience as free choice, in other words, women may experience as a forced choice.

Mothers, no more than fathers, do not want to see their children badly treated and badly raised. But mothers make employment decisions within assumptions that the quality of their child's early years depends on the mother's being the child's caretaker and not on her earning a lot of money. Fathers make employment decisions with a socially enforced belief that the child's well-being depends on the father's earning as much money as he can and not on how much time he spends with his children.[21] One might argue that institutionally and emotionally such beliefs limit human fulfillment and narrow the options for good child care. They certainly raise the question whether society can construct a non-sex discriminatory work policy without considering non-sex discriminatory means to raise children.

A Brief Note on Research Methods

During the last decade or so, feminist methodologists have begun to develop methods to understand subjective feelings and experiences as an alternative to (though not necessarily in place of) relying on objective questionnaires reporting predefined attitudes and behaviors.

In emphasizing the subjective side of what philosopher Sandra Harding has identified as the ideological dualisms of objectivity and subjectivity underlying contemporary science and social science,[22] feminist analysts have often disagreed with mainstream social scientists, who, in turn, have characterized women's voices telling their own stories as being too "soft" and too subjective. Feminist methodologists have generally preferred these more qualitative methodologies that try to learn how particular women construct their emotions, definitions, behaviors, life histories, and worlds under conditions that they do not necessarily choose.[23] The purpose of this kind of feminist research and methodology is not necessarily to create replicable generalizations or to test unvarying laws. Rather, the purposes are to raise women's consciousness and to increase their power to transform sexist society (Cook and Fonow, 1986).

The *Sears* case provides, once again, a good place to think about integrating methodologies that have been perceived as hostile. Though the EEOC and the Sears attorneys used mainstream social scientific statistical evidence and techniques to prove different truths—either that Sears had not hired women in the percentages in which they applied or that Sears had hired them appropriately—the statistics still show women ending up in different places in the Sears job inventory than men did. Such data, as with the data on occupational segregation, paint a picture of an employment landscape in which men and women inhabit different spaces. By including more qualitative, subjective experiential methodologies along with quantitative and statistical information, we can then seek to understand what brought women and men to their respective spaces and what processes could change the picture.

This chapter is intended to loosen up our intellectual muscles and to push for integration of a variety of disciplinary perspectives and methodologies on issues of major importance to women and men in our society. Our hope is to encourage more work across disciplinary differences and to remember that our goal is the search for dialogue and for policies that advance this country's historical commitment to nondiscrimination.

NOTES

1. Rosenberg (1986) cites much feminist psychological and sociological scholarship to bolster these points, such as articles written to support passage of Title IX of the Education Amendments of 1972 to guarantee girls a fair share of school athletic funds. In these, scholars argued that athletic programs were important because they developed "active, assertive, and self-assured social behavior."

2. Judge Nordberg states that the Kessler-Harris testimony lost impact because of its implication that "sweeping generalities can be accurately made about women . . . in the workplace" and her "unwillingness to qualify . . . generalizations by estimating some percentage of women with the interests or views being discussed."

3. "Negroes" files, RG 69, National Recovery Administration, contain many letters to this effect from African Americans describing the language employers used to justify "laying off" previously employed black workers and from white employers advocating a racial or regional (proxy for race) differential in the minimum wages required under NRA industrial codes. Similar statements are recounted by federal agents in the National Youth Administration, the FERA, and the WPA women's projects, (RG 69 NRA [National Archives]), as they sought to design and to fund projects from which women, white and black, and black youths, male and female, would be able to find nonrelief jobs.

4. Freeman (1978) discusses the *Griggs* v. *Duke Power Co.* (1971) case in terms of its recognition of the historical legacy of differential school graduation rates. Duke Power was forbidden from requiring "a high school education" for moving employees to any department other than the previously "black" one. Duke Power was allowed to draw up tests *related to job performance* in order to maintain production standards, but it could not use as a proxy the high school diploma that many black workers would have been discouraged from earning in

the previously segregated school system of North Carolina. The court specifically precluded "using diplomas or degrees as fixed measures of capability," since these often measured access more than "effective performance" (quoted by Freeman, 1978:1096).

5. As we move to more complicated questions about women's economic independence relative to men's, we should not underestimate the scope of simple discrimination (excluding women from men's places) that existed before passage of the 1960s legislation. As numerous histories of professional women document, women were systematically excluded from formal education programs and from various jobs and career ladders once they had struggled to achieve the necessary credentials. See, for example, Margaret W. Rossiter, *Women Scientists in America: Struggles and Strategies to 1940* (Baltimore, MD and London: The Johns Hopkins University Press, 1982); Mary Roth Walsh, *Doctors Wanted: No Women Need Apply. Sexual Barriers in the Medical Profession, 1835–1975* (New Haven, CT: Yale University Press, 1977); Paula Giddings, *When and Where I Enter: The Impact of Black Women on Race and Sex in America* (New York, NY: William Morrow and Company, Inc., 1984).

6. British courts, responding to suits from the Employment Opportunities Commission in Great Britain, have been less amenable to partial exclusion than have U.S. courts. For cases in the area of comparable worth, a notion more clearly supported in EEC law than in U.S. employment law, the British courts have ruled that if one man is employed in a predominantly female occupation, then the occupation is not liable to be compared to predominantly male occupations to determine if it is being undervalued relative to the skills and responsibility required by the two occupations. To be liable to charges of discrimination, employers must have placed only men in certain jobs and only women in others.

7. David L. Kirp, Mark G. Yudof, and Marlene Strong Franks parody this position in the first chapter of *Gender Justice,* calling those who want to remake the imaginary state of Civitas so that butchering and candle-making cease to be respectively "male" and "female" occupations the Levellers (1986:9–10).

8. Margaret Mead made a similar suggestion to reconcile post–World War II American women to the loss of wartime advantages; in a December 1946 *Fortune* article, she argued that if women were given the opportunity to choose between career and family, they would choose family much more happily than if they were denied the right to make the choice.

9. Thanks to our colleague Tim Brennan for introducing us to David Luban, ed., *The Good Lawyer: Lawyers' Roles and Lawyers' Ethics* (Maryland Studies in Public Policy, 1983). The question of the truth-ascertaining effectiveness of the adversarial system is challenged in the essays "The Adversary System Excuse," by David Luban, especially pp. 93–97, and "The Zeal of the Civil Advocate," by Murray L. Schwartz, especially pp. 157–160.

10. Michelle Rosaldo and Louise Lamphere, in *Woman, Culture and Society* (Palo Alto, CA: Stanford University Press, 1974), now a classic in anthropology and feminist theory, established the "public-private" distinction as a useful framework for analysis. In their introductory essay they argued, and most of the essays in the book demonstrated, that all societies divide human activities into

public (economic, political, formal institutional) life and private (familial, intimate, informal institutional) life. In all societies, those activities defined as public had more prestige and power than those activities labelled private. Men led and were identified with public life, while women inhabited and were identified with private life. Theorists and practitioners in various disciplines adopted this analytic framework, notably Eli Zaretsky, *Capitalism, the Family, and Personal Life* (New York, NY: Harper & Row Publishers, 1976) in history; Nancy Chodorow in sociology; and numerous feminist literary critics such as Patricia Spacks, Elaine Showalter, Susan Gubar, and Susan Gilbert. After using this analysis for a few years, theorists began to recognize its artificiality. Theorists writing now have not given up the dichotomous language, but they are describing how, for instance, state decisions affect family life, and sexuality affects the public arena of the workplace, and how the shifting boundaries of public and private are a topic for historical research. (See Jane Flax, "Feminist Theory, Post-Modernism, and Gender Relations in Contemporary American Culture," *Signs,* 12 (Summer 1987). Some feminist thought has never accepted the analytic usefulness of this distinction; they have, instead, pointed out that the experience of African American women leaving their own homes to do housework in the homes of others is a good example of how arbitrary the categories are. See, for instance, Angela Y. Davis, *Women, Race & Class* (New York, NY: Vintage Books, 1983); Bonnie Thornton Dill, "The Dialectics of Black Womanhood," *Signs,* 4 (Spring 1979):543–555; and Phyllis Marynick Palmer, "Black Women/White Women: Dualisms of Identity and Experience," *Feminist Studies,* 9 (Spring 1983).

11. "Privacy" became important to women as a positive defense after the Supreme Court abortion decision in *Roe* v. *Wade*, which protected women's right to abortion on the grounds of noninterference with women's right to privacy. A distinction made by feminist theorists is between "privacy" for the individual and "privacy" for the family, which may simply protect male authority over women and children. For a lucid explication of the difference in usage, see Rosalyn Petchesky, "Antiabortion, Antifeminism, and the Rise of the New Right," *Feminist Studies,* 7 (Summer 1981):206–246.

12. An inspiration to examine the "choice" issue in economics is the mind-opening work of Thomas C. Schelling, especially his *Choice and Consequence: Perspectives of an Errant Economist* (Cambridge, MA and London: Harvard University Press, 1984). Schelling points out that there may be many ways to protect free choices and that programs can be rethought as we juggle the alternatives being compared. Schelling's modesty in proposing economic reasoning as a means to assess goals and not a preeminent good in itself also can help noneconomists feel more friendly to this tool. ("Economic Reasoning and the Ethics of Policy," especially pp. 24ff).

13. Gary Becker, *A Treatise on the Family* (Cambridge, MA: Harvard University Press, 1981) is the best-known work about this position.

14. Lenore J. Weitzman, *The Divorce Revolution: The Unexpected Social and Economic Consequences for Women and Children in America,* cites data to the effect that "divorced women and the minor children in their households experience a 73 percent decline in their standard of living in the first year after divorce

[while] former husbands, in contrast, experience a 42 percent rise in their standard of living" (1985:xii).

15. This brief explication of socialization theory is clearly an oversimplified one and has been referred to by sociologist Dennis Wrong as the "oversocialized conception of man [sic]." See Dennis M. Wrong, "The Oversocialized Conception of Man," *American Sociological Review,* 26:183–193.

16. Feldberg and Glenn describe how sociologists have made the a priori decision to use a job model in analyzing male workers and a gender model to analyze female workers. A subset of assumptions are that: men's basic social relationships are determined by work and women's by family; men's connections to the family are as economic providers and women's are as wives/mothers; men's sociopolitical attitudes are derived from occupational status and women's from family roles.

17. Phyllis Palmer, *Dirty Work, Housework and Domestic Labor in the U.S., 1920–1945,* (manuscript in progress) describes vocational education programs in home economics partially funded by the Office of Education after passage of the Smith-Hughes Act in 1917 and work relief and training programs for unemployed women funded under various New Deal legislation, beginning with the Federal Emergency Relief Act of 1933. In these programs women were trained to be domestic workers, housewives, home economics teachers, sewers, and clerical workers. Only by accepting traditional concepts of work for women were relief authorities able to get Congress to authorize any money to assist women on relief, many of them heads of household. See Martha H. Swain, "ER and Ellen Woodward: A Partnership for Women's Work Relief and Security," in Joan Hoff-Wilson and Marjorie Lightman, eds., *Without Precedent: The Life and Career of Eleanor Roosevelt* (Bloomington: Indiana University Press, 1984).

18. Chapter 3 of Thomas Schelling's *Choice and Consequence,* "The Intimate Contest for Self-Command," gives a superbly humorous description of the variability of the human mind as it makes decisions for its person about whether or not to smoke a cigarette, eat a piece of chocolate cake, or skip the day's jogging.

19. The Texas debates about requiring a C average in order to participate in extracurricular activities, including the sacrosanct sport of football, have presented a particularly lively version of this social debate. Critics will argue that this is not an interference with free choice, because we do not typically allow such freedom to people under the age of 18. Cases such as the Texas one, and the recent University of the District of Columbia study raising an alarm about pressures exerted on adolescents in the District of Columbia not to be "brainiacs," suggest, however, that some social goods outweigh free choice. It is not usually argued that Texas or District of Columbia youths do not understand their interests and have the ability to make decisions; it is that society is not willing to tolerate the results of their wrong decisions. Texas, as a competitive economy, needs educated citizens to work in high-tech industries. The District, as the center of the federal government and a showcase for the nation, cannot allow black youngsters to decide to fail academically, endangering not only the D.C. economy and their own future as earners, but also the reputation of the United States as a racially

just society. (This example is especially poignant to one of the authors who as a young girl lived in Texas; little energy was felt to be needed to keep young girls from not succumbing to the pressures to believe that marching in the Kilgore Rangerettes or the Apache Belles was a much more worthy goal than being a "brain" at Rice University.)

20. That fathers face the same dilemma as mothers has become the staple of popular journalism. Was this story not "sexy" until it had a male protagonist? A *Fortune* cover story, "Executive Guilt: Who's Taking Care of the Children?" (February 16, 1987) began its account with a 37-year-old vice-president of a sportswear company who couldn't concentrate on his work for worrying about his one-year-old child—until his parents moved next door and became full-time baby-sitters.

21. Cancian (1986) describes as a difference in female-male perceptions of love that women interpret talking and "sharing feelings" as signs of love, while men see "instrumental help" as a love message.

22. The others include culture versus nature, rational mind versus prerational body, and irrational emotions and values, public and private. Masculinity is linked to one side of this set of dualisms and femininity to the other. See Sandra Harding, *The Science Question in Feminism*, Ithaca, NY: Cornell University Press, 1986, especially p. 136.

23. In her recent paper, "Feminist Methodology, Quantitative Data and the Decline of Family-Wage Patriarchy," Spalter-Roth identifies three feminist methodological positions: (1) those who argue that there are feminist research questions but no distinct feminist methods (defined as tools, techniques, and protocols); (2) those who argue that there is a distinct feminist methodology and it is the polar opposite of conventional quantitative methodology; and (3) those who argue that if critically used and driven by feminist questions and purposes a range of tools, techniques, and protocols are part of what can be called "feminist methodology" and that an important purpose of this methodology is to seek alternatives to existing sexist tools, techniques, and measures.

REFERENCES

Becker, G. (1981). *A treatise on the family*. Cambridge, MA: Harvard University Press.

Cancian, F. M. (1986). The feminization of love. *Signs,* 11 (Summer).

Carothers, S. C., and Crull, P. (1984). Contrasting sexual harassment in female- and male-dominated occupations. In K. B. Sacks and D. Remy (eds.), *My troubles are going to have trouble with me: Everyday trials and triumphs of women workers*. New Brunswick, NJ: Rutgers University Press.

Cook, J. A., and Fonow, M. M. (1986). Knowledge and women's interests: Issues of epistemology and methodology in feminist sociological research. *Sociological Inquiry,* 56:2–29.

Feldberg, R. L., and Glenn, E. N. (1982). Male and female: Job versus gender models in the sociology of work. In R. Kahn-Hut, A. K. Daniels, and R. Colvard. *Women and work*. New York, NY: Oxford University Press.

Freeman, A. D. (1978). Legitimizing racial discrimination through antidiscrimination law: A critical review of Supreme Court doctrine. *Minnesota Law Review,* 62:1093ff.

Harding, S. (1986). *The science question in feminism.* Ithaca, NY: Cornell University Press.

Kessler-Harris, A. (1986). Written testimony of Alice Kessler-Harris. *Signs,* 11, Summer:767–779.

Kirp, D. L., Yudof, M. G., and Franks, M. S. (1986). *Gender justice.* Chicago, IL and London: The University of Chicago Press.

Marini, M. M., and Brinton, M. C. (1984). Sex typing in occupational socialization. In B. F. Reskin (ed.).

O'Farrell, B., and Harlan, S. L. (1984). Job integration strategies: Today's programs and tomorrow's needs. In B. F. Reskin (ed.).

Palmer, P. *Dirty work, housework and domestic labor in the U.S., 1920–1945.* (manuscript in progress).

Palmer, P. M. (1983). Black women/white women: The dualism of female identity and experience. *Feminist Studies,* 9, Spring.

Reskin, B. F. (ed.) (1984). *Sex segregation in the workplace: Trends, explanations, remedies.* Washington, DC: National Academy Press.

Roos, P. A., and Reskin, B. F. (1984). Institutional factors contributing to sex segregation in the workforce. In B. F. Reskin (ed.).

Rosenberg, R. (1986). Offer of proof concerning the testimony of Dr. Rosalind Rosenberg. *Signs,* 11, Summer:757–766.

Santa Clara County, CA. (1987). *Johnson v. Transportation Agency* (480 U.S.).

Schelling, T. C. (1984). *Choice and consequence: Perspectives of an errant economist.* Cambridge, MA: Harvard University Press.

U.S. District Court for the Northern District of Illinois, Eastern Division (1986). *EEOC v. Sears, Roebuck & Company* (Civil Action 79-C–11373; 39 FEP Cases, 1703).

Weitzman, L. J. (1985). *The divorce revolution: The unexpected social and economic consequences for women and children in America.* New York, NY: The Free Press.

PART TWO

Learning Her Place:
Sex and Race Stereotyping
in the Schools

5

Sexism in American Education: The Hidden Curriculum

DAVID SADKER AND MYRA SADKER

Visit any school in the United States—elementary, secondary, or higher education—and ask for a copy of the curriculum. You will be given a hefty copy of the objectives and goals of the school: from developing reading skills to sharpening analytical objectives, from preparing future citizens to developing an appreciation of the arts. Undoubtedly, they also include several objectives devoted to preparing students for the world of work—learning about a variety of occupations, making career choices, visiting work sites, and eventually taking courses and programs to prepare them for specific occupations. Whether academic or vocational, our nation's educational objectives are plainly and publicly available for all to see. It is our national curriculum.

But it would be a mistake to believe that our official curriculum is our only curriculum. Below the surface of our official curriculum is an unofficial one, a hidden curriculum that prepares students to enter a world of mores, norms, and biases that go unannounced to the public and sometimes unnoticed by educators themselves. It is this world of the hidden curriculum that prepares girls and women for second-class citizenship in the world of work.

To discover the power and persuasiveness of the hidden curriculum, we shall look at several areas of school life, from the classroom to the principal's office. We shall begin our unofficial tour by visiting the heart of any school, the classroom. Classroom life is quite central to formal education, and the interactions between student and teacher are critical in shaping the academic and career goals of students. Yet the hidden curriculum creates two worlds in each classroom and two different educational environments: one male and central, the other female and peripheral.

INEQUITIES IN THE CLASSROOM:
TEACHER ATTENTION

Recent research on teacher effectiveness indicates that direct instruction appears to be very important in increasing student achievement. Direct instruction involves active teaching; it includes setting goals, assessing student progress, making active and clear presentations of the concepts under study, and giving clear instruction both for class and individual work (Good, 1979). The literature suggests that sex differences in active teaching attention may characterize the interaction process. For example, in one large study involving twenty-four fourth and sixth grade classes, teachers interacted more with boys on four major categories: disapproval, approval, instruction, and listening to the child (Spaulding, 1963). In another study at the junior high school level, boys received more academic contacts and were asked more complex and abstract questions (Sikes, 1971).

Similar findings were uncovered at the high school level. Boys were asked more direct questions and more open-ended questions; they received more teacher-initiated work contacts and more total positive teacher-student contacts (Jones, 1971). This pattern continues for gifted students; a study of 105 gifted students revealed that teachers initiated more talk with boys, discriminated significantly between boys and girls in favor of boys, and were more restrictive toward girls (Cosper, 1970; Sadker and Sadker, 1986).

Research at the preschool level showed that teachers gave attention over 1.5 times more frequently to boys than to girls who were participating in classroom activities. They praised boys more frequently and were 2.5 times as likely to engage in extended conversation with them. Further, teachers were twice as likely to give male students extended directions and detailed instructions on how to do things "for oneself." In contrast, teachers were less likely to explain things to girls; they tended to "do it for them" instead (Safilios-Rothschild, 1979). Serbin and O'Leary (1975) offered a graphic description of how this pattern operated:

> In one classroom, the children were making party baskets. When the time came to staple the paper handles in place, the teacher worked with each child individually. She showed the boys how to use the stapler by holding the handle in place while the child stapled it. On the girls' turns, however, if the child didn't spontaneously staple the handle herself, the teacher took the basket, stapled it, and handed it back to her.

One of the largest studies on classroom interaction was conducted by Sadker and Sadker (1986). With funding from the National Institute of

Education (NIE), researchers trained in classroom observation techniques to assess teacher-student interactions collected data in more than 100 fourth, sixth, and eighth grade classrooms in four states and the District of Columbia. The sample included urban, suburban, and rural classes; classes that were predominantly white, predominantly African American, and predominantly integrated. The teachers observed in this study were both male and female and both white and people of color; they taught language arts, social studies, and mathematics. While the sample reflected some of the diversity of U.S. students and teachers, the observations revealed the pervasiveness of sex bias.

The findings from studies of the 1960s and 1970s, which first documented the nature and extent of sexism in classroom interaction, continue to be valid in the 1980s. Despite the increased knowledge of sex bias and the passage of Title IX, the day-to-day activity of classroom life remains fundamentally unchanged. In America's classrooms, boys and girls continue to receive very different educational experiences.

In the Sadkers' study conducted in the early 1980s, at all three grade levels and in all subjects, male students were involved in more interactions with teachers than were female students. It did not matter whether the teacher was black or white, female or male; the pattern remained the same. Male students received more attention from teachers. The quality of classroom interaction also differed; boys and girls received different kinds of evaluative comments for different kinds of accomplishments. One of the outcomes of this differential treatment is a phenomenon termed "learned helplessness."

TEACHERS' VERBAL EVALUATION
OF STUDENTS' WORK

"Learned helplessness" exists where failure is perceived as insurmountable. Children who exhibit learned helplessness attribute failure to factors that they cannot control, such as lack of ability. After receiving negative evaluations, children characterized by learned helplessness are likely to show further deterioration in performance. In contrast, children who emphasize factors that can be modified or changed, such as effort, tend to see failure as surmountable. After negative evaluation, these children often will show improved performance. Girls are more likely than boys to exhibit learned helplessness. They are more likely to blame poor performance on a lack of ability rather than a lack of effort. They are also "more prone than boys to show decreased persistence or impaired performance following failure, the threat of failure or increased evaluative pressure" (Dweck, Davidson, Nelson, and Enna, 1978). While the research is not conclusive, some studies suggest that teachers' evaluative feedback regarding the intellectual quality of academic work may be a factor in causing sex differences in learned helplessness. In observing fourth and fifth grade classrooms, Dweck and her colleagues (1978) found that approximately 90 percent of the praise boys received for their academic work was directed at intellectual competence. In contrast, less of girls' work-related praise—approximately 80 percent—was for intellectual competence. The other 20 percent of the praise girls received for their work was directed at papers following the rules of form. In terms of work-related criticism, the sex differences are even more striking. Approximately half of the work-related criticism boys received was for intellectual inadequacy and half was for failure to obey the rules of form. In contrast, almost 90 percent of work-related criticism girls received was specifically directed at intellectual inadequacy. Girls received little criticism pertaining to violation of the rules of form. A similar pattern was originally identified in a study by Spaulding (1963) involving twenty-one fourth and sixth grade classes which found that the boys received more total blame and disapproval, but this criticism was largely for inappropriate conduct rather than for lack of knowledge or skill. Girls received almost twice as much teacher disapproval as did boys.

As Dweck and her colleagues analyzed differences in the ways teachers criticized the academic work of girls and boys, they discovered another very important pattern. When teachers criticized boys, they tended to attribute boys' academic inadequacies to lack of effort; however, when teachers criticized girls, they seldom attributed intellectual inadequacy to lack of effort.

To determine whether these differential evaluation patterns were related to sex differences in learned helplessness, Dweck and her colleagues conducted the following experiment with sixty fifth grade children (1978). Ten boys and ten girls were randomly assigned to each of three experimental conditions. In one experimental condition, the boys and girls were taken individually to a testing room where they were presented with word puzzles. The children were given two kinds of failure feedback on their performance. One kind of feedback was specifically addressed to the correctness of the solution, while the other was explicitly addressed to a nonintellectual aspect of the performance. This was called the "teacher-boy condition" because it approximated the kind of negative evaluation that boys are more likely to receive in classrooms. In the other two experimental conditions, the children also worked individually on word puzzles in a testing room. However, the failure feedback these children received was addressed specifically to the correctness of the solution. These children did not receive failure feedback addressed to a nonintellectual aspect of the performance, such as neatness. These were called the "teacher-girl conditions" because they approximated the kind of negative evaluation girls are more likely to receive in classrooms.

At the end of the word puzzle trials, the children in all three conditions were given written questions that assessed whether they attributed failure to the instructor's unfairness, to their own lack of effort, or to their own lack of ability. Most of the children in the "teacher-boy condition" did not view failure on the word puzzles as reflecting a lack of ability. Both boys and girls in this condition indicated that insufficient effort was the cause of failure. In sharp contrast, both girls and boys in the two "teacher-girl conditions" overwhelmingly interpreted the failure feedback as indicating lack of ability. This research led the experimenters to conclude that "the pattern of evaluative feedback given to boys and girls in the classroom can result directly in girls' greater tendency to view failure feedback as indicative of their level of ability" (Dweck, Davidson, Nelson, and Enna, 1978).

The Sadker and Sadker study (1986) also revealed some interesting sex differences regarding teachers' evaluative feedback. Teacher interactions involving precise feedback were more likely to be directed to male students. There were three types of precise teacher reactions: praise (positive reactions to a student's comment or work), criticism (explicit statements that an answer is incorrect), and remediation (helping students to correct or improve their responses). A fourth, less-specific teacher reaction consisted of simple acceptance of student comments, including such teacher comments as "okay" or "uh-huh." More than half of the teachers' comments fell into this category. When teachers' reactions were more precise, remediation comments designed to correct or improve students' answers were the most common, accounting for about one-third of all teacher comments. Praise constituted approximately 10 percent and criticism 5 percent of teacher interactions. Male students received significantly more remediation, criticism, and praise than female students. There was more equity in the distribution of acceptance responses—the ones that pack the least educational wallop.

Several studies indicate that male students receive more teacher disapproval contacts directed at classroom misbehavior and that boys are reprimanded more harshly as well as more often (Jackson and Lahaderne, 1967; Meyer and Thompson, 1963; Sadker and Sadker, 1986). A possible explanation of sex differential patterns of classroom management is that socialization patterns cause boys to misbehave more in schools and, consequently, males are deserving of negative teacher attention. However, one study of fifteen preschool classrooms showed that when teachers were faced with disruptive behavior, particularly aggressive behavior from both boys and girls, the teachers were over three times as likely to reprimand the boys as the girls.

Further, they more frequently punished the boys through a loud and public reprimand. When they did reprimand girls they did it quickly and quietly in a way that other members of the classroom could not hear (Serbin, O'Leary, Kent, and Tonick, 1973). So, even when both girls and boys are exhibiting inappropriate behavior, boys are reprimanded more frequently and more harshly. Several other studies at different grade levels indicate that when girls and boys have participated equally in classroom misconduct, boys are reprimanded more loudly and are given harsher penalties. Low achieving boys are most likely to receive this negative teacher attention (Brophy and Good, 1974).

While it is difficult to draw direct cause-and-effect links between teacher behavior and student outcomes, it is pertinent and intriguing to speculate about potential outcomes. Clearly, the frequent, intense public reprimand is a disciplinary approach at odds with the major themes of research concerning effective classroom management (Weber, 1989). It is even possible that the methods teachers frequently use to discipline boys are more likely to intensify inappropriate behavior than to terminate it. It is interesting that the patterns that emerge from the observational literature are also reflected in comments teachers make about students in interviews. Content analysis of these comments indicates far more personal involvement with male than with female students. Boys also receive more negative comments, mostly for sloppy work, not trying hard enough, and classroom misbehavior (Jackson, Silberman, and Wolfson, 1969).

SEX-SEGREGATED PROGRAMS AND CLASSES

Most Americans have first-hand knowledge of program and course segregation. Female students are less likely to be enrolled in math, science, and computer science courses in high school and college (Peng, Fetters, and Kilstad, 1981; Sells, 1973; Tobias, 1978; PEER, 1984). Their occupational and career horizons are severely limited by self-selection, counseling, or peer pressure dissuading girls and women from enrolling in math and science courses. Forty percent of college-bound men enroll in three or more years of high school mathematics, compared to only 28 percent of college-bound women (Peng, Fetters, and Kilstad, 1981). For college-bound and non-college-bound women, the lack of preparation in math serves as a "critical filter," inhibiting or preventing girls from many careers in science, math, and technology (Sells, 1973). There is evidence that non-college-bound students who take geometry and algebra receive substantially higher scores on civil service, federal, and private sector entry tests than students who do not take these math courses (Tobias, 1978). Researcher Lucy Sells estimated that a student with one year of high school math receives a starting salary that is $3,000 higher than a student with no high school math (Tobias, 1978).

Career and occupational programs are also marked by severe sex segregation. Women constitute approximately 12 percent of the enrollment in secondary-level technology programs. At two-year postsecondary institutions, women earn 88 percent of the degrees and certificates in health-related careers but only 6 percent of those in mechanical and engineering technologies (Randour, Strasburg, and Lipman-Blumen, 1982). Surveys conducted in California, Michigan, and Maryland reveal that boys outnumber girls 2 to 1 in computer science courses offered at the high school level. However, in clerical business education courses, the enrollment ratio is reversed, with twice as many girls enrolled in these courses (PEER, 1984). In vocational programs and schools, carpentry, electronics, and automotive training programs are dominated by males, while cosmetology and clerical training are attended overwhelmingly by females. School programs and courses, both academic and vocational, are marked by significant sex segregation. But even within integrated classrooms, with equivalent numbers of males and females, sex segregation remains a barrier.

In-class segregation provides physical evidence of the disparate educational environments experienced by girls and boys, who still spend large periods of time in segregated environments decades after the *Brown* decision outlawing racial segregation in schools. Segregation emerges through students' decisions (and the attraction of the peer group) as well as through teacher decisions.

Children learn early to value the opinions of their peer group (Campbell, 1964). The importance placed on this opinion increases as children mature, resulting in a high degree of conformity during the preadolescent and adolescent years. In his classic study of students in ten urban and ten rural high schools, Coleman (1960) found that students typically valued popularity more than academic success. This peer group pressure for social rather than academic success was shown to be especially potent and stressful for the adolescent girls. Other studies (Fox, 1977; National Science Foundation, 1988) indicate that the adolescent peer group can have a negative effect on female participation in math and science. Many young women in high school perceive strong peer pressure against enrolling in advanced math courses, and mathematically gifted women show reluctance to skip grades for fear of peer disapproval and rejection. Matthews and Tiedeman (1969) found that a decline in career commitment by high school women was related to their perceptions of male peers' disapproval of a woman using her intelligence. This traditional belief that men are threatened by intelligent women may still persist into the 1990s.

Peer groups that are segregated by sex characterize the elementary school years. Sometimes teachers create this segregation by categorizing students on the basis of gender; they may form separate boy and girl lines, teams for contests, and groups for various classroom tasks and assignments (Frazier and Sadker, 1973; Sadker and Sadker, 1985). Teachers may also influence peer groups and sex segregation by assigning more leadership roles in the classroom to male students (Lockheed, Finkelstein, and Harris, 1978). However, even when this teacher interference does not occur, children tend to self-select into same sex peer groups. Clement and Eisenhart (1979) found that 10- to 12-year olds sorted themselves into gender-segregated groups whenever the opportunity arose. Within these sex-segregated groups, different values and roles were emphasized for boys and for girls. Girls' groups stressed the importance of being "popular," "cute," and "sweet." Boys' groups placed higher value on being "strong," a "good student," and a "good basketball player."

Several other researchers note that same-sex interactions are more common than cross-sex interactions among elementary school children; children are more likely to cross racial lines than sex lines in classroom interaction (Bossert, 1979; Willia and Recker, 1973; Nelson-Le Gall and DeCooke, 1987; Webb, 1984; Warring, Johnson, Maruyama, and Johnson, 1985). Grant (1982) conducted ethnographic observations of urban first grade classrooms and found that girls often fulfilled a caretaker or helping role for boys (helping with academic work, tying shoes), but boys were far less likely to demonstrate these behaviors for girls. In contrast, girls received more hostile remarks in cross-sex interaction and were more likely to be the victims of criticism, racist and sexist remarks, and physical and verbal aggression (Grant, 1982).

A variety of negative outcomes may result from this sex-segregated peer grouping. Girls and boys who interact primarily in sex-segregated groups may have limited opportunities to learn about and engage in the interests and activities of the other gender group. Further, sex-segregated grouping may make it more difficult for teachers to interact equitably with male and female students in classrooms. Moreover, this sex segregation may create barriers to women and men working cooperatively together, not only during school, but potentially during the adult years as well. While there have been many reports that teacher behavior may increase sex segregation, there is, at this point, limited research concerning interaction patterns teachers may use to encourage cooperative cross-sex work and play. However, Serbin and her colleagues (1977) found that cooperative cross-sex play in a preschool setting can be increased through the use of contingent teacher attention. Teacher praise of cooperative cross-sex play produced a clear increase in this type of student behavior. It is important to note that this increase was generally achieved without a reduction in same-sex or solitary play. Instead, children's range of playmates expanded; they did not tend to change from one set of playmates to another. This study at the preschool level may have implications for intervention at the upper elementary grades.

Finally, Lockheed and Harris's (1982) research in twenty-nine fourth and fifth grade classrooms found that students often do not appear willing to work on science projects with cross-sex classmates. However, students held significantly less stereotyped attitudes in classrooms where there was more opportunity for peer collaboration and interaction; but Sadker and Sadker (1986) found that approximately 50 percent of elementary and secondary classes were characterized by heavy sex segregation.

Sex segregation probably contributes to classroom inequities, in part because teachers gravitate to the boys' section of the room and are more likely to interact with them. The inequitable distribution of the teacher's time and attention, the most valuable resources in the classroom, is a central feature of the hidden curriculum. But it is not the only feature.

SEXIST LESSONS IN THE CURRICULUM

Several researchers have studied bias in the content of written language usage and a variety of findings have emerged. For example, there are ten times as many sexual terms applying to females as to males (Nilsen, 1972). Women are often compared to plants (clinging vine, shrinking violet), animals (biddy, chicken, pig), and foods (sweetie, honey, dish). There are, in general, far more negative terms for women than for men. Most of the research on sex bias in written language has focused on the potential impact of the use of supposed generic terms such as "he" and "man" to refer to all people. Studies indicate that elementary, secondary, and college students *literally* envision males when these generic terms are used, even when the context implies both men and women (Eakins and Eakins, 1978). In a study by Schneider and Hacker (1973), students illustrated supposedly generic references to "urban man" with pictures of males; they were less likely to illustrate with male pictures when the references were neutral (such as, "urban life"). Other researchers found that female students indicated that the job of psychologist was less attractive to them when it was described with male generic nouns and pronouns than when sexually neutral terms were used. Cole, Hill, and Dayley (1983) conducted six experiments to explore whether the pronoun "he," when used as a supposed generic, might increase the likelihood that people would think of male referents. They found no empirical evidence that the pronoun "he" alone gave rise to increased male imagery. They also found that the use of egalitarian pronouns ("he or she," "they") did not increase the likelihood that the subjects would visualize women. However, when the word "man" was used as a generic and linked with the pronoun "he" used generically, the responses of both men and women reflected more thoughts of men than when subjects were exposed to the alternative pronoun "they" with "man." Further, women who are exposed to the female generic ("she" to include everybody) reported feelings of pride, importance, and power (Brannon, 1978).

Far less research has been conducted on the use and impact of supposedly generic words in spoken communication, particularly classroom interaction. However, research by Richmond and Dyba (1982) conducted with 452 elementary and secondary teachers showed that they used sexist language frequently. This research also demonstrated that major changes in the behavior of teachers can be achieved in controlled situations so that teachers will use less sexist terminology and more nonsexist language.

ADMINISTRATION: WHERE HAVE ALL OUR LEADERS GONE?

The most visible career ladder to promotion for classroom teachers (most of whom are women) is the principalship. In the early part of the twentieth century, more than half of these leadership positions in supervision and administration were held by women (Howard, 1975: Jones and Montenegro, 1982). In 1928, 55 percent of the elementary school principals were women (Jones and Montenegro, 1982; Byrnd, Hines, and McLeary, 1982) and two-thirds of the county superintendents in the West and Midwest were female (Gribskov, 1980). The significant representation of women in educational administration declined precipitously during the next half century. It was not until the late 1970s and early 1980s that this decline was checked. By the early 1970s, less than 1 percent of school superintendents were women; women were only 13 percent of elementary school principals, 3 percent of junior high school principals and a mere 1.4 percent of high school principals (Jones and Montenegro, 1982; Smith, Mazzarella and Piele, 1981; Howard, 1975). Although recent years have shown a slow improvement in the representation of women in educational administration, barriers still persist.

Study after study conducted over the last quarter of a century shows that when faced with a choice between an equally qualified man and woman, superintendents and school board members generally hire the man. Women must have skills and qualifications superior to male candidates to secure administrative appointments (American Association of School Administrators [AASA], 1979; Makulski, 1976; Niedermayer, 1974; Smith, Kalvelage, and Schmuck, 1982); many informal barriers hinder the entrance and promotion of women in educational administration, including a lack of access to informal information channels, the absence of role models, male screening committees, lack of influential sponsors, and "preadministrative experience" such as coaching (Timpano, 1976; Weber, Feldman, and Poling, 1981). Some studies indicate that sexist attitudes still characterize the thinking of key decision makers (Baltzell, 1983). Studies indicate that board members and male superintendents frequently regard women as too emotional, indecisive, unable to manage budgets, and less desirable as employees because of pregnancy, menstruation, and family responsibilities (AASA, 1981; Makulski; 1976; Tripple, 1972).

Women teachers still get the message that the offices of principal and superintendent are not their domain. One study showed that untenured female teachers who expressed administrative aspirations had difficulty getting tenure. And those women who persisted were encouraged to fill personnel, counselor, and other nonleadership vacancies (Bach, 1976; Ortiz and Covel, 1978).

The loss of women in leadership positions in education is unfortunate for several reasons. Boys and girls are deprived of the daily exposure to women leaders as role models, perhaps resulting in a negative impact on girls' career aspirations and boys' ability to relate to women as leaders. Moreover, research indicates that schools are losing the services of talented leaders; studies indicate that female administrators excel in human relations skills, are more aware of problems facing teachers, more likely to focus on instructional challenges, more effective in working with the community, and more likely to establish a democratic school climate (Fischel and Pottker, 1974; Meskin, 1974; Hemphill, Griffiths, and Frederickson, 1962; Gross and Trask, 1965; King, 1978; Adkinson, 1981). Studies suggest that female principals put more emphasis on monitoring pupil participation and that students achieve more in schools headed by women (Meskin, 1974; Hemphill, Griffiths, and Frederickson, 1962; Gross and Trask, 1965).

THE COST OF SEXISM

The preceding examples of the hidden curriculum are not meant to be inclusive. Limits of space preclude a discussion of bias in athletics, higher education counseling, testing (See Rosser, 1989) and other areas of school life. But the facets of the hidden curriculum already discussed teach powerful lessons that inhibit the career and academic potential of females. Although schools publish their official curriculums, their hidden curriculums are more difficult to discern. Also difficult to uncover is the cost of this hidden curriculum—the cost of sex bias in schools. Although the following findings are unlikely to appear on any report card, these findings do indicate the cost of the hidden curriculum.

When elementary school girls are asked to describe what they want to do when they grow up, they are able to identify only a limited number of career options, and these fit stereotypic patterns. Boys, on the other hand, are able to identify many more potential occupations (Looft, 1971; Hidgems, 1987).

Starting at the junior high school level, girls say that mathematics is less important and useful to career goals. The majority of girls enter college without completing four years of high school mathematics. This lack of preparation in math serves as a "critical filter" inhibiting or preventing girls from entering many science, math, and technologically related careers (Sells, 1973; Parsons et al., 1983).

Girls from lower socioeconomic backgrounds are less likely to have plans for college than those from more affluent families. But family finances are less likely to affect the college options of males. In fact, one study showed that when families were forced to make a financial decision as to whether to send their daughter or their son to college, 80 percent chose the boy (Peterson et al., 1982).

Many girls see motherhood as both their primary and exclusive career in the future. Traditional sex-role stereotyping encouraging girls to pursue this path into motherhood can lead to severe economic consequences, especially when begun early (Earle, Roach, and Frasier, 1987).

Teenagers who become mothers earn only about half the income earned by women who delay childbearing. When families are headed solely by young mothers, they are six times as likely to be in poverty. The National Research Council indicates that it costs $18,130 a year to support a 15-year-old mother and her baby (Earle, Roach, and Frasier, 1987; Buie, 1987).

In urban areas, 43 percent of young men who drop out of school are likely to return to school. For young women who drop out, the return rate is only 25 percent (Kolstan and Owings, 1986).

One in ten teenage girls becomes pregnant every year. For over 40 percent of all adolescent girls who drop out of school, the cause is pregnancy. Teenage pregnancy is related to a constellation of factors including poverty, low self-esteem, academic failure, and the perception of few life options (McClellan, 1987).

The preparation and counseling girls receive in school contribute to the economic penalties they encounter in the workplace. Over 90 percent of the girls in today's classrooms will work in the paid labor force for all or part of their lives (National Commission on Working Women [NCWW], 1986; U.S. Department of Labor, 1989), but a woman with a college degree will typically earn less than a man who is a high school dropout, and the typical working woman will earn 64 cents for every dollar earned by a male worker; women of color earn even less, averaging approximately 50 percent of the wages earned by white males. Women must work almost nine days to earn what men earn for five days of work. Approximately 77 percent of employed women are in nonprofessional jobs. Only 11 percent are in traditionally male-dominated occupations. A majority of women work because of economic necessity: nearly two-thirds of all women in the labor force are single, widowed, divorced, or separated, or are married to spouses earning less than $10,000 a year.

Although women earn higher grades than men, they are less likely to believe they can do college work and they exhibit lower self-esteem than men during secondary and postsecondary education (Richman, Clark, and Brown, 1985). Girls have less confidence than boys in their mathematical ability. The sex-typing of mathematics as a masculine discipline may also be related to low female confidence and performance (Sherman, 1980). Girls also have less positive attitudes toward science than do boys. High school girls view science, especially physical science, as a masculine activity (Vockell and Lobone, 1981).

Girls start out ahead of boys in speaking, reading, and counting. In the early grades, their academic performance is equal to boys' in math and science. However, as they progress through school, their achievement test scores show significant decline. The scores of boys, on the other hand, continue to rise and eventually reach and surpass those of their female counterparts, particularly in math and science. Girls are the only group in our society that begin school ahead and end up behind (Maccoby and Jacklin, 1974).

Girls are more likely to be invisible members of classrooms. They receive fewer academic contacts, less praise and constructive feedback, few complex and abstract questions, and less instruction on how to do things for themselves (Sadker and Sadker, 1985; Wirtenberg, 1979). Girls who are gifted are less likely to be identified than are gifted boys. Those girls who are identified as gifted are less likely to participate in special or accelerated programs to develop their talent. Girls who suffer from learning disabilities are also less likely to be identified or to participate in special education programs than are learning disabled boys (Fox, 1977; Davis, 1978; Lietz and Gregory, 1978; Caplan, 1977).

In athletics, women and girls also face sex bias. For example, although there has been some progress, women's athletics budgets in the nation's colleges are only a modest percentage of men's budgets (Sadker and Sadker, 1982; Trunzo and Wolfe, 1985).

CONCLUSIONS AND RECOMMENDATIONS

The persistence of sex and race bias does not mean that there are not positive signs of change on the horizon. Although girls and boys continue to forecast stereotypic careers for themselves, girls are beginning to see themselves in less stereotypic and more lucrative occupations (Lenerz, 1987). A quarter of a century ago, women composed only a third of the students in higher education; today they constitute a slim majority (Randour, Strassberg, and Lipman-Blumen, 1982). A similar increase is reflected in America's workforce, where women are slowly making gains into higher-level positions (NCWW, 1987). And perhaps the brightest hope for the future comes from young children themselves. Responding to a national survey sponsored by *Weekly Reader,* an overwhelming majority of children predicted that the future would be characterized by equality of the sexes (Johnson, 1987).

These hopeful seeds can grow to create a more equitable future if educators and parents work together to promote change and ensure funding for equity efforts: (1) Curricular materials could be analyzed to insure that females and persons of color are included in a fair and realistic manner. Different texts or supplementary materials can be adapted to remediate curricular bias. (2) Pre and inservice teacher training should reflect the research and skills related to equitable classroom interaction. College and university programs should incorporate this new knowledge base and educators already in schools should be provided with professional inservice training. (3) School boards should review their policies and practices, ranging from recruiting and selecting educational leaders to curriculum and textbook adoption policies. School boards will need to take a hard look at strategies to attract more women and persons of color to manage-ment-level positions, to provide inservice training programs for faculty and staff, and to ensure the selection of equitable and effective curricular materials. (4) School superintendents and school boards will need to record and analyze standardized test scores to follow the progress of students. If female and minority students continue to lag behind white male students, as current scores indicate, or if any group shows an achievement deficit, remedial steps should be considered, including development of alternative methods of student evaluation (See Rosser, 1989). (5) Counseling pro-cedures, vocational interest tests, extracurricular activities, athletics—all facets of the school experience—must be evaluated to assure that educa-tional opportunities are not being denied to any group.

When educators and parents, schools and communities, cooperatively address the barriers imposed by bias, these barriers can be removed. When that happens, tomorrow's children will enjoy a future of greater promise and America will benefit from a more productive society.

REFERENCES

Adkinson, J. (1981). Women in school administration: A review of the research. *Review of Educational Research,* 51 (3).

American Association of School Administrators (1981). *Survey: Attitudes toward women as school district administrators.* Newton, MA.: WEEA Publishing Center.

————— (1979). *Survey of attitudes toward women as school district administrators: Summary of responses to a survey of superintendents and school board presidents.* Washington, DC: AASA.

Bach, L. (1976). Of women, school administration, and discipline. *Phi Delta Kappan,* 57 (7).

Baltzell, C. (1983). *Selecting American school principals.* Washington, DC: Abt Associates and NIE, Jan.

Bem, S. (1975). Sex role adaptability: One consequence of psychological andro-gyny. *Journal of Personality and Social Psychology,* 31.

Benton, C. (1987). *Sex related differences in mathematical reasoning ability among intellectually talented adolescents: Their characterization, consequences, and possible explanations* Paper presented at the American Educational Research Association.

Bossert, S. (1979). *Tasks and social relationships in classrooms.* Cambridge, MA: Harvard University Press.

Brannon, R. (1978). *The consequences of sexist language.* Paper presented at the American Psychological Association, August.

Brody, L. (1987). *Gender differences in standardized examinations: Cause and consequences.* Paper presented at the American Educational Research Association, Washington, DC.

Brophy, J., and Good, T. (1974). *Teacher-student relationships: Cause and con-sequences.* New York, NY: Holt, Rinehart and Winston.

————— (1973). Feminization of American elementary schools. *Phi Delta Kappan,* 54.

Buie, J. (1987). Pregnant teenagers: New view of old solution. *Education Week,* April 8.

Byrnd, D., Hines S., and McLeary, L. (1982). *The senior high school principalship.* Reston, VA: National Association of School Principals.

Campbell, J. D. (1964). Peer relations in childhood. In M. L. Hoffman, and L. L. Hoffman (eds.), *Review of child development research.* New York, NY: Russell Sage Foundation.

Caplan, P. (1977). Sex age, behavior and school subject as learning determinants of report of learning problems. *Journal of Learning Disabilities,* 10.

Clement, D., and Eisenhart, M. (1979). *Learning gender roles in a southern elementary school.* (Final Report). Chapel Hill, NC: Spencer Foundation.

Cole, D., Hill, F., and Dayley, L. (1983). Do masculine pronouns used generically lead to thoughts of men? *Sex Roles,* 9.

Coleman, J. D. (1960). The adolescent subculture and academic achievement. *American Journal of Sociology,* 65.

Cosper, W. (1970). *An analysis of sex differences in teacher-student interaction as manifest in verbal and nonverbal cues.* Unpublished doctoral dissertation. The University of Tennessee.

Crosby, F., and Nyquist, L. (1977). The female register: An empirical study of Lakoff's hypothesis. *Language in Society,* 6.

Cross, P. (1963). College women: A research description. *Journal of National Association of Women Deans and Counselors,* 32.

Dauber, S. (1987). *Sex differences on the SAT-M, SAT-V, TSWE and ACT among college bound high school students.* Paper presented at the American Educational Research Association, Washington, DC.

Davis, W. E. (1978). A comparison of teacher referral and public self-referral measures relative to perceived school adjustment. *Psychology in the Schools,* 15.

Duke, D. L. (1976). Who misbehaves? A high school studies its discipline problems. *Educational Administration Quarterly,* 12.

Dweck, C., Davidson, W., Nelson, S., and Enna, B. (1978). Sex differences in learned helplessness: II. The contingencies of evaluative feedback in the classroom. III. An experimental analysis. *Developmental Psychology,* 14.

Eakins, B., and Eakins, R. (1978) *Sex differences in human communication.* Boston, MA: Houghton, Mifflin.

Earle, J., Roach, V., and Frasier, K. (1987). *Female dropouts: A new perspective.* Alexandria, VA: National Association of State Boards of Education.

Etaugh, G., and Harlow, H. (1975). Behavior of male and female teachers as related to behaviors and attitudes of elementary school children. *The Journal of Genetic Psychology,* 127.

Felsenthal, H. (1970). Sex differences in expressive thought of gifted children in the classroom. *ERIC,* 039–106. American Educational Research Association.

Fennema, E. (1984). Girls, women and mathematics. In E. Fennema and M. J. Ayer (eds.), *Equity or equality: Education for women.* Berkeley, CA: McCutchan.

Fischel, A., and Pottker, J. (1974). Women in educational governance: A statistical portrait. *Educational Researcher,* 3 (7).

Fox, L. (1977). The effects of sex role stereotyping on mathematics participation and achievement in women and mathematics: Research perspectives for change. In National Institute for Education (1977). *Papers in Education and Work,* 8. Washington, DC: NIE.

Frazier, N., and Sadker, M. (1973). *Sexism in school and society.* New York, NY: Harper and Row.

Good, T. (1979). Teacher effectiveness in the elementary school. *Journal of Teacher Education,* 33.

Grant, L. (1982). *Sex roles and statuses in peer interactions in elementary schools.* Paper presented at the American Educational Research Association, New York, NY, March.

Gribskov, M. D. (1980). Feminism and the woman school administrator. In S. Biklen and M. Branningan (eds.). *Women and educational leadership.* Lexington, MA: D.C. Heath.

Gross, N., and Trask, A. (1965). *Men and women as elementary school principals.* Cambridge, MA: Harvard University Press.

Guttentag, M., and Bray, H. (1976). *Undoing sex stereotypes: Research and resources for educators.* New York, NY: McGraw Hill.

Hemphill, J. K., Griffiths, D. E., and Frederickson, N. (1962). *Administrative performance and personality.* New York, NY: Teachers College Press.

Henley, N., and Thorne, B. (1977). Womanspeaks and manspeaks: Sex differences and sexism in communication, verbal and nonverbal. In A. Sargent (ed.), *Beyond sex roles.* St. Paul, MN: West Publishing Co.

Hidgems, E. L. (1987). *A study of the relationship between study skills and aspiration level of high school seniors.* Unpublished doctoral dissertation, Washington, DC: The George Washington University.

Howard, S. (1975). *Wanted: More women. Why aren't women administering our schools?* Arlington, VA: National Council of Administrative Women in Education.

Hoyle, J. (1969). Who shall be principal—a man or a woman? *National Elementary Principal,* 48 (30).

Jackson, P., and Lahaderne, H. (1967). Inequalities of teacher-pupil contact. *Psychology in Schools,* 4.

Jackson, P., Silberman, M., and Wolfson, B. (1969). Signs of personal involvement in teachers' description of their students. *Journal of Educational Psychology,* 60.

Johnson, L. (1987) Children's visions of the future. *The Futurist,* 21.

Jones, E., and Montenegro, D. (1982). *Recent trends in the representation of women and minorities in school administration and problems in documentation.* Arlington, VA: American Association of School Administrators.

Jones, V. (1971). *The influence of teacher-student introversion, achievement, and similarity on teacher-student dyadic classroom interactions.* Unpublished doctoral dissertation. Austin: University of Texas.

King, P. J. (1978). *An analysis of teachers' perceptions of the leadership styles and effectiveness of male and female elementary school principals.* Doctoral dissertation. University of South Carolina.

Kolstan, A. J., and Owings, J. A. (1986). *High school dropouts who change their minds about school.* Washington, DC: U.S. Department of Education, Office of Educational Research and Improvement.

Kramer, C., Thorne, B., and Henley, N. (1983). Perspectives on language and communication. *Signs,* 3.

Lakoff, R. (1976). *Language and women's place.* New York, NY: Harper Colophon Books.

Leinhardt, G., Seewald, A., and Engel, M. (1979). Learning what's taught: Sex differences in instruction. *Journal of Educational Psychology,* 71.

Lenerz, K. (1987). *Factors related to educational and occupational orientations in early adolescence.* Paper presented at the American Educational Research Association, Washington, DC.

Lietz, J., and Gregory, M. (1978). Pupil race and sex determinants of office and exceptional education referrals. *Educational Research Quarterly,* 3.

Lippitt, R., and Gold, M. (1959). Classroom social structure as a mental health problem. *Journal of Social Issues,* 15.

Lockheed, M., Finkelstein, K., and Harris, A. (1978). *Curriculum and research for equity: A training manual for promoting sex equity in the classroom.* Princeton, NJ: Educational Testing Service.

Lockheed, M., and Harris, A. (1982). Classroom interaction and opportunities for cross-sex peer learning in science. *Journal of Early Adolescence,* 2.

Looft, W. R. (1971). Sex differences in the expression of vocational aspirations by elementary school children. *Developmental Psychology,* 5.

Makulski, M. J. (1976). *Case studies of the attitudes of superintendents and school board members of selected school districts in the state of Michigan toward the employment of women as school administrators.* Doctoral dissertation. University of Michigan.

Matthews, E., and Tiedeman, D. (1969). Attitudes toward career and marriage in the development of life styles of young women. *Journal of Counseling Psychology*, 11.

Maccoby, E., and Jacklin, C. (1974). *The psychology of sex differences.* Palo Alto, CA: Stanford University Press.

McClellan, M. (1987). Teenage pregnancy: Practical applications of research, *Phi Delta Kappan*, 68.

Meskin, J. (1974). The performance of women school administrators: A review of literature. *Administrator's Notebook*, 23 (1).

Meyer, W., and Thompson G. (1963). Teacher interactions with boys as contrasted with girls. In R. Kuhlems and G. Thompson (eds.), *Psychological studies in human development.* New York, NY: Appleton-Century-Crofts.

Mullis, I. (1987). *Trends in performance for women taking the NAEP reading and writing assessment.* Paper presented at the American Educational Research Association.

National Association of Elementary School Principals (1981). *A statistical report.* Arlington, VA: NAESP.

National Center for Education Statistics (1987). Unpublished data. Washington, DC: NCES.

National Commission on Working Women (1987). *An overview of women in the workforce.* Washington, DC: NCWW.

———— (1986). *An overview of minority women in the workforce.* Washington, DC: NCWW.

National Science Foundation (1988). *Women and minorities in science and engineering.* (NSF 88–301). Washington, DC: NSF.

Nelson-Le Gall, S., and DeCooke, P. (1987). Same-sex and cross-sex help exchanges in the classroom. *Journal of Educational Psychology*, 79.

Niedermayer, G. (1974). *Women in administrative positions in public education.* Washington, DC: U.S. Department of Education.

Nilsen, A. (1972). Sexism in English: A feminist view. In C. Hoffman, C. Secor, and A. Tinsley (eds.), *Female Studies*, 4. Old Westbury, NY: The Feminist Press.

Ortiz, F. I., and Covel, J. (1978). Women and school administration: A case analysis. *Urban Education*, 13 (2).

Parsons, J. E. et al. (1983). Expectancies, values, and academic behavior. In J. T. Spence (ed.). *Achievement and achievement motives: Psychological and sociological approaches.* San Francisco, CA: W.H. Freeman.

PEER Computer Equity Report (1984). *Sex bias at the computer terminal—How schools program girls.* Washington, DC: Project on Equal Education Rights.

Peng, S., Fetters, W., and Kilstad, A. (1981). High school and beyond: A national longitudinal study for the 1980s. *National Center for Education Statistics.* Washington, DC: U.S. Government Printing Office.

Peterson, G. W. et al. (1982). Social placement of adolescents: Sex role influences on family decisions regarding the careers of youth. *Journal of Marriage and Family,* 44.

Randour, M., Strasburg, G., and Lipman-Blumen, J. (1982). Women in higher education trends in enrollments and degree earned. *Harvard Educational Review,* 52.

Richman, C. L., Clark, M. L., and Brown, K. (1985). General and specific self esteem in late adolescent students: Race × gender × SES effects. *Adolescence,* 20.

Richmond, V., and Dyba, P. (1982). The roots of sexual stereotyping: The teacher as model. *Communication Education,* 31.

Robovits, P., and Maehr, M. (1973). Pygmalion black and white. *Journal of Personality and Social Psychology,* 25.

Rosser, P. (1989). *The SAT gender gap: Identifying the causes.* Washington, DC: Center for Women Policy Studies.

Sadker, M., and Sadker, D. (1986). From grade school to graduate school: Sex bias in classroom interaction. *Phi Delta Kappan,* April.

—— (1985). Sexism in the schoolroom of the 80s. *Psychology Today,* March.

—— (1982). *Sex equity handbook for schools.* New York, NY: Longman.

Safilios-Rothschild, C. (1979). *Sex-role socialization and sex discrimination: A synthesis and critique of the literature.* Washington, DC: National Institute of Education.

Schneider, J., and Hacker, S. (1973). Sex role imagery and use of the generic man in introductory texts: A case in the sociology of sociology. *American Sociologist,* 8.

Sells, L. (1973). *High school mathematics as the critical filter in the job market: Developing opportunities for minorities in graduate education.* Proceedings of the Conference on Minority Graduate Education at the University of California. Berkeley: University of California.

Serbin, L., and O'Leary, D. (1975). How nursery schools teach girls to shut up. *Psychology Today,* 48.

Serbin, L., O'Leary, D., Kent, R., and Tonick, I. (1973). A comparison of teacher response to the preacademic and problem behavior of boys and girls. *Child Development,* 44.

Serbin, L., Tonic, K., and Sternglanz, S. (1977). Shaping cooperative cross-sex play. *Child Development,* 48.

Sherman, J. (1980). Mathematics, spatial visualization, and related factors: Changes in girls and boys grade 8–11. *Journal of Educational Psychology,* 72.

Sikes, J. (1971). *Differential behavior of male and female teachers with male and female students.* Unpublished doctoral dissertation. Austin: University of Texas.

Silviera, J. (1972). Thoughts on the politics of touch. *Women's Press,* 7 (13).

Smith, M. A., Kalvelage, J., and Schmuck, P. (1982). *Women getting together and getting ahead.* Washington, DC: Women's Educational Equity Act Program.

Smith, S. C., Mazzarella, J. A., and Piele, P. K. (eds.) (1981). *School leadership: Handbook for survival.* Eugene, OR: University of Oregon Clearinghouse on Educational Management.

Sommer, R. (1969). *Personal space*. Englewood Cliffs, NJ: Prentice Hall.

Spaulding, R. (1963). *Achievement, creativity, and self-concept correlates of teacher-pupil transactions in elementary school*. (Cooperative Research Project No. 1352) Washington, DC: U.S. Department of Health, Education and Welfare.

Swacker, M., The sex of the speaker as a sociolinguistic variable. In B. Thorne & N. Henley (eds.), *Language and sex: Difference and dominance*. Rowley, MA: Newbury Homes.

Timpano, D. (1976). *Sex discrimination in the selection of school district administrators: What can be done?* Washington, DC: National Institute of Education.

Tobias, S. (1978). *Overcoming math anxiety*. New York, NY: Norton and Co.

Tripple, M. (1972). *The attitude of superintendents and board members toward women in school administration in the state of Michigan*. Doctoral dissertation. University of Michigan.

Trunzo, T., and Wolfe, L. R. (1985). *Like she owns the Earth: Women and sports*. Washington, DC: Project on Equal Education Rights.

United States Department of Labor, Women's Bureau (1979). *The earnings gap between men and women*. Washington, DC: U.S. Department of Labor.

Vockell E. L., and Lobone, S. (1981). Sex role stereotyping by high school females in science. *Journal of Research in Science Teaching*, 18.

Warring, D., Johnson, D., Maruyama, G., and Johnson, R. (1985). Impacts of different types of cooperative learning on cross-ethnic and cross-sex relationships. *Journal of Educational Psychology*, 77.

Webb, N. (1984). Sex differences in interaction patterns and achievement in cooperative small groups, *Journal of Educational Psychology*, 76.

Weber, M., Feldman J., and Poling, E. (1981). Why women are underrepresented in educational administration. *Educational Leadership*, 38 (4).

Weber, W. (1989). Classroom management. In J. Cooper, (ed.), *Classroom teaching skills: A handbook*. Lexington, MA: D.C. Heath.

Willia, C., and Recker, C. (1973). *Race-mixing in the public school*. New York, NY: Praeger.

Wirtenberg, T. J. (1979). *Expanding girls' occupational potential: A case study of the implementation of Title IX's anti-segregation protection in seventh grade practical arts*. Unpublished doctoral dissertation. University of California.

Zimmerman, D., and West, D. (1975). Sex roles, interruptions and silences in conversation. In B. Thorne and N. Henley (eds.), *Language and sex: Difference and dominance*. Rowley, MA: Newbury Homes.

6

Honoring Cultural Diversity and Building on Its Strengths: A Case for National Action

BERYLE BANFIELD

Women of color continue to be clustered in low-paying, low-status jobs. They are underrepresented in managerial and executive positions and, with the exception of Asian American women, are grossly underrepresented in the scientific, engineering, and technical professions. This is not mere happenstance. The unfavorable economic condition of women of color is the inevitable consequence of historical inequities they have experienced as a result of discrimination based on race and gender.

People of color in the United States have traditionally suffered social, political, and economic discrimination based on race and ethnicity. These discriminatory practices evolved to accommodate the economic and political interests of the nation and became institutionalized as they were supported by judicial decisions and the activities of business and political organizations. Well-defined negative stereotypes were developed for the express purpose of justifying the continuing inequitable treatment of African Americans, Asian Americans, Hispanics, and Native Americans.

While a specific set of negative characteristics was ascribed to each group as a whole, within each group certain traits were cited as typical of the women and men. Thus, the classic stereotypes of the African American woman emerged as the "mammy," the dominating matriarch, the tragic octoroon, the woman of easy virtue, and the buxom, good-natured, dependable cook. Asian American women were stereotyped as the sinister "Dragon Lady," the female counterpart of Dr. Fu Manchu, the sexy China Doll, or the geisha girl; they were also depicted as overly passive, domestic, obedient, and subservient. Hispanic women were stereotyped as hot tempered and troublesome on the one hand and passive and submissive to male family members on the other. Native

American women have been stereotyped either as Pocahontas, the beautiful "Indian Princess," or as the dull, uncomplaining "squaw" who does all the hard work while her "brave" enjoys his leisure.

These stereotypes of women of color have no basis in historical reality. Throughout their history in this nation, African American women have worked in "nontraditional" occupations; they have smelted iron, laid railroad tracks, and made bricks. They were among the organizers and developers of the new African American towns in the Southwest; they were some of the earliest doctors in the country and many operated successful small businesses. Native American women have a proud history of political leadership and active roles in shaping their societies prior to European contact. Asian American women, Chicanas, and Puertorriqueñas have belied the stereotype of passivity and submissiveness by their demonstrated courage in working and organizing for better pay in the sweatshops, factories, and agricultural fields to which they were consigned.

These stereotypes of women of color were perpetuated and reinforced by popular literature, children's tradebooks, textbooks, and the electronic media. The net result was an almost universal acceptance of these stereotypes as valid by members of the dominant society; to a large extent, acceptance of these stereotypes has translated into limited employment and educational opportunities for women of color (Jackson, 1973; King, 1974; Witt, 1974; Yoshioka, 1974).

Acceptance of stereotypes based on race and gender also has helped create an educational climate that fails to foster the social and intellectual development of women of color and the ethnic groups to which they belong. The high dropout rate of African Americans, Hispanics, and Native Americans is causing grave concern in their respective communities. For those students who remain throughout high school the outlook is less than encouraging in terms of the skills and competencies that will be demanded by the highly technological society of the coming decades. African American, Hispanic, and Native American youths continue to be underrepresented in mathematics and science courses in junior and senior high school; a similar situation obtains on the college level, where they are greatly underrepresented in science, engineering, and mathematic courses even though they constitute one-half of the student population.

The extent to which biased attitudes that evolved from the internalization of racial stereotypes can impact on the educational experience of youth of color bears some examination. Educational institutions must of necessity reflect the values and beliefs of the societies they serve. And at one point in U.S. history, social thought and institutions were greatly influenced by such doctrines as "social Darwinism," "manifest destiny," and "the white man's burden." Each of these theories justified inequitable treatment of people of color on the basis of their supposed inferiority. These theories—with the stereotypes developed to support them—also found their way into history books and children's literature in common use in U.S. schools.

The Bobbsey Twins series, one of the most popular and enduring works of literature ever devised for children, made its appearance in 1904 and introduced Dinah, the family cook, to thousands of young readers as the ultimate stereotype of the contented slave and the superstitious, watermelon-eating, eye-rolling, thieving African American. The doctrine of "manifest destiny," which justified the capture of Native American lands, was supported by Laura Ingalls Wilder's *Little House on the Prairie* and *The Matchlock Gun* by Walter D. Edmonds. Both works, which have enjoyed enormous popularity through the years, depicted Native Americans as fierce, marauding savages, greatly to be hated and feared. *The Five Chinese Brothers* written by Claire Huchet Bishop and illustrated by Kurt Wiese, received wide critical acclaim when it was first published in 1933 and became one of the most popular children's books in the United States. This "classic" helped to perpetuate the perception that all Chinese looked alike, had sickly yellow skin, slit and slanted eyes, and dubious moral values.

The social and political doctrines of social Darwinism and "the white man's burden," received wide exposure through the original "Dr. Doolittle" series by the British author Hugh Lofting. In his various adventures, the good doctor visits the lands of benighted savages such as "Red Indians" and Africans. He brings these ignorant natives the benefits of his superior knowledge; at their request, he consents to remain in their land and rule over them. All people of color were portrayed as grotesque, abysmally ignorant, and ridiculous in the extreme. The themes of "the white man's burden" and social Darwinism appeared in several children's books produced in the 1950s. The story line usually centered on a family of color beset by numerous difficulties, who found themselves totally incapable of coping. They were usually rescued by a benevolent white social worker, teacher, or librarian.

Textbooks, in many instances, were less subtle than tradebooks in perpetuating these theories and stereotypes. As late as the 1970s, textbooks were depicting Native Americans as warlike, African Americans as unskilled and dependent, Asian Americans as compliant, and Puerto Ricans as violence prone and contributing to urban unrest. The following quotations are indicative: "The Iroquois were a fierce and warlike people" (*America: Its People and Values,* Harcourt, Brace, Jovanovich, 1975, page 68); "Many former slaves did not know how to live without their former masters" (*The Pageant of American History,* Allyn and Bacon, 1975, pages 281–282); "In San Francisco, the historically compliant Chinese aggressively resisted attempts to bus their children to schools outside of Chinatown"

(*The American Experience,* Addison-Wesley, 1975, page 643); "groups such as the Puerto Ricans in New York City . . . form additional sub-urban populations which keep the nation's cities seething with discontent and conflict" (ibid., page 646).

It was not until the Civil Rights Movement of the 1960s that concerned organizations, notably the Council on Interracial Books for Children (CIBC), alerted the general public to the dangers inherent in these materials. Working closely with educators and librarians, CIBC developed criteria for evaluating tradebooks and textbooks for racism and sexism and published the landmark *Stereotypes, Distortions and Omissions in U.S. History Textbooks* (1979), a critical analysis of twelve history textbooks all published in the 1970s and widely used in U.S. schools. Through its quarterly *Bulletin,* the council provided reviews of children's literature and educational materials focusing on issues of race and gender; CIBC also developed curriculum packages designed to reduce race and gender bias. The New York–based Asian Americans for Fair Media produced a booklet, *The Asian Image in the United States: Stereotypes and Realities,* (n.d.) that identified and refuted the stereotypes of Asians spread by print and nonprint media.

Contributing to the inhospitable educational atmosphere for youth of color were the theories of "cognitive deficit" and "cultural deprivation" that gained common acceptance in urban classrooms. These theories were rooted in the perception that youth of color were lacking in qualities essential for educational success. These "deficit" theories were projected by educators and social scientists who used white Anglo culture as the norm. Goldberg (1963) paints a devastating picture of a student from a "disadvantaged" home who comes to school with few of the experiences considered necessary to prepare one for academic success. Deutsch (1963) likewise posited that the home environment of "disadvantaged" students contributed to psychological deficiencies which presaged school failure. "Compensatory education" programs were developed for those students, largely poor, largely students of color, who were determined to be in need of remediation of these deficiencies. These programs, designed to compensate for the knowledge gap between "disadvantaged" students and their Anglo counterparts, emphasized basic skills and teaching strat-egies that included constant drill and repetition. Many instructional packages for younger children developed on this theoretical base found favor in inner-city schools, to the dismay of many African American educators who felt that these programs were designed to train, not educate, students of color.

The perceptions of cultural and cognitive deficiencies determined many of the experiences provided for youths of color in counseling, course assignment, and grade placement. Oakes (1983) refers to Anderson's findings that from the very beginning of vocational education programs, African American youth have been prepared only for those jobs traditionally held by African Americans. To ensure their continued aspirations to these jobs, African American youths were counseled to make "realistic" career choices. Oakes (1986) also noted that special barriers existed in the case of women of color, as school practices and policies reflected biased societal attitudes. Perceived as innately lacking in ability, they were consistently tracked into low-ability classes and diverted from the study of math and science, which were seen as the province of the white male.

Teacher expectation is a critical factor in pupil success or failure. Studies have shown significant relationships between teacher expectations and academic achievement—even when those expectations were based on spurious information (Mazer, 1971; also see Sadker and Sadker, Chapter 5). Research has also shown that teacher attitudes vary by the race and gender of the learner (De Nys and Wolfe, 1985) and that the race of the pupil tends to be the most important variable in teacher perception (Washington, 1982). Teachers behave differently toward different students—communicating high expectations to some and low expectations to others.

Frazier and Sadker (1973) observed that teachers' and counselors' lower expectations for girls have an impact even when they are not explicitly stated. Their work substantiates the earlier findings of Sears (1963) that girls in elementary schools tend to have a lower opinion of their abilities than do boys. Kenneth Clark (1965), whose ground-breaking work on the deleterious effects of discrimination on the African American child contributed to the historic 1954 Supreme Court decision outlawing school segregation, has commented that stimulation and teaching based on positive expectations are much more important to a child's school achievement than the environment provided by the community.

Socioeconomic status is also a factor influencing teacher expectations of pupil achievement. Gollub and Sloane (1978) assert that certain inequalities of opportunity exist among classes and races of people. Rist (1970) found a decided difference in the quality of treatment accorded to pupils. Teacher interest was greatest in those students perceived to have high socioeconomic status and possessed of "desirable" behavior traits. Yee (1968) found that while teachers were warm and sympathetic toward middle-class children, they were cold toward lower-class children and tended to blame and fault them.

This differentiated behavior has a substantial impact on the self-concept of the student and, over time, impacts on achievement motivation and levels of aspiration. In the end, high expectations elicit high performance, low expectations, poor performance (Good, 1981). Those teachers who hold stereotypic perceptions of persons of color will inevitably communicate these to the students with the resultant negative effect.

In career counseling, race and gender stereotypes may also operate in ways harmful to students of color. Teachers, counselors, and students themselves, for example, accept the stereotyped image of the scientist as white and male. This stereotype is spread through the media and textbooks and may adversely affect the expectations that students of color, particularly girls, have for themselves (Rowe, 1977). These images also serve to reinforce stereotypic perceptions held by teachers and counselors. Consequently, many young people of color do not receive the type of counseling that would inspire and adequately prepare them to enter science, mathematics, and engineering courses in college.

African American and Hispanic students also are consistently underrepresented in programs for the gifted and talented. They are more frequently enrolled in programs that train students for low-level occupations such as building maintenance, commercial serving, and institutional care (Oakes, 1986). Many Native American youths report that they have been counseled *not* to take mathematics courses, as math is seen as being "too difficult" for them (Cheer, 1984). Matthews (1984) reports that early tracking of students of color into vocational and remedial classes is a continuing problem.

Female students are victimized by counseling practices based on sexist assumptions and practices. Quite often they are channelled into home economics, secretarial, or beauty culture courses. Their occupational choices are thus effectively limited since the net result of such counseling is to direct female students to low-paying, sex-segregated jobs.

Low self-esteem has been cited as a major factor in the failure of persons of color to opt for courses in mathematics and science. Indeed, low self-esteem is an inevitable result of stereotyping; persons victimized by such negative perceptions tend to internalize these perceptions. The result is a poor self-image, lower aspirations, and pursuit of limited educational and occupational options. This problem must be addressed far more widely, given the urgent need for technically skilled personnel during the coming decades. The need to enhance the self-concept of children of color has been a focus of concerned educators for decades. These educators were stimulated by the works of psychologists who had concluded, on the basis of studies, that what individuals feel about themselves is determined by their perceptions of what others think and feel about them. Within a given culture, this perception of self is influenced by the role and status that the society assigns to an individual. In a society in which racist and sexist stereotypes persist, they will continue to have a negative impact upon the self-concept of women and of men of color.

The theory of self-concept received wide circulation among educators and the general public as a result of the famous black doll/white doll study of Kenneth Clark (1963) which indicated that African American children had internalized the negative attributes ascribed to their blackness by white society. In an effort to determine the relation between self-concept of ability and school achievement, Brorboner, Erickson, and Joiner (1967) conducted a longitudinal study of students in one secondary school, from the seventh through eleventh grade. Their research indicated that others' evaluations of students' ability affected their perceptions of their academic ability and set limits on their academic achievement. Practically none of the students with lower self-concepts achieved at a high level.

The underachievement and underrepresentation of students of color in the critical areas of science, mathematics, and engineering is now cause for national concern. By the year 2000, the greatest number of entrants into the job market will be women, people of color, and immigrants (See Lott, Chapter 2). Yet these are the very students who are failing to receive the type of education that will enable them to compete successfully in math- and science-related fields. If this state of affairs is allowed to continue, a large and valuable pool of talent will have gone to waste, and the nation will have surrendered its position as a leader in the technological world of the future. The effect upon our economy could be disastrous. Every effort must therefore be made to ensure excellent education for youth of color in an educational atmosphere that is hospitable and free of racism and sexism.

Many educational institutions and professional organizations have already begun to address the problem of underachievement and under-representation of persons of color in science and engineering courses. The National Action Council for Minorities in Engineering (NACME) has developed programs designed to provide better academic preparation for students of color and to increase their self-confidence. NACME encourages secondary schools and colleges to cooperate in establishing engineering programs that combine advanced preparation in math and science with a strong system of student counseling and support. Other institutions reporting success in recruiting and retaining women and men of color cite similar programs of intervention prior to college entrance (Richardson, Simmons, and de los Santos, 1987). The essential elements of such programs appear to be student tutoring, the creation and maintenance of a hospitable campus atmosphere, and teacher education. In spite of these efforts, however, progress has been limited. There are simply not enough men and women of color currently in the pipeline. Too many become educational casualties in or before high school.

Therefore, serious consideration must be given to the quality and nature of education provided for children of color from the earliest grades.

Concern over the quality of education provided for children of color reached a peak during the Civil Rights Movement of the 1960s and early 1970s. Asian Americans, African Americans, Native Americans, Chicanos, and Puerto Ricans began to protest vigorously against the stereotypic presentations of their lives, histories, and cultures in educational materials. The "melting pot" concept was rejected as an inappropriate guiding principle for a pluralistic society and a strong movement toward multicultural education was launched. This reform effort was assisted by federal, state, and local policies that supported educational equity.

The federal Ethnic Heritage Program operated under Title IX of the Elementary and Secondary Education Act (ESEA) of 1965 provided funds for the development and operation of ethnic heritage programs. The program also provided funds for the development of curriculum materials based on the history and geography of various cultural groups. These materials were intended for use in elementary and secondary schools and in institutions of higher learning. On-site curriculum development projects were supported in various parts of Africa and Latin America. The Women's Educational Equity Act (WEEA) of 1974 program supported the development of model projects designed to ensure educational equity for girls and women. Many of these projects addressed the issues of math avoidance and anxiety, science education, and nontraditional occupational choices for girls and women. The Indian Education Act led to the development of curriculum materials relevant to the lives, histories, and cultures of various Native American societies. Many states and local educational agencies created similar programs on a smaller scale.

Teacher educators began to develop criteria for courses that would be required for the preparation of all teachers (Klassen and Gollnick, 1977; National Council for Accreditation of Teacher Education, 1977). Many of the proposed courses addressed such issues as racism and sexism, the histories and cultures of various racial and ethnic groups, and intergroup relations. These recommendations assume greater urgency for teachers in the 1990s in view of changing school demographics. Other institutional and programmatic arrangements also must be revised to meet the needs of a changing school population. Increased emphasis must be placed on the preparation of teachers who can be effective in culturally diverse learning environments. Adequate preparation for teachers should afford them the opportunity to: recognize their own conscious and unconscious racist and sexist attitudes; analyze the ways in which racism and sexism operate in society; become reasonably well informed concerning the role of women of color in our society and the role they have played and continue to play in shaping the history of their own communities and nations; and become reasonably well informed concerning the history and culture of various racial and ethnic groups.

It is also important that teachers be equipped with the skills both to evaluate instructional materials for racist and sexist content and to use potentially destructive materials in a constructive fashion. Teachers also need to be aware of the ways in which cultural influences may affect the ways in which students process information. In addition they should be equipped with the skills to utilize cultural materials in developing suitable curricular approaches and teaching strategies (Braun, 1977; Cummins, 1986).

The preparation of teachers to educate an increasingly culturally diverse population requires sharper focus than it has previously received. For this reason, it will be necessary for teachers and prospective teachers to move from a purely intellectual understanding of racism and sexism in our society to a more personal examination of their own attitudes and behaviors. No one is entirely free from stereotypic perceptions of members of other racial/cultural groups. When held by teachers, these misconceptions can be damaging to their students because of the way in which stereotypes influence teacher expectations and treatment of children based on race and gender. Racism and sexism awareness training thus becomes an imperative for all teachers. This is a serious and painful process; it may also be threatening, as it requires the examination of racism and sexism from a personal as well as an intellectual point of view. Participants in such training are helped to see how their acceptance of racist and sexist stereotypes can have an impact on their teaching behavior to the detriment of their students. Because of the emotion and sensitivity surrounding such training, it should be conducted only by highly skilled trainers. Once helped to confront their own biases on a personal level, teachers may undertake an intellectual analysis of the ways in which institutional racism and sexism have operated to limit the educational and occupational options of people of color.

The history of racial and ethnic minority groups in the United States has generally been told from a Eurocentric point of view, which has generally served to perpetuate stereotypes about people of color. Teachers need adequate and accurate information concerning the role of African Americans, Asian Americans, Chicanos, Puerto Ricans, and Native Americans in United States history. Information concerning the values and belief systems that undergird cultural traditions and practices should also be provided. This type of information is especially important if teachers are to be equipped to counteract the stereotypes that still are projected in many works of literature and textbooks.

To Kill a Mockingbird by Harper Lee (Lippincott, 1960) and *The Double Life of Pocahontas* by Jean Fritz (Putnam, 1983) are two works that are widely used in public and private schools in the United States. But both works perpetuate negative stereotypes of women of color. Lee's "junior" novel not only presents a stereotyped portrayal of the African American family housekeeper but portrays African Americans as superstitious people with a deficient speech pattern. Fritz's *Pocahontas,* written for nine and ten year olds, is a fanciful retelling of the discredited myth of the beautiful "Indian Princess." Teachers equipped with accurate information about the historic role of Native American and African American women and the value and belief systems that informed their cultures and traditions would be able to guide students in exploring the basis of these stereotypes and in identifying the historical inaccuracies. Further, recently published textbooks still depict the Iroquois nation as warlike. Teachers with accurate information would be able to discuss the Iroquois Confederacy as a union of nations desiring peace, thus counteracting this negative view and also explaining how the Iroquois Confederacy influenced the "founding fathers," who were seeking a mechanism to weld the colonies together; such efforts would develop in all students an appreciation of the ways in which Native Americans helped shape U.S. history and government.

A culturally diverse student body requires the use of instructional techniques and curricular materials that are congruent with the culturally influenced learning styles and curriculum needs of the students. In order to devise the appropriate teaching strategies and make the necessary curricular adaptations, teachers need to develop an appreciation and understanding of the values and belief systems of their students. They also need to be aware of the cultural diversity that exists within these groups.

For example, there are between 350 and 400 Native American societies. While there are similarities in language and culture in some groups, there are many societies with widely differing customs and languages. The people of these Native American societies prefer to be known by their national names—Iroquois, Lakota, or Navajo, for instance. Asian Americans may be Chinese, Filipino, Korean, Japanese, Indian, Vietnamese, or Thai—all with different histories and traditions. The countries from which they came have different historical relations to the United States and to each other. Their experiences in the United States may have been similar in some respects and vastly different in others. In addition, there are ethnic Asians from the Caribbean who relate to Caribbean culture. Among people of African ancestry, there are those who were born in the United States, those who came from the Caribbean islands of Jamaica, Trinidad, and Barbados, and those who came from countries in South and Central America. Hispanics may be Puerto Rican, Cuban, Mexican American, Dominican, or Salvadoran, for example. In each of these individual groups there is wide variation based on income, class, education, race, and attitude toward the dominant culture. There is also wide variation in the historical role of women.

Many Native American women wielded great economic power because of their relationship to the land. In some nations, women derived power as clan mothers, who selected the rulers. The African American woman, while playing an important role in the shaping of American society, was nevertheless victimized by sexism both within her own society and in the dominant culture; she has had to fight such negative stereotypes as the dominating matriarch and the castrating female. Asian women, particularly those reared under the principles of Confucius, have had to cope with the structures of a sexist society. Similarly, Hispanic women have had to cope with a society that favored male domination.

Cultural values influence the way pupils respond to authority, whether they work better in groups or as individuals, and whether they prefer competitive activities or activities that require group cooperation. Thus, teachers preparing to teach African Americans, Asian Americans, Hispanics, and Native Americans should be provided with the opportunity to study the key elements of these cultures.

Students of color, their parents, and members of their communities are once more beginning to raise demands for a culturally sensitive curriculum. Research studies would seem to support the validity of their claim that such curricula would increase the students' chances of academic success. Cummins (1986) cites research that indicates that students' performance improves when culturally based materials are incorporated into the curriculum. Cheer (1984) reports on Greene's (1978) study, which found that none of the Native American students described as having math anxiety had ever heard of the Mayan or other advanced mathematical systems of Indians of pre-Columbian Mexico.

Very explicit recommendations concerning the type of curricular approaches that may be employed have been made in recent years. For example, Bradley (1984) suggests that the beadwork of Native Americans has properties that illustrate mathematical concepts of geometry, number theory, and measurement. Moore (1988) has employed a culturally based approach to mathematics using petroglyphs created and carved on the surfaces of caves, cliffs, and stones by ancestors of Native Americans. Zaslavsky (1973) has written in detail concerning the construction of numeration systems based in African societies' geometric forms in architecture, geometric form and pattern in African art, and the use of mathematics in games played by African peoples.

Closely related to the use of culturally based curricula is the adaptation of instructional techniques to accommodate culturally influenced learning styles. There is a body of evidence indicating that considerable improvement in student performance occurs when instructional techniques respond to culturally conditioned learning styles (Cummins, 1986). Much classroom instruction today, for instance, depends on verbal communications.

But this may disadvantage Native American students who come from cultures in which highly sophisticated nonverbal communication is valued (Bradley, 1984). African American students come from a society with a strong oral tradition and their mode of communication often is oral and dramatic. This may pose difficulties when they are confronted with the silent writing tasks that are a major focus of the school day (Gilbert and Gay, 1985). Instructional techniques emphasizing competition may conflict with the values of students who come from cultures that prize cooperation and sharing. For these students, peer-mediated instruction and small group activities achieve better results. Adequate teacher preparation should prepare the practitioner to be responsive to the differences in culturally influenced learning styles and to be able to utilize a wider range of appropriate instructional techniques.

There is also the question of preparing girls to function at their maximum potential. Block (1984) asserts that girls are socialized to allow boys to dominate them in order to maintain harmonious relationships with them. School experiences encourage boys to experiment and problem solve and train girls to be unassertive and accommodating. This suggests that attention must be given to providing those educational experiences that would encourage girls to aspire to leadership and mastery.

Educational institutions have traditionally maintained administrative arrangements and policies that have served to inhibit the academic progress of students of color. Chief among these have been the practices of tracking and ability grouping. These practices serve to isolate and segregate students of color within a school, thus reinforcing negative stereotypes and contributing to their low self-esteem and aspirations. Often tracked into classes perceived as depositories for students of limited ability, students of color find their access to higher education effectively blocked, as they are denied the opportunity to acquire those skills and proficiencies that would equip them to pursue college careers. They then have no choice but to enter low-paying occupations.

Biased testing may also contribute to the negative educational experiences of students of color and girls. Standardized tests in common use for college admissions have been criticized as culturally biased, sex biased, and irrelevant to the experiences of students of color (Rosser, 1989). Other assessment instruments have been criticized because they have been normed on a group that is different in race and gender from the students in a particular classroom. Assigning or tracking students of color on the basis of such evaluation procedures is part of a process that limits their options. Ability grouping and tracking should be abandoned in favor of heterogeneous grouping. Different assessment measures that take into account cultural diversity and consciously eliminate biased items and approaches should be devised. Otherwise, large numbers of students of color will continue to be miseducated and poorly tested. Begle's 1972 study (cited in Beane, 1985) and Rosser's recent research (1989) indicate that there is already a body of evidence that standardized tests do not adequately predict the achievement of students of color, girls as well as boys.

By the middle of the next century, if current demographic trends continue, nearly half of the U.S. population will be people of color (see Chapter 2, "The New Demographics," by Lott). The significance of this prediction has not been lost on those concerned with the future technological workplace. Betty Vetter, executive director of the Commission on Professionals in Science and Technology, speaking at the National Association of Minority Engineering Program Administrators Institute in the summer of 1987, noted that: "In order to maintain our technological base, we will surely need more engineers than we can expect to draw from a dwindling white male population. We must therefore not only continue the effort to recruit U.S. minorities and women, we must do whatever is necessary to keep them in school until graduation. . . . Tomorrow is coming and if we don't plan, we won't be ready for it at all."

This defines the problem purely in terms of the national interest. What must also remain a primary concern is the need to educate students of color in an atmosphere that honors and values their diversity. This means rethinking and reshaping educational policies and practices that have operated largely to the advantage of white males. The folly of continuing to pursue these institutional arrangements becomes more and more evident as we compare the projections of the available pool of professional and technical talent with the staggering dropout rate of African Americans, Hispanics, and Native Americans. In addition, Asian American students are reporting negative experiences as a result of being burdened with the "model minority" stereotype (Odin, 1987). Indeed, Asian Americans are being harmed by the perceptions that they are being overrepresented as students at Ivy League schools and that they are narrow and technically oriented. This amounts to "blaming the victim" in a convoluted way. Asian American students are defined as successful and talented only at math and science and they have begun to believe this limiting stereotype. Thus they tend to opt for professions in the scientific and technical fields, remaining underrepresented in other areas.

The students preparing to live and work in the twenty-first century will come largely from populations of color. From the very beginning of their schooling, they should be exposed to an equitable educational atmosphere in institutions whose commitment to cultural diversity is obvious. Such institutions would be characterized by the following: an educational manifesto that affirms a commitment to cultural diversity; a staffing pattern that reflects the pupil population on all levels; administrative procedures that avoid the use of such sorting devices as tracking and ability grouping; and school-home relationships that reach out to parents and involve them in school activities. Such institutions would also be characterized by allocation of sufficient resources, both human and financial, to provide necessary equipment and services. Counseling practices would focus on guiding pupils to reach their maximum potential, advising them of all available options, guiding them toward proper course selection, and providing them with essential information concerning available services. Curriculum experiences would reflect an emphasis on the diverse lives, histories, and cultures of U.S. racial and ethnic groups. Curricula would be evaluated for evidences of race and gender bias as well as other types of bias. Teachers would be provided with continuous opportunities to sharpen their teaching skills and to acquire valid information about the history and culture of the various groups represented among their student population.

Until the major restructuring of the educational system that commitment to cultural diversity demands has been achieved, there are several immediate steps that individual teachers, school administrators, and superintendents can take:

On the classroom level, the individual teacher can begin immediately by rearranging the classroom environment to reflect a commitment to cultural diversity. Action can be taken to enhance pupils' self-concept. From the earliest grades, students can be taught to recognize harmful stereotypes and be helped to understand how and why these stereotypes developed. Historical information, proverbs, folklore, and literature from the groups involved may be used to refute these stereotypes. It is within the power of the individual teacher to adopt instructional techniques that avoid doing violence to the cultural values of the students. Most important of all, the individual teacher must consciously communicate high expectations to all students, provide positive reinforcement to their learning attempts, and treat females and males equally.

School principals and local superintendents have the power to allocate resources and provide opportunities for teachers to gain new information and sharpen their teaching skills. In most cases, however, they do not have the authority to eliminate such negative procedures as ability grouping, tracking, and the use of standardized testing. They may, however, encourage the development of other procedures that would lessen the impact of these practices. Both principals and superintendents can extend their outreach into the community to involve parents and community members in school activities and programs, thus validating them as important participants in their children's education.

There is some indication that people of color are themselves beginning to call for an end to those practices that are limiting educational opportunities for their children. Yet at the same time, students of color, particularly in urban areas, now are being labeled as "children at risk." This term, originally employed to indicate the severity of the problems faced by these youth, is now being employed in educational circles much as the terms "disadvantaged" and "culturally deprived" were used in previous decades. The plight of these children is the direct result of decades of race and sex discrimination and they represent potential dropouts and a tragic waste of human potential. Many professional educators who are people of color view this, quite correctly, as an educational crisis that requires governmental intervention on all levels. In some instances, alliances have been formed with legislators, community agencies, and community members in order to ensure the broadest possible support for such intervention.

It is futile to discuss the need for a pool of "minority" engineers, scientists, and technicians, unless steps are taken to ensure that students of color remain in school through high school and beyond. The broad restructuring of educational programs required can be achieved only with solid governmental support.

Many low-income students and children of color in our cities and towns attend schools that are in advanced states of disrepair. Many of their schools lack the necessary equipment to provide a sound foundation in science. What is needed is a massive infusion of funds from state and federal agencies that would remedy these situations. Government funding of the type formerly provided by the Elementary and Secondary Education Act of 1965 (ESEA) program should be reinstated. These funds could be used to provide stipends for teachers to allow them to return to universities for additional training. They also would provide for the employment of persons from various cultures to serve as consultants to individual schools and school districts. Funding also could provide financial assistance to the students themselves, and if necessary, their families, many of whom cannot easily provide students with the type of assistance (computers at home, for instance) that would allow them to participate in extracurricular activities and even homework important to their academic success. Also worthy of consideration are special incentives for teachers of demonstrated skill to teach in schools with large numbers of students of color; these incentives might include the opportunity to study for a higher degree at a cooperative university. An infusion of funds would also permit the development and dissemination of bias-free texts and curriculum materials that reflect the most current research in curriculum development and evaluation of materials for bias and accuracy of presentation of the lives, histories, and cultures of the nation's various racial and ethnic groups. Students who have special aptitudes and talents could be identified at an early age and be carefully nurtured throughout their educational courses.

The business community has responded to the need for increased minority participation in the scientific professions by instituting "Adopt A School" programs. Concerned individuals have instituted their own incentive programs for youth of color. Much more is needed. In this era of reduced government spending, it is almost heresy to call for massive funding in any area. But the truth is that we will pay now or we will pay later—dearly.

REFERENCES

Beane, D. B. (1985). *Mathematics and science: Critical filters for the future of minority students*. Washington, DC: The American University, Mid-Atlantic Center for Race Equity.

Block, J. H. (1984). *Sex role identity and ego development*. San Francisco, CA: Jossey-Bass.

Bradley, C. (1984). Issues in mathematics education for Native Americans and directions for research. *Journal for Research in Mathematics Education,* 15 (2):96–106.

Braun, M. (1977). Toward teacher training for desegregated schools: Organization, content, and subculture context. *Education and Urban Society,* 9 (3):353–369.

Cheer, H. H. (1984). Increasing the participation of Native Americans in mathematics. *Journal for Research in Mathematics Education,* 15 (2):107–113.

Clark K. (1965). *Dark ghetto*. New York, NY: Harper & Row.

––––––. (1963). *Prejudice and your child*. 2nd ed. Boston, MA: Beacon Press.

Cummins, J. (1986). Empowering minority students: A framework for intervention. *Harvard Educational Review,* 56 (1).

De Nys, M., and Wolfe, L. R. (1985). *Learning her place: Sex bias in the elementary school classroom*. Washington, DC: Project on Equal Education Rights.

Deutsch, M. (1963). The disadvantaged child and the learning process. In H. H. Possow (ed.), *Education in depressed areas*. New York, NY: Teachers College Press.

Frazier, M., and Sadker, M. (1973). *Sexism in school and society*. New York, NY: Harper and Row.

Gilbert, S. E., II, and Gay, G. (1985). Improving the success in school of poor black children. *Phi Delta Kappan,* 67 (2):133–137.

Gollub, W., and Sloane, E. (1978). Teacher expectations and race and socioeconomic status. *Urban Education,* 13 (1):95–106.

Good, T. L. (1981). Teacher expectations and student perceptions: A decade of research. *Educational Leadership,* 38 (5):415–422.

Jackson, J. J. (1973). Black women in a racist society. In C. V. Willis, B. H. Kramer, B. S. Brown (eds.), *Racism and mental health.* Pittsburgh, PA: University of Pittsburgh Press.

King, L. M. (1974). Puertorriqueñas in the United States. *Civil Rights Digest,* 6 (3):20–27.

Klassen, F. H., and Gollnick, D. (eds.) (1977). *Pluralism and the American teacher: Issues and case studies.* Washington, DC: American Association of Colleges for Teacher Education.

Matthews, W. (1984). Influences on the learning and participation of minorities in mathematics. *Journal for Research in Mathematics Education,* 15 (2):84–93.

Mazer, G. E. (1971). Effects of social class stereotyping on teacher expectations. *Psychology in the Schools,* 8:373–398.

Moore, C. G. (1988). Mathematics-like principles inferred from the petroglyphs. *Journal of American Indian Education,* 27 (2):30–36.

National Council for Accreditation of Teacher Education (1979). *Standards for the accreditation of teacher education.* Washington, DC: NCATE.

Oakes, J. (1987). Curriculum inequity and school reform. *Equity and Excellence,* 23 (2).

—— (1986). Keeping track, part I: The policy and practice of curriculum inequality. *Phi Delta Kappan,* 68 (1):12–17.

—— (1983). Limiting opportunity: Student race and curricular differences in secondary vocational education. *American Journal of Education,* 91 (3):328–355.

Odin, P. (1987). Asian American enrollments: A dilemma of competing values. *Black Issues in Higher Education,* 4 (15):8–9.

Richardson, R. C., Jr., Simmons, H., and de los Santos, A. C., Jr. (1987). Meeting the needs of minority students. *Change,* 19 (3):20–27.

Rist, R. C. (1970). Students' social class and teacher expectations: The self-fulfilling prophecy in ghetto classrooms. *Harvard Educational Review,* 40:411–451.

Rosser, P. (1989). *The SAT gender gap: Identifying the causes.* Washington, DC: Center for Women Policy Studies.

Rowe, M. B. (1977). Why don't Blacks pick science? *Science Teacher,* 44:34–35.

Sears, P. (1963). *The effect of classroom conditions on the strengths of achievement, motive and work output of elementary school children.* Washington, DC: U.S. Government Printing Office.

Washington, V. (1982). Racial differences in teacher perceptions of first and fourth grade pupils on selected characteristics. *Journal of Negro Education,* 51 (1).

Witt, S. H. (1974). Native women today. *Civil Rights Digest,* 6 (3):29–35.

Yee, A. H. (1968). Interpersonal attitudes of teachers and advantaged and disadvantaged youth. *Journal of Human Relations,* 3 (3):327–345.

Yoshioka, R. B. (1974). Asian American women: Stereotyping Asian women. *Civil Rights Digest,* 6 (3):43–47.

Zaslavsky, C. (1973). *Africa counts.* Boston, MA: Prindle, Weber and Schmidt.

PART THREE

New Careers: Preparing Women for the Professions, for Technical Jobs, and for the Skilled Trades

7

Equitable Computer Education for Girls and Boys of Color

CAROL EDWARDS

THE PROBLEM

Computers are creating profound changes in every aspect of life. The way we work, communicate, and spend leisure time have all been affected by computers. They have ushered in a new age—the Information Age—that already is a household word. Although the role of computers in the postindustrial United States has been vilified by some and exalted by others, all agree that the workplace will never be the same. Computers have played a role in the decrease of manufacturing jobs and the increase of service jobs; they have contributed to the increased rate of job obsolescence, the elimination of low-skill jobs, the generation of very low and very high wage occupations, and the increased ease of some jobs and the increased difficulty of others. The productivity of computers, especially in the workplace, means that they are not just another fad. Because part of education's mission is to prepare youth to successfully meet the future, schools must deal with the tools of the Information Age.[1]

COMPUTERS IN ELEMENTARY AND SECONDARY SCHOOLS

Prior to the 1980s, computers were too expensive for most schools to use as instructional devices. Since the invention of the microcomputer, however, enthusiasm among educators for their instructional use has been tremendous. The earliest groundswell developed in communities where men used computers on their jobs and recognized their significance early. In such communities, expertise, financial support, and general clout worked together. Their children's schools acquired microcomputers. By

1983 the rush to acquire microcomputers had spread throughout the suburbs. Perhaps it is not an exaggeration to say that microcomputers acquired some of the Yuppie mystique of designer handbags; it became chic to have them. Fortunately, other, more substantive, reasons also fueled the acquisitive urge.

The growth of microcomputers used for instructional purposes has been substantial in a relatively short time. In 1981, 16.5 percent of schools had at least one instructional microcomputer; by 1983, 66.8 percent of schools used microcomputers and in 1988, the rate was up to 94.9 percent (Quality Education Data, 1988). The installed base of microcomputers in schools increased from less than 1 million in 1984 to 3 million in 1987; in 1990 it was expected to be 5.6 million (Ritchie, 1988). In 1983, there was an average of 125 students to 1 machine, but by 1987 the ratio had dropped to about 30 to 1 (QED, 1988).

The early history of instructional computing was largely "entrepreneurial." Interest in microcomputers was often championed by an enthusiastic teacher, usually a high school math teacher, who proselytized the virtues of microcomputers in his or her school. Enlisting a few of their precocious students of high math ability, these teachers pioneered the introduction of microcomputers. Most of the enthusiast teachers were self-taught through independent study and trial and error; they devoted many hours of their own time and money to their new love. Because of the knowledge and visibility this early use afforded them, they became the first computer coordinators, making important administrative decisions that shaped school and district acquisition and use of microcomputers.

Most pioneer computer teachers were white males, as were their computer students. Districts with few resources, such as large urban and small rural ones, had neither the funds nor the expertise to acquire and use instructional microcomputers as quickly as suburban districts did. Traditional patterns of relationships between low-income parents, especially parents of color, and educators did not lead to the intensity of community pressure to acquire microcomputers that was exerted and heeded in wealthy districts.

Moreover, it was during these early years, 1980 to 1984, that the Reagan administration began its substantial reduction in federal support to education. Chapter 2 of the Education Consolidation and Improvement Act of 1981 (ECIA), the "block grant," redirected Emergency School Aid Act of 1972 (ESAA) resources away from their former targets, students who were educationally disadvantaged as a result of years of segregation. Chapter 1, which replaced the former Title 1, also reduced the amount of funding many educators of educationally disadvantaged students had anticipated. Often newly eligible Chapter 2 schools used their federal block grant funds to purchase microcomputer hardware and software.

For example, from 1982 to 1983, 56 percent of 2,500 schools responding to a survey conducted by the American Association of School Administrators indicated that they used Chapter 2 funds for hardware or software (Boes, 1984). Some Chapter 1 Migrant Education and Special Education funds also were used to provide microcomputers; however, regulations restricted their use to eligible children and often meant that the computers and software had to be physically separated from the equipment or materials used by the rest of the school.

By 1983 an alarming pattern was beginning to develop in microcomputer access. Affluent districts were more likely to have computers than were the poor urban districts that schooled about one-third to one-half of African American and Hispanic children. In 1983, 44 percent of schools in which less than 5 percent of the students were classified as poor had microcomputers, compared to only 12 percent of schools with over 25 percent poor students. In 1984, rich schools had one microcomputer for every fifty-four students, economically disadvantaged schools, one for every seventy-three. Worse, the gap grew from an average of 2.2 microcomputers to 3.8 between 1983 and 1984 (Hood, 1984). The south, with its large African American population, was the region least likely to have microcomputers in the schools. Although 97 percent of inner-city schools had at least one microcomputer in 1988, the per student ratio still showed a gap when compared to affluent schools.

People of color also were less likely to have access to microcomputers in the home. Profiles of home computer owners in 1983 showed that they were most often college-educated males with incomes over $35,000.[2] In 1985, 26 percent of families with incomes over $40,000 owned home computers, while only 3 percent of those with incomes less than $10,000 owned computers (Ancarrow, 1986). According to a survey of southern, predominantly economically disadvantaged and African American students conducted by the Southern Coalition For Educational Equity, 17.5 percent owned home computers compared to 32.8 percent owned nationally among a predominantly white group of similar age (Edwards and Irvine, 1987). Even in affluent families, however, parents were less likely to purchase home computers for girls and less likely to send their daughters to computer camp (Project on Equal Education Rights [PEER], 1985).

To obtain a complete picture of microcomputer use, factors such as instructional patterns, teacher expertise, and counseling should be considered. A 1983 study of microcomputer use revealed that at the elementary school level, students averaged twenty minutes per week of hands-on time (Becker, 1983–1984). These users primarily engaged in computer literacy, that is, learning to operate a microcomputer. Their second most frequent use was drill and practice, or computer-aided instruction (CAI). Few children used microcomputers for applications (such as word processing), programming, or higher-order thinking skills. Students of color received drill and practice exclusively (Becker, 1983–1984). This use pattern was underscored by the results of the first national assessment of computer competence, in which students scored highest on questions about computer operation, compared to questions about computer applications (such as spreadsheets) or programming; and ethnic and gender scoring gaps appeared favoring white boys (Martinez and Mead, 1988).

At the high school level, use patterns differed. Fewer students used microcomputers but with more hands-on time, about 45 minutes per week. It was not unusual to find the most intense use of microcomputers among students in advanced math or computer science courses where girls and students of color were underrepresented. Secondary school students of color were more likely to use microcomputers for drill and practice, and less likely to use them for programming, applications, or higher-order thinking skills (Becker, 1986).

A 1985 follow-up study found increased and somewhat different use patterns (Becker, 1986). While elementary students' hands-on time had increased to about 35 minutes per week, it was still small. Another study found similarly that at least 56 percent of seventh graders and 61 percent of eleventh graders spent less than 30 minutes per week using computers to aid subject matter instruction and less than 10 minutes on computer applications (Martinez and Mead, 1988). However, time spent on computer applications was growing compared to computer operation and CAI, especially at the secondary level. Elementary schools, where CAI was still relatively high, showed no difference in use by race. At the high school level, however, students of color continued to use microcomputers disproportionately for drill.

The National Assessment of Educational Progress (NAEP) study conducted by Martinez and Mead, the largest national computer assessment conducted to date, contained findings similar to those of several previously cited studies. It found that African American and Hispanic students had less access to computers than whites. For example, 20 percent of African American and Hispanic eleventh graders had never used a computer compared to 11 percent of white eleventh graders. Since the study concluded that computer competence was strongly related to computer experience, the lower level of computer competence reported among African American and Hispanic students across all grade levels, about 5 to 8 percent on average compared to white students (Martinez and Mead, 1988), was partially due to the "access gap."

The study showed that there was little difference in the level of computer competence by *where* computer experience was attained. Therefore, children who used computers at home but not in school achieved results similar to or slightly higher than those who had school, but no home, access. Those who had access both at home and school reported the highest competence. The advantage of home computer use compounded the disadvantage for children of color, because they were 4.7 to 10.7 percent less likely to come from families that owned home computers (Martinez and Mead, 1988).

However, home and school access alone does not account for the differences in computer competence among children of color and whites. Even among African American and Hispanic students who had comparable school use and home ownership rates compared to whites, the study reported slightly lower computer competence scores. Future research may explore reasons for these differences, such as bias in assessment instruments, low teacher expectations for children of color, and unavailability of role models. A finding confirmed by this study was that expert computer teachers were substantially less likely to be found in schools with large numbers of students of color and that people of color as role models were extremely rare. It reported only 4.4 percent of African American and 1.1 percent of Hispanic computer coordinators worked at the eleventh grade level (Martinez and Mead, 1988). Seventh grade percentages were comparable. Although no data exist that document the extent of biased and/or poor computer-related counseling, informal observations among educational computing educators indicate that there may be a problem.

The NAEP study showed small gender-related differences in computer competence favoring boys. Although these differences were less than 1 percent for third graders, they grew to almost 3 percent at the seventh and eleventh grades. Girls were almost as likely as boys to use computers in school classes, although boys began to use computers earlier than girls. However, the greatest differences occurred in the home, where girls were 5.6 percent to 10.1 percent less likely to have access to a home computer than boys (Martinez and Mead, 1988). This gap increased with age.

Although none of these studies reported data by gender within race and ethnic group, the implication for girls of color is clear. They are most likely to experience the least amount of computer access because of relatively large race and ethnic gaps at school and relatively large gender gaps at home. This lack of access correlates directly to their opportunity to achieve computer competence, especially in areas that require long and intensive computer use, such as programming.

COMPUTERS IN COLLEGE

At the postsecondary level a similar pattern of problems is evident. Historically black colleges and other colleges with large enrollments of students of color are less well equipped and staffed than affluent, white colleges and universities (International Association for Computing in Education, 1984). Furthermore, people of color are more likely to attend proprietary schools which often provide inadequate instruction, offering high-tech hype but dead-end courses and poor counseling. Women are overrepresented in word processing and data entry, men in computer technician courses. Lack of transportation and affordable child care restrict the access of women of color to the best of these institutions and contribute to a high dropout rate.

Reductions and eligibility changes in financial aid, enacted during the Reagan administration, paralleled a yearly decrease in the number of students of color attending college from 1980 to 1986. Financial aid cuts exacerbated the traditional problems that women and people of color face in pursuing mathematics and science; further, colleges with no computer science major often place computer courses under the mathematics or engineering departments.

One bright note is that because it is still relatively new as an academic discipline, a lack of high school computer science does not preclude it as a college major. On the other hand, computer science courses require long and often solitary laboratory hours in uninviting surroundings (frequently windowless basements). At best, since most graduate assistants and professors have not received equity training, they can be culturally insensitive and, at worst, downright abusive. Women of color face additional gender-related problems, such as sexual harassment.

A combination of these factors results in few people of color seeking and completing college or graduate degrees in computer science (see Table 7.1; NCES, 1986). The one encouraging exception is among Asian American men. In 1985, one American Indian, one African American and one Hispanic—all men—were awarded Ph.D.s in computer science. At the masters level, 13.5 percent of the degrees conferred in computer and information science were awarded to people of color, about 40 percent of whom were Asian American, including about one-third women. In 1986, 15 percent of the persons who took the Graduate Record Examination with the intention of majoring in computer science were people of color, about half of whom were Asian American. Only 11.2 percent of the computer science bachelor's degrees were awarded to people of color, two-thirds to Asian Americans.

WORKPLACE PROBLEMS—TWO OCCUPATIONS

The growth of microcomputers in education, as in business, has created new jobs. Two occupations and related equity problems are considered here: computer coordinator and educational software developer.

Table 7.1 Computer and Information Science Majors

	Men	Women	Total
Bachelor's Degrees			
White	20,188	11,133	31,321
Black	1,036	1,107	2,143
Hispanic	484	342	826
Asian	1,158	886	2,044
Amer. Indian	76	63	139
Nonresident	1,444	672	2,116
All	24,386	14,203	38,589
Master's Degrees			
White	3,052	1,251	4,303
Black	108	72	180
Hispanic	65	29	94
Asian	414	201	615
Amer. Indian	28	13	41
Nonresident	1,269	440	1,709
All	4,936	2,006	6,942
Doctoral Degrees			
White	131	19	150
Black	3	0	3
Hispanic	2	0	2
Asian	13	1	14
Amer. Indian	1	0	1
Nonresident	66	4	70
All	216	24	240

Source: U.S. Dept. of Education, National Center for Education Statistics (1986). *Degrees and Other Formal Awards Conferred Survey.* Washington, DC: U.S. Government Printing Office.

Computer Coordinator

Computer coordinators are responsible for microcomputers in education at the state, local district, or individual school level. Their responsibilities generally include identifying and assessing computer-related needs, selecting and purchasing hardware and software, training faculty and other personnel, teaching students, maintaining hardware and software, installing or managing the installation of computer equipment, writing computer programs, and developing computer-related curriculum. They may work with computers to facilitate administrative information processing, such as district-wide attendance reporting, instructional management, student learning, or any combination of the three. Generally, there are computer coordinators at both the school and district levels.

According to a 1987 survey (McGinty, 1987), two-thirds of instructional computer coordinators at the school level had part-time teaching responsibilities. (In a 1989 survey [Bruder, 1990], men outnumbered women by 55 percent to 44 percent, and the proportion of men had grown 8 percent from the previous year.) There were more women coordinators at the elementary level, more men at the high school level. District-level coordinators were less likely to teach as many classes and more likely to have larger computer-related budgets than were school-level coordinators. District-level coordinators also were somewhat more likely to be employed full time and generally earned higher salaries. The gender disparity among district-level coordinators was even greater; 68 percent were male and only 32 percent were female. Men at both the district and school levels earned higher salaries than women. Comparative data on earnings of computer coordinators who are people of color were unavailable.

Although the majority of computer coordinators possess master's degrees, very few have degrees in computer science or educational technology. Most computer coordinators emerged from the grassroots, with math or business education backgrounds. It is unlikely that many computer coordinators have had equity training. Because their backgrounds are in areas where women and people of color are either underrepresented or highly stratified, it is easy to ascertain why many problems in microcomputer equity remain unaddressed.

Most computer coordinators (77 percent) reported being satisfied with their jobs, although some problems were cited, including inadequate salaries, a condition that characterizes education generally. National average salaries were $38,000 for district-level coordinators and $27,200 for school-level coordinators. In 1987, a systems analyst with comparable experience (15 years) could expect to earn about $39,000. Computer coordinators also reported disliking the long work hours that resulted from understaffing.

The other most commonly stated concern among computer coordinators was an inadequate budget. In 1987, schools spent approximately $2,000–$5,800 on instructional technology, depending on size and geographic region. Although the cost of computer hardware was declining, it was still relatively expensive, at $500–$1,500 per unit. The cost of software was rising. Security, maintenance, and training were also major cost factors. Computer coordinators found that budget constraints frustrated their efforts to deliver a high-quality program to all students.

Computer coordinators who are people of color primarily serve in districts and schools that contain large numbers of children of color. They face serious challenges and pressures. For example, in large urban districts where decision making is bureaucratic, computer coordinators sometimes lack the flexibility and authority to respond creatively to the opportunities offered by this new technology. In small rural districts serving African American, Hispanic, or Native American communities, computer coordinators lack even the most basic resources, in both money and expertise. However, educational leaders and the concerned public in such districts often possess unrealistic expectations concerning what educational computing can accomplish and are tempted to view the microcomputer as a neat, tangible panacea to "fix" schools.

No one knows how these factors affect the attractiveness of the job to people of color. Given other occupational experiences, it is more likely that other factors, such as institutional racism, lack of computer experience, fewer computers in schools with the highest numbers of teachers of color, and lack of role models and mentors have more significance in keeping the number of computer coordinators who are people of color small. The future looks discouraging. As computer science and educational computing degrees become a more important prerequisite for computer coordinators, underrepresentation of people of color will probably increase. In 1989, schools spent an average of $2,450 on instructional technology, which is less than the school-level budgets of previous years (Bruder, 1990).

Educational Software Developer

A software developer designs and creates new software, often as part of a team. Some software developers also market their products, while others sell their software to publishers. Most early CAI software was designed to tutor or drill the learner in basic skills, was relatively easy to program, and fit the math background of many programmers. As the number of microcomputers began to grow, however, so did the diversity, sophistication, and educational value of software. Some educators felt that teaching programming was not the best use of computers for all students at every level. They wanted subject-specific and tool software. Teachers, therefore, began to write programs and sell them to others and a cottage industry began to develop. Composed of former teachers who fell in love with computing, computer professionals involved with educational computing on mainframes in the 1960s and the 1970s, and young, interested college graduates, the educational software development field was overwhelmingly white and predominantly male.

Communities of educational software developers began to solidify in the Silicon Valley, California, Minneapolis, the Boston-Washington corridor, and a few other areas, mostly located in the suburbs or near universities. State-of-the-art research and thinking occurred in these places, making them desirable places to work. However, their racial and ethnic isolation made them unattractive to many people of color. Although there are no data on the percentage of software developers who are people of color, it would be surprising to find more than 1 or 2 percent.

As the industry matures, the amount of capital needed to start a software firm is increasing. Competition is keen, and the industry is experiencing a shakeout; large publishing vendors also are beginning to enter the market. These factors contribute to the difficulties faced by people of color who would like to start software companies, but whose resources are limited.

Methods for developing good software are becoming more complex, usually requiring a team of persons with a variety of specialties including an instructional design expert, a programmer, a technical writer, a graphic artist, and a software engineer. These occupations are all fields in which people of color are underrepresented (Green and Epstein, 1988). Companies engaging development teams for software projects generally rely on word-of-mouth recommendations to hire staff or consultants. This informal "old boys and girls" network is de facto closed to minorities and minority-owned firms. Limited marketing experience, lack of access to distribution networks, and the high-risk nature and financial instability of the product compound the likelihood that people of color will continue to be underrepresented as software developers.

The existing situation in both professions, computer coordinator and software developer, illustrates the problems that people of color, particularly women of color, face in high technology. As these occupations grow and become more mainstream, they begin to exclude women at the highest levels. Institutional racism reinforces a vicious cycle of exclusion of people of color from educational computing as consumers, producers, and a part of the product. Not only does it limit access to lucrative, exciting, and rewarding new occupations but it also robs educational technology of the very people who are likely to bring diversity, vitality, richness, creativity, and advocacy to serve children of color.

EDUCATIONAL COMPUTING AS TODDLER

To complicate quantitative and qualitative access problems, the field of educational computing also suffers from relative immaturity and fluidity. Early in the development of microcomputers, limited memory, slow processing speed, novelty, and cost considerations contributed to the focus of computer usage on programming and drill CAI. As computer hardware changed so did computer software. Attributes often were added to software because hardware advances made them possible, but their instructional value was not objectively considered. Rather, features were attributed value because they were technically spectacular. More graphics and sounds, color, and other features were added to instructional software which appealed to the senses but contained no redeeming educational value. All too often technology drove reason, not reason, technology. Instances of this phenomenon are still common today.

However, computer educators have begun to define those characteristics that meet learning objectives effectively. For example, a series of national field studies on effective microcomputer use is being conducted at the Johns Hopkins University. Several meta-analyses of educational computing research are being conducted. More and better evaluations are being carried out as part of computing instruction. These evaluations have raised many questions: What is a critical mass of hands-on time? What are valuable uses of microcomputers? To whom are they valuable? How should and can educational institutions change to reap the full instructional benefits of microcomputers? What are the characteristics of effective software? Can microcomputers help in the teaching of problem solving and critical thinking? What will the next evolutionary breakthrough mean,[3] and how can it be made beneficial to teaching and learning? Where does teacher training fit in the instructional computing equation? Will the cost/value ratio of microcomputers increase in the near future? Can microcomputers reduce teaching-related costs? The answers to these and similar questions will improve the effectiveness of microcomputers as instructional tools.

A note of caution is appropriate, however. A popular poster of the 1960s pictured an orangutan slapping its forehead with the heel of its hand, a puzzled expression on its face. The caption read, "Just when I thought I had all the answers, they came up with new questions!" And so it goes in the world of educational computing. Technological breakthroughs, a better understanding of cognitive science, instructional design, and software engineering, and the speed of change and social acceptance of computers—all add new questions.

Today's educational computing professionals are parents to a developing toddler. As they try to cope with the changing environment caused by this toddler, the needs of learners who are girls and young women of color must not be overlooked.

THE SOLUTIONS

Changing the Perpetrator

It has become common for people to blame the victim rather than the criminal—the perpetrator in police lingo. For instance, a man leaves his wallet in a supermarket cart while shopping, and the wallet is stolen. Customers who witness the scene fault the man for inviting the thief to take the wallet by leaving it unattended in the cart. Similarly, society often blames women of color, the victims, for the practices and results of racism and sexism. In education, the various environmental and cultural differences of minority, economically disadvantaged, female, and disabled children all too often form a ready excuse for poor instructional practices, inadequately designed instructional materials, and the sociocultural prejudices of educators. Indeed, the "failure" of these children to conform to white, male, upper-middle-class norms is seen as a fault of the children and their race and/or gender rather than as a sign that these norms—and the classroom environment they have produced—are limited, insufficient, and in need of change.

To eliminate educational inequities, profound change must occur in the *will* of educators to succeed with populations they are currently failing. School officials and policymakers must stop blaming and devaluing parents, home life, and the children themselves. Successful solutions follow from asking and answering the right questions. The lesson is clear for the development of instructional computing; the question for educators is not how they can correct *learning* deficiencies with microcomputers, but rather how they can correct *teaching* deficiencies with microcomputers. It is this spirit, changing the *perpetrator,* that characterizes the solutions proposed in the remainder of this chapter.

The Federal Level

The federal government can make a significant contribution to the reduction of qualitative and quantitative inequities. Since 1980, legislation has been proposed in Congress that would specifically assist local school districts to acquire computers, either through direct grants or tax incentives to the computer industry for gifts to schools (Stedman, 1988). Much of this legislation is targeted toward economically disadvantaged schools and some includes funds for software and teacher training. None of this legislation has ever been passed.

Federal funds for microcomputer acquisition have come through legislation that allowed schools to purchase instructional supplies. Such provisions were broadly interpreted so as not to prevent their use for the purchase of hardware and software. Legislation to improve math, science, and technology education has also allowed the limited purchase of microcomputers as a means to develop programs in those areas.

It is time to fund direct legislation to help schools in economically disadvantaged communities purchase computers. With such assistance boys and girls of color, who are overrepresented in economically disadvantaged schools, will gain the critical mass of hardware,[4] software, and training needed to achieve equitable, excellent technology usage. This legislation could take the form of a combination of tax incentives to the industry and direct grants to schools, with support services in the form of teacher training (including equity training) required.

Another approach to this problem is to substantially reduce hardware costs, while continuing to provide state-of-the-art computing power. Federal incentives to computer manufacturers toward that end could make a significant contribution. Federally sponsored research and development in establishing standards for hardware and operating system compatibility also possess great potential for cost reduction. Federal incentives to cut the cost of upgrades, such as tax incentives to industry for deeply discounted buy-back programs for economically disadvantaged schools, should also be considered. Programs through which schools lease hardware and software from third parties should be piloted.

Legislation has also been proposed regularly, but never passed, that would fund educational software research and development. Most federally funded software development is agency specific. For example, the National Science Foundation makes grants to support development of science education software. Nonscientific subjects, particularly the humanities, receive little federal assistance. Much of the federally funded advanced research in software development, such as the development of expert systems, occurs through military-related funding and may take a long time to reach the general public. In neither case are there incentives to include people of color and women in the development process. Typically, federally supported software is developed by and field tested with few or no people of color and with minimal concern for its impact on women.

Federal support should be provided for all areas of software development but only to those efforts that meet exemplary equity standards. A federal center comprised of equity experts, instructional specialists, programmers, cognitive psychologists, software and human factors engineers, teachers, instructional designers, arts and graphics designers, writers, and others should be established to develop both exemplary software and a model *process* for creating software. As a part of its software research effort, the U.S. Department of Education should support evaluations of software for equity; these evaluations should be widely distributed.

Federal funding for assessment in all areas of educational computing is recommended. Little legislation that would specifically fund educational computing assessment has been passed by Congress. Indeed, most research in educational computing outside the military, especially at the precollege level, although improving, has been sparse, short term, and involved small samples.

A federal role in assessment is appropriate in two ways. Federal funding for educational computing in any form should include reporting and evaluation requirements for *disaggregated* data by race, ethnicity, sex, and disability. Such reporting should eventually include federal funds that are used for all instructional materials, so that programs such as Chapter 2, widely used for computer-related purchases, are included. Second, women and people of color should be well represented among assessors in all federally sponsored evaluations. Federally supported assessment should include instrument development as well as qualitative and quantitative assessments.

Direct and indirect federal funding and policy leadership could assist in the prevention of further inequities in educational computing. Federal funding should support the development, dissemination, and replication of good computer equity models, teacher training in educational computing in economically disadvantaged schools, and computer-related vocational and technical programs targeted toward girls and women of color. A larger share of the funds for postsecondary-level work in educational computing should be granted to minority colleges and universities. Federal policy should also support equity for women and people of color in educational computing indirectly, by supporting strong child care legislation, restoring aid to higher education, strongly enforcing civil rights laws, and providing strong executive leadership in advocating equity.

The State Level

States have varied in their support of educational computing; however, every state has played some role. Most states have or are computerizing the reporting and administration of educational data; and some states have provided computers to local districts for that purpose. States have contributed to precollege, local school instructional computing primarily in three ways. First, they have enacted legislation to fund the acquisition of hardware and/or software for local schools. But generally these distribution formulas do not correct for district wealth. Second, some states have developed curricula to teach about computers (computer literacy) and/or have developed certification standards for faculty who teach with computers. Third, states have provided technical assistance to local districts to implement educational computing. This assistance usually takes the form of training for teachers or teacher trainers, reduced rates for the purchase of hardware, software, and supplies, software preview centers, state-wide educational technology conferences, and the like. At the postsecondary level, some states have updated and added microcomputers in vocational schools and community colleges. Several states have also begun to regulate proprietary schools more closely.

States should provide more assistance for hardware and software acquisition and teacher training to economically disadvantaged urban and rural schools and community colleges. Allocation of state-controlled federal funds should be weighted toward educationally disadvantaged learners.

State trainers should provide equity training to local schools and disseminate good equity models to local districts. State-sponsored conferences and other professional development opportunities should always include equity as an important component of each part of the program, *not* as a separate session.

States should make equity standards part of the criteria for state contracts. For example, software vendors should be required to provide evidence that their product was field tested with people of color and women and includes sensitive portrayals of people of color and women in all graphic representations of people. If large states such as California, Texas, New York, and Florida had such criteria in place, changes in software would occur more rapidly. All states should affirmatively seek to increase the number of minority vendors, especially women of color, seeking and being awarded computer-related contracts. Evaluations and recommendations at state software preview facilities should highlight equity. Indeed, more men and women of color should be promoted to key jobs, such as state computer coordinator and assistant commissioner for technology.

States should also assist in achieving equity by collecting disaggregated data by race, ethnicity, sex, and disability. Equity behaviors should be included in state assessments of district programs. Equity should be an integral part of state-developed assessment instruments.

Finally, states that choose to establish a computer curriculum should build in specific learning objectives related to equity. Curriculum field tests should include equity criteria, particularly for new computer programming and computer repair courses. Computer-related certification requirements should be assessed as they are developed to ensure they do not adversely impact minority and female teachers.

The Local Level

At the local precollege level, most school districts have a long-range technology plan. Generally the computers purchased according to these plans are distributed equally among schools, regardless of need. School districts often allow school or parent-generated funds to be used as the school wishes. Therefore, some schools have a substantial number of community-generated microcomputers. In some communities, volunteers or businesses that have "adopted" a school provide teaching or teacher training assistance. Although comprehensive long-range technology planning is beginning to change this pattern, at both the precollege and community college level the quality of microcomputer use, and to a lesser extent, the quantity of microcomputers, depend on having a strong local advocate. The result of these practices is great variation in the availability of microcomputers and the quality of educational computing available to individual students. As a rule, high-ability students at wealthy schools have the most hands-on time and use microcomputers the most for higher-order thinking; "slow learners" have the least amount of both (Becker, 1983–1984).

School districts and postsecondary institutions should adopt effective computer equity models. Individual schools or departments should be assessed for their equity practices. Data collection should be disaggregated, as previously recommended. Equity training should not only be provided to computer-using teachers and computer science professors, but also to principals, counselors, and graduate assistants. Counselors and principals often have the greatest impact on student course selection and scheduling. Their awareness of the influence they can have in encouraging students of color, especially girls, could make a positive difference in the composition of intermediate and advanced computer science courses.

There are many actions that local schools and postsecondary institutions can take to promote equity for boys and girls of color. They can allocate a greater percent of technology funds to teacher training. In order to integrate computers into learning and emphasize higher-order thinking skills a great deal of training is necessary. Good equity practices should be an integral part of this training.[5]

As curriculum is developed on the local level, equity should be consciously included. Manuals and materials used should be selected only if they address equity concerns. Programming courses should be redesigned to draw from the diverse cultures and environments of the students. For example, programming should be collaborative; beginning programming activities should be meaningful, not boring data entry exercises, and research should be conducted to ascertain which programming languages appeal most to boys and girls of color. Once good programming instruction is developed, it should be made an essential part of the curriculum. In order not to be excluded from some of the most lucrative jobs of the future, all students should be required to take enough programming to be able to enter the computer science pipeline.

Two non-computer-specific practices that will foster equity at the precollege level are: eliminating the widespread practice of tracking and encouraging parental involvement. Tracking is a very serious problem emerging in the use of microcomputers. At all levels teachers perceive microcomputers to benefit high-ability students most. Because a disproportionate number of students of color, especially boys, are assigned to and remain in the lowest tracks, they receive less hands-on time and more remedial drill. Low teacher expectations with regard to the ability of students of color to benefit academically from microcomputers for uses other than remedial CAI poses one of the most severe threats to learning that economically disadvantaged students of color—both male and female—continue to face.

An increasing number of school districts are establishing computer lending libraries. After attending a training workshop, parents can borrow a computer and software for home use for a specified period of time. Such programs have been highly popular, with very little loss or damage to equipment. Parents who are least likely to participate in microcomputer lending programs, however, are those with limited literacy skills; coupling adult literacy programs with home lending programs is one way to involve parents who are hard to reach.

Professional Associations and Unions

Professional educational associations and unions can encourage equity for boys and girls of color in several ways. They can advocate for federal, state, and local policies that foster equity in educational computing. They can sponsor conferences, seminars, and other professional development opportunities for members that emphasize computer equity. Finally, they can support the hiring and promotion of more people of color and women to key positions in educational computing.

Hardware Vendors

Hardware vendors should test new products with boys and girls of color. Advertising should include more people of color in nontraditional, active roles. They should encourage people of color to become third-party developers, use minority vendors, and conduct more joint research on minority college campuses. Hardware vendors should locate facilities inside large city limits, so that tax dollars and jobs are available to benefit urban youngsters and their parents.

By allocating a larger percentage of the company's philanthropic dollars to projects that bring boys and girls of color into the pipeline, hardware vendors support their own future productivity. The skills necessary to maintain leadership in the computer industry will only be available to the degree that knowledgeable, bright, confident, and creative young people continue to join the work force. If today's youth, so many of whom are children of color, are not prepared to keep the nation's technology on the cutting edge, the vendors themselves will be hurt. The elimination of many children of color begins with early tracking practices. Vendors can provide leadership to reverse this trend by targeting grants to early intervention programs. Most importantly, they must change the structure and practices of their corporations to hire and promote women and people of color equitably. Establishing rewards in the corporate culture for equity, providing equity training for all workers, using affirmative personnel practices, and replacing the "old boys" network with a more open system that encourages diversity and risk taking are some of the ways they can correct underrepresentation of people of color, especially women, in their companies.

Software Vendors and Developers

The recommendations made for hardware vendors apply to software developers and publishers as well. For example, providing equity training to staff, a practice that could be instituted immediately, would help in the development of high-quality software. Field and outcome testing of software with people of color would add significantly to the validity of products. More importantly, software developers can become proactive in the inclusion of diverse ethnic cultures and environments in the themes, graphics, and design of their software products. More people of color should be hired and promoted in software companies. Joint ventures with partners who have equity expertise would improve software products. The advertising and philanthropic sensitivity recommended for hardware vendors also applies to software vendors.

Parents and Communities

Parents and interested community citizens should monitor educational computing practices in schools for qualitative and quantitative equity (PEER, 1985). They should become active consumer advocates, evaluating hardware and software, and communicating their critiques to vendors. For example, when parents purchase hardware and software, equity should be a part of their selection criteria. Moreover, they should express their equity concerns to vendors. Parents and others can volunteer as computer aides in schools and enlist the participation of role models in the community. Parents can respond to the double jeopardy of girls of color by encouraging them to use computers outside of school.

CONCLUSION

Currently there is a great opportunity to create success with populations that educators have traditionally failed. In the process, the quality and relevance of schools can be improved for all learners. The key to success is risk taking. Educators must be willing to substantively change schools to take advantage of microcomputers as learning tools. This means altering the very structure of schools. The notion of education as a five-day-per-week collection of six fifty-minute periods, during which a knowledge expert, the teacher, imparts a collection of right or wrong answers determined by white, male norms to selected students, must be discarded. The view of education that replaces it must be a flexible day in which teachers, serving as facilitators of learning, can value various ethnic cultures and environments and stress higher-order thinking for all students, using a wide variety of teaching/learning strategies and tools.

With the excitement and motivation that educational technology has caused, educators have a unique opportunity to revolutionize and restructure many institutional practices. They should use this opportunity to make education work for boys and girls of color. Given demographic projections, educating people of color to become thoughtful problem solvers and decision makers who use technology knowledgeably could well mean the difference between power or weakness for the United States in the twenty-first century. In the words of an anonymous proverb, "When the chickens come home to the roost, may foresight have made it warm, dry, full of corn, and sweet music."

NOTES

1. One of the greatest difficulties in describing the nature and extent of the problem of access to educational and recreational computing by girls and women of color is the way in which data are collected. Virtually no data are available in a disaggregated format. Therefore, data in this paper will generally appear by race or by sex, but rarely by sex within racial or ethnic group.

2. Home computer data by race and ethnicity are not available for 1983; however, data by income is relevant because almost half of children of color live in families at or below the poverty line.

3. These breakthroughs include sophisticated voice input, intelligent integrated multimedia, and transparent interface.

4. Although there has not been enough research to suggest the definitive critical mass, some experts suggest that it is reached when enough microcomputers are present to permit each student at least four hours hands-on time per week, or about one computer for every four students.

5. For examples of effective equity training models for women and girls, see materials produced through the Women's Educational Equity Act, available through the WEEA Publishing Center, 55 Chapel Street, Newton, MA 02160.

REFERENCES

Ancarrow, J. (1986). *Use of computers in home study* (OERI Report No. 86–403). Washington, DC: U.S. Government Printing Office.

Becker, H. J. (1988). *The impact of computer use on children's learning.* Baltimore, MD: The Johns Hopkins University Center for Research on Elementary and Middle Schools.

———— (1986). *Instructional uses of microcomputers: Reports from a national survey* (No. 1–4). Baltimore, MD: The Johns Hopkins University Center for Social Organization of Schools.

_____ (1983–1984). *School uses of microcomputers: Reports from a national survey* (No. 1–4). Baltimore, MD: The Johns Hopkins University Center for Social Organization of Schools.

Boes, S. (ed.) (1984). *High tech for schools.* Arlington, VA: American Association of School Administrators.

Bruder, I. (1990). The third computer coordinator survey. *Electronic Learning,* 9 (5).

Collis, B. (1988). Research window. *The Computing Teacher,* 16 (1).

Edwards, C. E., and Irvine, J. J. (1987). Project MiCRO: Prior student computer use. *Proceedings of National Educational Computing Conference.* Eugene, OR: International Council For Computers In Education.

Green, G., and Epstein, R. (eds.) (1988). *Employment and earnings.* U.S. Department of Labor, Bureau of Labor Statistics. Washington, DC: U. S. Government Printing Office.

Hood, J. (ed.) (1984). *Microcomputers in schools.* Westport, CT: Market Data Retrieval.

International Association For Computing in Education (1984). Unpublished raw data presented at the Minority Computer Awareness Workshop.

Martinez, M. E., and Mead, N. A. (1988). *Computer competence: The first national assessment.* Princeton, NJ: Educational Testing Service.

McGinty, T. (1987). Growing pains: A portrait of an emerging profession. *Electronic Learning,* 6 (5).

Oakes, J. (1985). *Keeping track of how schools structure inequity.* New Haven, CT: Yale University Press.

Project on Equal Education Rights (1985). *Programming equity into computer education: Today's guide to the schools of the future.* Washington, DC: PEER.

Quality Education Data (1988). *Market target: Microcomputer usage in schools: A QED Update.* Denver, CO: QED.

Ritchie, D. (ed.) (1988). Make computers "indispensable" to teachers, educator advises. *Education Computer News,* 5 (19).

Solomon, G. (1988). The role of the federal government in educational technology. *Electronic Learning,* 8 (2).

Stedman, J. B. (1988). *Computers in elementary and secondary schools: An analysis of recent legislation.* Washington, DC: Congressional Research Service.

U.S. Congress, Office of Technology Assessment (1988). *Power on! New tools for teaching and learning* (OTA-SET–379). Washington, DC: U.S. Government Printing Office.

U.S. Department of Education, National Center for Educational Statistics (1986). *Degrees and other formal awards conferred survey.* Washington, DC: U.S. Government Printing Office.

8

Hispanic Women in College and Careers: Preparing for Success

LAURA I. RENDÓN AND AMAURY NORA

Despite dramatic changes in the social and economic lives of women in recent decades, Hispanic women remain in a secondary economic status. They often trail men and women of other ethnic groups in salary scales and remain concentrated in relatively low-paying jobs. In spite of claims that sex and race discrimination in the labor force have declined, Hispanic women still remain concentrated in the lowest-paying occupations and earn less than white and African American men and women. In 1986, for every $1 paid to white men:

.72 was paid to African American men
.68 was paid to Hispanic men
.67 was paid to white women
.61 was paid to African American women and
.53 was paid to Hispanic women (U.S. Department of Labor, 1986).

Reducing pay and occupational disparities remains a challenge to the women's movement, to Hispanic leaders and policymakers, as well as to leaders of the U.S. economic, political, and social system. In a nation that is witnessing the dynamic growth of ethnic minorities, it has become not only morally but also politically wise to provide mechanisms and infrastructures to ensure that Hispanics, African Americans, Native Americans, and Asian Americans receive the education and training to participate fully in a labor force needed to sustain the country's economic stability and national security. In a nation that takes pride in granting all of its citizens equal opportunity, it becomes imperative to reduce wage and occupational disparities that have historically divided men and women. Hispanic women merit full participation in a globally competitive society, but to do so, they must acquire the education and training needed to move into "nontraditional" careers.

This chapter has several purposes: (1) to examine the context in which the problems related to Latina participation in the labor force occur, including demographic trends and differences among Hispanic subgroups, (2) to review the research literature that has identified barriers to the educational progress of Hispanic women, (3) to highlight the major factors believed to have an influence on participation of Hispanic women in nontraditional careers, and (4) to outline recommendations for preparing Latinas for higher education and nontraditional careers.

As would be expected in a study of a group that has only recently been the subject of research and policy attention, this analysis has several limitations. First, the scholarship on Hispanic women is very limited, and much of the literature is fugitive. Second, data often are not disaggregated by gender and ethnicity, making it difficult for researchers and policy analysts to make assumptions from a generic to a specific group. Third, most studies or analyses about Latinas are not theory based, and the findings tend to be descriptive or anecdotal, as opposed to inferential. These limitations notwithstanding, it is possible to draw a rough, though useful, profile of the Hispanic population and to define critical issues associated with the participation of Hispanic women in nontraditional fields.

PROFILE OF THE HISPANIC POPULATION

To understand the economic and social status and needs of Hispanic women, it is necessary to first understand the Hispanic population at large and then to address gender differences within the Hispanic community. According to the *Current Population Survey* (CPS) (U.S. Department of Commerce, 1987), there were 18.8 million Hispanics in the United States in March 1987, constituting 7.9 percent of the nation's population. This figure represents a 30 percent increase between the 1980 census and the March 1987 CPS, compared to a 6 percent increase for the non-Hispanic population. Women are approximately half of the total Hispanic population.

Mexican Americans represent the largest of the five principal Hispanic population groups, composing 63 percent of all Hispanics; Puerto Ricans compose 12 percent; Central and South Americans, 11 percent; other Hispanics, 8 percent; and Cubans 5 percent. Hispanics are much younger than the non-Hispanic population, with a median age of 25.1 years, compared to 32.6 years for non-Hispanics. Hispanics also constitute a larger proportion of individuals who are either in school, preparing to enter school, or who should be in school. In 1987, more than one Hispanic in ten (10.6 percent) was a child under the age of five; roughly 25 percent of Hispanics were 5 to 17 years of age, compared to 18 percent of the non-Hispanic population. Further, a large proportion of Hispanics were of college-going age in 1987; about 14 percent were 18–24 years old, compared to about 11 percent of non-Hispanics.

Hispanic median annual income was $19,995 in 1986, an increase of only $91 from 1981. By contrast, the income of non-Hispanics increased from $27,480 in 1981 to $30,231 in 1986, a jump of $2,751. Cuban Americans' median income ($26,770) most closely approximated that of non-Hispanics, while Puerto Ricans' income ($14,584) was about half of white income.

As a whole, Hispanics have made small but significant gains in educational attainment. The median number of school years completed increased from 10.8 in 1982 to 12 in 1987. Similarly, while 45.4 percent had completed four years of high school or more in 1982, by 1987 the figure was 50.9 percent. In 1982, 7.7 percent of Hispanics had completed four or more years of college, compared to 8.6 percent in 1987. Despite these gains, Hispanics have not reached parity with non-Hispanic whites; in 1987, roughly 77 percent of young non-Hispanic white adults were high school graduates, and 21 percent had completed four years or more of college. There are also striking differences in educational attainment among young adults of different Hispanic origin groups. About 62 percent of Cubans were high school graduates, compared to 54 percent of Puerto Ricans and 45 percent of Mexican Americans.

These increases, while encouraging, need to be viewed with caution, for several reasons. First, between 1972 and 1984, the 18- to 24-year-old Hispanic population increased by about 51 percent, compared to growth in the general population of 18- to 24-year-olds of only 14 percent. Consequently, the Hispanic population of high school graduation age has been growing faster than the rest of the population. The growth in the numbers of Hispanics attending college therefore may be attributed to the sheer growth of the Hispanic population rather than to an increased propensity for Hispanics to either complete high school or to attend college. Second, the figures obscure the fact that often these numbers have not kept pace with the dynamic Hispanic population growth that this country has witnessed within the last decade. Third, it remains doubtful that large numbers of Hispanics will attend four-year colleges to pursue undergraduate majors that will lead to the pursuit of graduate and professional study since the growth in college enrollment has occurred primarily in the two-year college sector where disappointing retention and transfer rates also have been reported (Duran, 1986).

Further, the *poverty rate* for Hispanic families in 1986 was 24.7 percent, a slight increase over the 1982 poverty rate of 23.5 percent. Because of the growth of the Hispanic population, about 200,000 more Hispanic families were living in poverty in 1986 than in 1981. Of the 1.1 million

Hispanic families living below the poverty level in 1986, 51.2 percent were in female-headed households, compared to 33 percent for non-Hispanic white families. In families headed solely by Puerto Rican women, 67 percent were living below the poverty level; 49 percent of Mexican American households headed by women lived below the poverty level in 1986. Further, 62.5 percent of the Hispanic families living below the poverty level in 1986 were headed by individuals 25 years and older who were not high school graduates.

PROFILE OF HISPANIC WOMEN

In 1986, according to a CPS survey (U.S. Department of Commerce, 1987), Hispanic females earned roughly 69 percent of Hispanic males' median salaries and 42 percent of non-Hispanic white males' median salaries. Hispanic males earned a median salary of $11,958 in 1986, compared to $8,258 for Hispanic women. Earnings for non-Hispanic white males were $19,588 and for females, $10,110. Among Hispanic women, Mexican American females had the lowest median salaries ($7,446) and Cuban American females had the highest ($11,664).

And these women now are more likely to be supporting their families alone. As with other population groups, the percentage of Hispanic families maintained by women alone has increased. In 1970, about 15 percent of families were maintained by Hispanic women, while 11 percent were maintained by non-Hispanic white women. By 1987, the figure rose to 23.4 percent, compared to 15.7 percent for white women. By contrast, in 1987 only 5.7 percent of families were maintained solely by Hispanic males, and 3.8 percent were maintained solely by white males. Puerto Rican women maintained 43.3 percent of all Puerto Rican families, and Mexican American women maintained 19.2 percent of all Mexican American families (U.S. Department of Commerce, 1987).

Further, these women also have increased their labor force participation; the proportion of Hispanic women in the labor force grew from 41 percent in 1973 to 49 percent in 1982. In 1987, Hispanic women represented 51 percent of Hispanics in the civilian labor force. By contrast, Hispanic men's participation decreased slightly, from 81 percent in 1982 to 79 percent in 1987. Since 1973, when annual data on the unemployment of Hispanics first became available, Hispanic unemployment rates have been consistently higher than those for non-Hispanic whites. In 1987, about 11 percent of Hispanic males were unemployed, compared to 7 percent of non-Hispanic white males. About 10 percent of the Hispanic female population was unemployed, compared to 6 percent of the non-Hispanic white female cohorts (U.S. Department of Commerce, 1987).

HISPANIC WOMEN AND
OCCUPATIONAL SEGREGATION

Occupational statistics paint different portraits for Hispanic and non-Hispanic males and females. CPS data (U.S. Department of Commerce, 1987) reveals the concentration of Hispanic males in operative occupations such as precision production, craft, and repair (21 percent) and operators, fabricators, and laborers (28 percent). While 27 percent of non-Hispanic males were employed in managerial and professional specialties, only 11 percent of Hispanic males held these jobs.

About 41 percent of Hispanic females were concentrated in technical, sales, and administrative-support occupations, about the same as for non-Hispanic women (46 percent). However, nearly twice as many non-Hispanic women (26 percent) were employed in managerial and professional occupations than Hispanic women (15 percent). Cuban American women's participation in professional specialties was roughly the same as that for non-Hispanic women and men. Among the major Hispanic subgroups, Mexican American men and women were least represented in managerial and professional specialties.

Hispanic women are most underrepresented in all occupations associated with high salaries where college degrees are required. For example, in 1986, 698,000 women scientists and engineers were employed in the United States, representing 15 percent of all scientists and engineers, up from 9 percent in 1976. About 5 percent (34,500) were African American women; 5 percent were Asian American (36,300); 3 percent were Hispanic (19,600); and less than 1 percent were Native American (2,700) (National Science Foundation, 1988). In higher education, few Hispanics were in the professoriate. In 1983, of all full-time faculty in higher education, only 0.2 percent of Hispanas were professors, 0.4 percent were associate professors, and 0.5 percent were assistant professors. By comparison, 9.9 percent of white women faculty members were professors, 19.8 percent were associate professors, and 30.4 percent were assistant professors (Equal Employment Opportunity Commission, 1983). Only about 1.2 percent of the professoriate is comprised of Latinos (Jacobson, 1985).

In the area of degrees earned in the total population (see Table 8.1), women appear to have reached parity at the undergraduate and master's levels but not in the number of doctorates and first professional degrees earned. Moreover, it is interesting to note that while Hispanic women now earn slightly more bachelor's and master's degrees than Hispanic men, Hispanic men earn nearly twice as many doctorates and first professional degrees as Hispanic women.

The participation of Hispanics in selected fields in 1984–1985 is portrayed in Table 8.2. A cursory glance at the data reveals the under-

Table 8.1 Degrees Earned by Hispanic Men and Women, 1984–1985

	Total	Percent
Bachelor's Degrees		
All	968,311	100.0
Men	476,148	50.8
Women	492,163	49.2
Hispanic	25,874	2.7[a]
Men	12,402	2.6[b]
Women	13,472	2.7[c]
Master's Degrees		
All	280,421	100.0
Men	139,419	49.7
Women	141,004	50.3
Hispanic	6,864	2.4
Men	3,059	2.2
Women	3,805	2.7
Doctorate Degrees		
All	32,307	100.0
Men	21,296	65.9
Women	11,011	34.1
Hispanic	677	2.1
Men	431	2.0
Women	246	2.2
First Professional Degrees		
All	71,057	100.0
Men	47,501	66.8
Women	23,556	33.2
Hispanic	1,884	2.7
Men	1,239	2.6
Women	645	2.7

Notes: [a]Degrees awarded to this group as a percentage of all degrees awarded at this level.

[b]Degrees awarded to men in this group as a percentage of all degrees awarded at this level.

[c]Degrees awarded to women in this group as a percentage of all degrees awarded at this level.

Source: Wilson, R., and Melendez, S. (1987). *Minorities in higher education*. Washington, DC: American Council on Education.

representation of Hispanics in all fields and the minute numbers of Hispanic women in engineering and biological/life sciences. Nonetheless, a comparison of both genders reveals that women are overrepresented in fields traditionally defined as "women's" professions; education, for example, continues to draw more Hispanic women than men. Further, four times as many Hispanic women as men are earning bachelor's degrees

Table 8.2 Degrees Conferred by Selected Field to Hispanic Men and Women, 1984–1985

	Hispanic Bachelor's		Hispanic Master's	
	Total	*Percent*	*Total*	*Percent*
Education				
Total	2,533[a]	2.9	2,519	3.3
Men	597[b]	2.8	668	3.2
Women	1,936[c]	2.9	1,851	3.4
Business				
Total	5,616	2.5	1,172	1.8
Men	2,928	2.4	811	1.8
Women	2,688	2.7	361	1.7
Social Sciences				
Total	2,846	3.1	272	2.7
Men	1,557	3.1	159	2.5
Women	1,289	3.2	113	2.9
Health Professions				
Total	1,550	2.4	296	1.7
Men	309	3.2	89	2.2
Women	1,241	2.3	207	1.6
Engineering				
Total	1,775	2.3	337	1.7
Men	1,501	2.3	296	1.6
Women	274	2.5	41	1.9
Public Affairs				
Total	NA		568	3.8
Men	NA		188	3.5
Women	NA		380	3.9
Biological/Life Sciences				
Total	1,241	3.3	NA	
Men	681	3.4	NA	
Women	560	3.1	NA	

Notes: [a] Degrees awarded to this group as a percentage of all degrees in this field.
[b] Degrees awarded to men in this group as a percentage of all degrees awarded to men in this field.
[c] Degrees awarded to women as a percentage of all degrees awarded to women in this field.
NA Not available

Source: Wilson, R., and Melendez, S. (1987). *Minorities in higher education.* Washington, DC: American Council on Education.

in the health professions. About twice as many Hispanic women are earning master's degrees in public affairs. Moreover, at the bachelor's degree level, the participation of Hispanic women closely approximates that of Hispanic men in nontraditional fields such as business, social sciences, and biological/life sciences, although large gaps separate the groups at the master's degree level in business and social sciences. The largest gap is found in engineering, where Hispanic men greatly outnumber women at both the bachelor's and master's degree levels.

In summary, the demographic profile of the Hispanic population reveals that the cohort may be characterized by the terms growth, diversity, and youthfulness. While Hispanics continue to register dramatic growth, they continue to be afflicted by poverty and low levels of educational attainment. This situation is particularly true in families headed by Puerto Rican and Mexican American women.

While Hispanic women have increased their participation in the work force, they still earn about $3,700 less than Hispanic men, $11,330 less than non-Hispanic white men, and $1,852 less than non-Hispanic white women, reflecting the impact of sex segregation of women of both groups in lower-paying jobs. Indeed, it is likely that the concentration of Hispanic women in technical, sales, and administrative-support occupations may account for their lower salaries. Finally, while there have been encouraging gains in educational attainment, overall Hispanic participation in higher education and degrees earned in selective fields remains low. Hispanic women appear to be most represented in education and health professions; their participation in public affairs appears to be moving upward. Hispanic women are least represented in engineering and biological/life sciences.

BARRIERS TO EDUCATIONAL PROGRESS: FIVE EMPIRICAL STUDIES

Although barriers to educational advancement for Hispanic women have been identified in numerous studies, there are few theoretically based studies that have examined the relationships among these factors. A review of the literature reveals that while a concern for Hispanic women in higher education is prevalent, only a handful of studies have focused on and tested the causal relations among factors believed to have an impact on the educational progress of Hispanic women at different institutions. This review of the literature instead focuses on five empirical studies that have specific, identifiable conceptual frameworks or have at least incorporated a theoretical perspective based on social theory suggested by previous studies of Hispanic women.

A Study of the Chicana Experience in Higher Education

In "A Study of the Chicana Experience in Higher Education," Muñoz and Garcia-Bahne (1978) identified a set of social and educational predictors suggested by the literature. Significant factors in this quantitative study included: (1) academic performance (grade point average, GPA), (2) levels of parental education and occupation, (3) socioeconomic status of the family, (4) family income, (5) dropping out behavior, (6) motivation, (7) self-expectations, and (8) self-esteem. A discriminant analysis was performed that identified canonical functions that maximally separated the groups in the study. The findings both supported notions held about the academic performance of Hispanic women compared to Hispanic men and contradicted what was found in other studies regarding parental educational and occupational attainment and the educational progress of Hispanics.

The study revealed that Hispanic women received higher grades than Hispanic men both in high school and college. However, although women were found to outperform men academically, Muñoz and Garcia-Bahne (1978) noted that the rate of persistence to graduation is much lower for Hispanic women than for Hispanic men. Further, the study found no significant differences between college grade point average received by Hispanic males and females and the socioeconomic standing of the family, as measured by parents' educational and occupational attainment. This finding was significant because it differed from previous studies by Vasquez (1978), Pantages and Creedon (1978), Astin (1971, 1975), Astin, Astin, Bisconti, and Frankel (1972), and Cope and Hannah (1975). However, Muñoz and Garcia-Bahne did find a negative relationship between the income level of the family and attrition or dropping out behavior: Hispanic students from low-income families were more likely to drop out of college than were those Hispanics who came from families with higher income levels. However, dropping out was not associated with academic performance at their respective institutions.

Findings related to motivation and self-expectations demonstrated that over half (55 percent) of all Hispanic students surveyed did not begin to consider attending an institution of higher education until the eleventh grade or later and that more than 26 percent of these Hispanic students did not consider going to college until the twelfth grade or later. Muñoz and Garcia-Bahne concluded that for first generation Hispanic students, expectations to attend a higher education institution occur later than for the nonminority population. Therefore, it is necessary for high school teachers, counselors, and significant others to begin earlier to encourage Hispanic women with potential for success to attend college, prior to their junior and senior years in high school.

Chicana and Anglo University Women

In another quantitative study, "Chicana and Anglo University Women: Factors Related to Their Performance, Persistence and Attrition," Vasquez (1978) also identified a set of social and educational predictors of academic success theoretically supported in other studies. These factors were similar to those identified by Muñoz and Garcia-Bahne (1978): (1) grade point average, (2) persistence, (3) attrition, (4) parental educational and occupational levels, (5) family income, (6) motivation, (7) self-expectation, and (8) self-esteem. Contrary to what Muñoz and Garcia-Bahne found, however, Vasquez's findings support the notion that socioeconomic status discriminates between "successful" Hispanic and Anglo women and "nonsuccessful" Hispanic and Anglo women. Moreover, persisters from both ethnic groups were found to come from families with higher parental educational, occupational, and income levels. While similarities between Hispanic and Anglo persisters were noted, differences in socioeconomic status between Anglo and Hispanic women were found for the total sample. Anglo women came from higher socioeconomic levels than did Hispanic women. Again, these findings differed from those of Muñoz and Garcia-Bahne.

An important finding of this study, which was later substantiated by Gandara (1982), was that maternal support and encouragement to do well in college was one of the most influential factors that separated persisters and nonpersisters. No other factors were found to distinguish between the groups in the study.

High-Achieving Chicanas

Gandara's 1982 study, "Passing Through the Eye of the Needle: High-achieving Chicanas," utilized quasi-qualitative methodology to examine categories related to academic persistence of Hispanic women. Factors identified in previous studies that were believed to influence retention provided the theoretical framework for the study. These factors included: (1) childrearing practices, (2) peer-related factors, and (3) school variables. Similar to Vasquez (1978), Gandara found that the role the Hispanic mother plays in fostering an educational drive for high-achieving Hispanic female students is consistent with that of Anglo mothers and high-achieving Anglo female students.

Moreover, Gandara concludes that Hispanic mothers were either equally or more influential than Hispanic fathers on their daughters' educational aspirations. Gandara's ethnographic study also found that Chicanas and offspring of immigrant families had in common a hard-work ethic; as Gandara suggested, "an emphasis on quality of performance in school and elsewhere appears to have been an important part of their upbringing."

Consistent with other studies of high academic achievement in the majority population, these Hispanic female students described their parents as nonauthoritarian in their discipline and as having placed a strong emphasis on independent behavior. Gandara found that the ability to move with ease between two cultures was probably related to earlier school experiences; about three-quarters of the women had attended high schools that were highly integrated, either at least 50 percent Anglo or virtually all Anglo, and high-achieving Hispanic females, more than high-achieving Hispanic males, tended to come from more integrated schools. Gandara also noted that: "There is [an] intriguing possibility also that the women had less traditional role models in their mothers since significantly more women than men reported that their homes were not kept very neat and orderly, presumably because their mothers placed their efforts elsewhere." Gandara concluded:

> Although there are hints of many factors that contributed to [Hispanic women choosing to attend college], . . . including such things as peers or neighborhoods, the emotional support of her family may be critically important to the educationally ambitious Mexican American woman, since she is not likely to find it in great abundance elsewhere. Second, it is probably time to review our stereotyped beliefs about the role and potential of the Chicana mother. Clearly, she is capable of having a powerful impact on the ambitions of her children. Given proper credit and a little more guidance, Chicana mothers may be able to facilitate the educational accomplishments of their offspring (pp. 177–178).

Barriers to Progress in Higher Education

In an extensive study, "Chicanas and Chicanos: Barriers to Progress in Higher Education," Chacon, Cohen, and Strover (1986) hypothesized causal relationships between factors identified in the literature. A hypothesized path model was tested to examine the direct effects of age, gender, socioeconomic status, type of campus, hours of domestic work, hours of paid work, and freedom from academic difficulties on academic progress. Other variables in the study included: (1) marital status, (2) parental support, (3) stress, and (4) number of children. The study population consisted of Hispanic males and females in four different types of institutions: private universities, University of California campuses, community colleges, and rural and urban state universities. Not surprisingly, Hispanic males and females in private universities were found to have the highest socioeconomic status rating, to be the youngest students (median age 19), to have ". . . put in much less time in paid work and domestic labor," and to be similar on all the variables. The group with the next highest socioeconomic status rating, the second youngest (median age 21) with the second fewest number of hours worked (both domestic and paid work) came from the University of California system.

The oldest group in the population, with the lowest socioeconomic status rating of all groups in the sample and with the most differences between males and females, came from the community colleges. Women averaged 22.25 hours per week in domestic labor as compared to 9.09 for men, averaged 26.06 hours per week of paid labor compared to 3.14 for men, and were older than the men (30.21 years versus 27.83). These findings differ in some respects from those derived from two separate studies by Rendón and Nora (1988) and Nora and Rendón (1987) which found that the mean age for Hispanic students in six community colleges in four states (California, Texas, Arizona, and New Mexico) was similar to that in the rural and urban state universities (median age 23). Moreover, the Hispanic female population was found to be younger than the Hispanic male population. However, both studies substantiated the finding by Chacon, Cohen, and Strover (1986) that there is no basis for arguing that Hispanic females on their respective campuses are older than the majority population.

With respect to domestic labor, this study revealed that women worked more hours than men in their home environment, a finding similar to Gandara's (1982). In a sample of 508 women, 148 were either married or divorced and only thirteen women had more than two children. But, single women, married women, and women with children nearly always put in double the amount of domestic labor as did men in similar marital or parental circumstances; and single women averaged 7.8 hours of work per week to single men's 4.7 hours, while married women averaged 23.0 hours to married men's 12.6 and women with children averaged 31.5 work hours per week compared to men with children, who averaged 12.8 work hours per week.

Other factors that were found to separate Hispanic males and females were parental support and stress. "Women reported less parental support for going to college than men, particularly support from their mothers. These differences were statistically significant despite the fact that over 60 percent of the sample reported their parents as very supportive and only a small fraction reported any parental opposition" (Chacon, Cohen, and Strover, 1986:314). More stress was reported by women than by men, but the authors cautioned that their finding regarding stress might not have reflected ". . . thinking that higher levels of reported stress [could] be due to a general tendency for women to be more willing than men to report psychic difficulties" (Klerman and Weissman, 1980). However, in an earlier study, Muñoz and Garcia-Bahne (1978) found sex differences for Chicanos but *not* for Anglos. The authors interpret the findings on stress as indicating that Chicanas do indeed experience more stress (p. 314).

Again, the multivariate analysis performed in the study tested the direct effects of exogenous variables on endogenous variables and of specific endogenous variables on other endogenous variables in a causal model. The last endogenous (or dependent) variable in the model was program progress. The variable was a measure of progress over time toward completion of a degree-granting or vocational program. Program progress was operationally defined by seven items: (1) self-assessment of whether one would drop out temporarily, (2) self-assessment of whether one would drop out permanently, (3) length of time away from school if education had already been interrupted, (4) frequency of postsecondary interruptions, (5) number of units taken the previous term if enrolled, (6) patterns of school enrollment, to include moving from school to school and "reverse" transfer from four-year to two-year schools, and (7) self-assessment of the likelihood of needing extra time to complete a respective program. The following outline represents the findings from the path analysis performed in the study:

I.   Paths from school type to hours of paid labor and hours of domestic labor

    A. Negative paths between hours of paid labor and hours of domestic labor and the private university, the University of California campus, and the rural state university campus.

    B. In contrast, the path coefficient between the community college and hours of paid work was positive (.17).

    C. No path from community college to hours of domestic work.

II. Paths from gender to other variables in the model

    A. No direct effect from gender to program progress.

    B. Direct effect (.35) from gender to domestic hours.

    C. Direct effect (.18) from gender to hours of paid work.

III. Paths from socioeconomic status (SES) to other variables in the model

    A. Direct effect (.27) from SES to freedom from academic difficulty.

    B. Direct effect (−.09) from SES to program progress.

IV. Paths from age to other variables in the model

    A. Direct effect (−.23) from age to program progress.

    B. Direct effect (.35) from age to domestic hours.

    C. Direct effect (.18) from age to hours of paid work.

V. Paths from hours of paid labor and hours of domestic labor to program progress

    A. Direct effect (−.14) from hours of paid labor to program progress.

    B. Direct effect (−.22) from domestic labor to program progress.

VI. Freedom from academic difficulty was found to be a powerful precursor (.24) of program progress.

In sum, the type of institution the student attended and the number of hours of paid work were found to be significant barriers to educational advancement for Hispanics. Although gender was not directly related to program progress, Chacon, Cohen, and Strover (1986) concluded that gender differences on the dependent variable were mediated through other intervening factors, namely hours of domestic work. This indirect effect and others, however, were never tested in the study.

Mathematics and Science Students in Community Colleges

In "A Discriminant Analysis of Math and Science Students in Community Colleges," Nora and Rendón (1987) identified a set of social, demographic, academic preparation, and attitudinal variables based on a theoretical model of race/gender inequities in education by Klein et al. (1985). Three variables were examined in the quantitative study: (1) precollege factors, including high school grades, academic rank, encouragement by others, high school mathematics preparation, high school science preparation, problems with mathematics and science courses; (2) college factors, including number of mathematics and science courses taken at the community college, attitudes about faculty involvement, attitudes about counselor involvement; and (3) status variables, including gender, age, ethnic origin, mother's and father's educational attainment.

The major purpose of the study was to discern the best combination of predictor variables (sociodemographic, academic preparation, and attitudinal) that maximized the differences among white and Hispanic male and female community college students enrolled in mathematics and science courses with varying levels of academic preparation. It was believed that community college students enrolled in mathematics and science courses were more representative of traditional transfer students.

The study population was drawn from community college students from six two-year institutions that make up the Border College Consortium and are located in border communities along the 2,000-mile United

States/Mexico border region. A total of 1,615 white and Hispanic community college students composed the student population.

A review of the descriptive findings for the total population revealed that Hispanic women who were enrolled in community college mathematics and science courses (and therefore were more representative of transfer students) were younger than the other groups in the study (white males and females and Hispanic males); the Hispanic population overall was found to be younger than the white population, with Hispanic females being the youngest and white females the oldest. Further, Hispanic males and females with either an adequate or good high school preparation were attending community colleges rather than four-year institutions, and Hispanic students enrolled in mathematics and science courses in community colleges had received higher grades in high school than had white students similarly enrolled in community college mathematics and science courses. Hispanic males and females enrolled in equal numbers in community colleges, but Hispanic females had earned higher grades in high school than had Hispanic males.

Two canonical discriminant functions were identified in the discriminant analysis, with a combined X^2 (96)=251.25, p<.001. After removal of the first discriminant function, the remaining discriminant function was highly significant, X^2 (77)=124.51, p=.0005. The between-group variances accounted for by the two canonical functions were 53.57 percent and 21.80 percent respectively. The first discriminant factor was parents' educational background. As expected, white males and females had parents whose educational attainment was higher than parents of Hispanic students of both genders. The findings suggested that even though Hispanic students' parents did not even graduate from high school, some Hispanic students interested in mathematics and science and who came from lower socioeconomic backgrounds were making extraordinary progress, despite the poverty and related economic and social hardships that often preclude satisfactory academic advancement. Also, the observation that Hispanic students were differentially concentrated in community colleges suggested that the brightest Hispanics were choosing to begin their college careers in mathematics and science education in community colleges and that two-year institutions were the primary collegiate vehicle Hispanics used to attain career, economic, and social mobility.

The second dimension related to grades earned at the precollege level, science preparation in high school, and encouragement received by significant others. Compared to all groups, white females without an adequate high school preparation received the lowest grades, had taken the fewest science courses in high school, and received the least amount of encouragement from significant others to attend college. While some Hispanic students coming from families where parents did not even graduate from high school appeared to be making extraordinary progress, attrition rates at two-year institutions remained exceedingly high and transfer rates exceedingly low for Hispanics. It was believed that although bright Hispanic students were attending community colleges to initiate mathematics and science careers, community colleges had not reduced either socioeconomic inequities or difference in mathematics and science participation between white and Hispanic students; participation disparities between men and women also remained. The minute share of degrees earned by Hispanics in mathematics and science fields suggests that there has been a talent drain and that the leak may have occurred at the community college level, where Hispanics were disproportionately concentrated. This was particularly true for Hispanic females—who earned higher grades than Hispanic males, but who remained grossly underrepresented in mathematics and science-based programs in higher education and, consequently, underrepresented in many occupational areas.

HISPANIC WOMEN'S PARTICIPATION IN NONTRADITIONAL CAREERS

Despite progress in educational achievement for Hispanic women, there is still no parity. The harsh reality is that there are few Hispanas with the necessary academic preparation to enter nontraditional fields such as medicine, engineering, physics, economics, law, dentistry, as well as leadership and policymaking positions. In addition to educational barriers, Hispanic women must often confront other barriers that may lower their aspirations or limit the extent to which they can fully participate or be considered as capable of participating in these careers.

Stereotyping

Stereotyping of Hispanic women is commonplace; the literature and the media have tended to portray Hispanas negatively as powerless and pathological. The victim is blamed for her victimization; consequently, Hispanas are assumed to focus only on home and family and to be subservient, dependent, dutiful daughters, wives, and mothers. Hispanas are portrayed as women who are content to be sex objects and decorative figures as opposed to well educated and career oriented; they are seen as ultra-religious, dependent on the Catholic church and God for change to come into their lives (Lewis et al., 1985; Marin, 1977). This monolithic image of Hispanas as powerless, pathological, backward, and prayerful has been perpetuated from generation to generation in textbooks, films, television, newspapers, and the mainstream of economic, political, and cultural Americana.

Discrimination

As both women and members of an ethnic minority group, Hispanas often confront double jeopardy when they attempt to enter a nontraditional occupation. Subtle discrimination occurs in fields that are primarily white male dominated, such as mathematics and science-related fields and the professoriate. For example, in higher education, few women of color pursue mathematics and science-based degrees. Fields such as medicine, engineering, statistics, and chemistry may not draw Hispanic women because they perceive that they cannot compete fairly with men in these professions. It may also be the case that women choose college majors and careers in which they are likely to be adequately represented because they perceive less discrimination and a greater opportunity for achievement and advancement. Many observers tend to believe that discriminatory practices, reflected in employment, salaries, and tenure are the most serious impediments to the goal of equity for women in mathematics and science education (Government-University-Industry Research Roundtable, 1987). Moreover, women of color entering the professoriate are often interviewed and have applications reviewed by male professors who do not understand or appreciate the significance of scholarship on women, including women of color. Consequently, Hispanas may be deemed unqualified, unprepared, or undesirable colleagues in these fields, and many decision makers still perceive women of color through stereotypical attitudes.

Multiple and Conflicting Roles

Entering nontraditional fields often requires Hispanas to operate between two cultures—neither fully part of the Hispanic culture from which they came nor a part of the Anglo culture in which they find themselves. Torn by multiple demands, they often function within a context of conflicting rules, values, attitudes, and behavior. "If, for example, they adopt Anglo values and attitudes, conflict arises within themselves, between themselves and Hispanic males who tend to prefer the traditionally assigned roles, and between themselves and the Anglo society, which generally endorses and perpetuates the myths and stereotypes of Hispanic women" (Lewis et al., 1985:378).

Cultural Influences

While change is occurring, many Hispanic women are still being raised in home environments that lower aspirations for women. In a study of community college students, Rendón, Justiz, and Resta (1988) found that Hispanic parents often expected their daughters to get married and raise a family, or at most, to become secretaries or receptionists, thus reinforcing the notion that a man's career was more important than a woman's. This type of social conditioning may discourage Hispanic women from setting their goals higher.

Family Responsibilities

Given the pressures of family needs with minimal spousal or societal support (child care, for example) Hispanic women often feel that they must choose lower-paying jobs with less responsibility and with fewer demands on their time, to allow them to have the benefits of flexible hours that will give them more time with their families. Further, while women have joined the work force in record numbers, working women with families still must juggle two jobs, often without a discernible reduction in their household and family responsibilities. Also, Hispanic men tend to be conservative about women's roles; they are often reluctant for their wives to work outside the home, especially when there are small children to care for in the family unit.

Despite these obstacles, there are encouraging signs of success for Hispanic women. Recently, the National Network of Hispanic Women sponsored a survey of 303 members who listed their occupations as managerial or entrepreneurial, including women in government, education, industry, communications, banking, finance, and other professional fields. The average respondent earned $45,000 a year. Eighty-two percent had earned college degrees. Eleven percent held doctorates; 5 percent law degrees; and less than 1 percent had earned medical degrees. The average respondent was 38 years of age, married with one to two children, and currently holding a middle/senior management position.

Nonetheless, virtually all successful Hispanas listed major obstacles they had faced in order to achieve their current position, including lack of mentors, lack of access to the mainstream society network, lack of opportunity for advancement, lack of an advanced degree, and the absence of affirmative action policies for Hispanic women. The value of this study was twofold: It demonstrated Hispanic women's potential for success in nontraditional careers, even with family responsibilities, and thus offered role models to other Hispanas. In addition, confirming the persistence of institutional barriers, the study also emphasized the need for affirmative steps to make both education and career options more available to young Hispanas ("Successful Hispanic Women," 1988).

RECOMMENDATIONS

The dynamic growth and dispersion of the Hispanic population is creating a nucleus of people who can enter the nation's work force. With proper education, training, and guidance, Hispanic women can be a significant part of this new work force, especially in nontraditional fields. The following recommendations are intended to assist educators, employers, researchers, and policymakers to prepare, recruit, and retain Hispanic women in preparation for nontraditional careers.

Recommendations for Educators

With more and more Hispanics entering the nation's educational system, intervention will be required at every level. In particular, early intervention in the form of guidance and counseling as well as special programs at the elementary and junior high school level should focus on the following: (1) moving Hispanic women and girls into academic tracks of study and encouraging them to take mathematics and science courses; (2) sponsoring early outreach programs to inform Hispanic women and girls about different careers and life options available to them and about the courses of study required; (3) counseling parents of Hispanic women and girls to provide them with information about different programs of study and to help them support and encourage their daughters to attend college and to enter nontraditional careers; (4) training faculty and counselors to understand the needs, problems, and cultures of the Hispanic population as well as to develop strategies to provide Hispanic girls and women with proper attention and encouragement needed to successfully maintain academic progress.

In community colleges, colleges, and universities, information, support, and encouragement may be provided through new or existing women's centers. For example, the Laredo (Texas) Junior College Women's Center has developed programs and strategies to help Hispanic women cope with stress, adapt to college life, and handle conflicting roles, life, and work in a multicultural society. Other essential programs include child care, mentorship/apprenticeship opportunities, mathematics anxiety reduction seminars that are culturally sensitive, financial aid, and financial planning seminars.

Currently, some innovative programs provide encouraging signs that access to postsecondary education can be widened. For example, Goddard College in Vermont enrolls single mothers in the regular residential program; welfare payments are used to defray room and board charges. The children of these "nontraditional" students live in a supportive environment with responsible young adults, receive on-campus day care, and interact with the children of other Goddard students. At Chatham College in Pittsburgh, on-campus housing for nontraditional students has been established, including space for single mothers with one child. These models and others (see Gittell, Chapter 11, and Kates, Chapter

12) can be expanded to other institutions and could meet the needs of many Hispanic women.

Recommendations for Employers

New strategies in the form of recruitment, incentives for participation, exposure to fields in which they are underrepresented, and child care are needed to bring Hispanas into the mainstream of nontraditional careers. Outreach and recruitment can take place in colleges and universities located in urban centers where most Hispanics reside. Recruiters should emphasize the company's commitment to employing women and minorities and the incentives offered by the company to its employees. Companies should train their recruiters to reach out to Hispanic women and make them feel comfortable during the interview process. Recruiters should allow interviewees to ask questions and recruiters should avoid patronizing comments and behaviors.

Incentives for participation could include flexible hours, salary bonuses, fringe benefits such as health care for the woman and her children, and opportunities for advancement. Further, specialized training for women needing to update or enhance their skills could be made available. Internships and mentorship programs that provide women with on-the-job training and a person to whom they can turn for assistance in getting the job done are needed. Similarly, it is important that employers provide child care facilities or resources and opportunities for family and medical leave, to accommodate parents' need to take time off on occasion to attend to their children.

Recommendations for Researchers

More gender-specific research about Hispanic women must be undertaken. For example, studies are needed on the educational experience of Hispanic women at the elementary, secondary, and postsecondary levels. We also need to understand what is happening to Hispanic women as they move into nontraditional careers. Important research questions include: (1) To what extent are Hispanic women socialized away from academic tracks and mathematics and science fields of study? (2) What factors account for the success or nonsuccess of Latinas in high school and college? (3) How are Hispanic women overcoming barriers to success in education and in the work force? (4) How are Hispanic women coping with multiple roles? and (5) What factors account for the success of Hispanic women in nontraditional fields?

Recommendations for Policymakers

State efforts can help improve Hispanic women's participation in education and work at every level. These efforts should include: (1)

funding of scholarships and fellowships for women of color wishing to enter nontraditional fields of study, (2) providing internship opportunities and conferences designed to alert women of color to new fields and the steps they need to take to enter these professions, (3) offering special educational programs such as women's centers, minority women's studies, counseling and guidance, early outreach, and the expansion of access to postsecondary education for nontraditional adult populations.

At the federal level, funded research and development should include attention to Hispanic women. For example, the Office of Educational Research and Improvement in the U.S. Department of Education should include a research priority focused on the participation of Hispanic women in various fields of study. Similarly, the Fund for the Improvement of Postsecondary Education should consider funding colleges to develop new and innovative strategies to attract and retain Hispanic women returning to college and to inform them about opportunities in nontraditional careers. The National Science Foundation should sponsor programs that attract and prepare Hispanic women to enter mathematics and science-based fields of study and should fund research that examines the factors that preclude or enhance their participation in scientific professions, both at the K–12 and college level.

Further, federal agencies, including the Census Bureau, should reassess their data-reporting policies and disaggregate data on Hispanics by different Hispanic subgroups and by gender. Given the scarcity of data about Hispanic women, more needs to be done to ascertain the educational and economic progress of this cohort.

In the area of work, federal and state policies are needed with regard to child care, pay equity, and equal opportunity. For example, states could offer incentives to employers who make day care available. States' equal opportunity requirements should include regular reporting of progress being made with regard to affirmative action and civil rights; and the federal government should offer incentives to those states that are making extraordinary progress in these areas.

CONCLUSION

American society is not yet accustomed to Hispanic women in nontraditional careers and leadership, but with more Hispanics going to school and entering college, it will become important to better understand this cohort, to design interventions to help them attain success in school and work, and to provide new and increased opportunities to facilitate their participation and leadership in nontraditional fields. The professional and social structure of America will be richer when Hispanas are afforded the opportunity to complete an education that leads to upward mobility, economic advancement, and career success. To undertake reform that builds equity in salary, education, and participation in nontraditional fields is to take a significant step in the direction of enhanced economic equality for Hispanic women and to embellish the economic health and sense of fairness and justice that characterize a democratic nation.

REFERENCES

Astin, A. W. (1975). *Preventing students from dropping out.* San Francisco, CA: Jossey-Bass.

———— (1971). *Predicting academic performance in college: Selectivity data for 2,300 American colleges.* New York, NY: The Free Press.

Astin, H. S., Astin, A. W., Bisconti, A. S., and Frankel, H. H. (1972). *Higher education and the disadvantaged student.* Washington, DC: Human Service Press

Chacon, M. A., Cohen, E. G., and Strover, S. (1986). Chicanas and Chicanos: Barriers to progress in higher education. In M. A. Olivas (ed.), *Latino college students.* New York, NY: Teachers College Press.

Cope, R. G., and Hannah, W. (1975). *Revolving college doors: The causes and consequences of dropping out, stopping out, and transferring.* New York, NY: Wiley Interscience.

Duran, R. P. (1986). Hispanic precollege undergraduate education: Implications for science and engineering studies. In L. Dix (ed.), *Minorities: Their under-representation and career differentials in science and engineering.* Washington, DC: National Academy Press.

Equal Employment Opportunity Commission (1983). *Job patterns for minorities and women in higher education.* Washington, DC: U.S. Government Printing Office.

Gandara, P. (1982). Passing through the eye of the needle: High-achieving Chicanas. *Hispanic Journal of Behavioral Sciences,* 4 (2):167–179.

Government-University-Industry Research Roundtable (1987). *Nurturing science and engineering talent.* Washington, DC: National Academy of Science.

Jacobson, R. L. (1985). New Carnegie data show faculty members uneasy about state of academe and their own careers. *The Chronicle of Higher Education,* 21:24–28.

Klein, S. et al. (1985). Examining the achievement of sex equity in and through education. *National Science Foundation News.* Washington, DC: National Science Foundation.

Klerman, G., and Weissman, M. (1980). Depressions among women: Their nature and causes. In M. Guttentag, S. Salasin, and D. Belle (eds.), *The mental health of women.* New York, NY: Academic Press.

Lewis, S., et al. (1985). Achieving sex equity for minority women in education. In S. Klein (ed.), *Achieving sex equity through education.* Baltimore: Johns Hopkins University Press.

Marin, R. (1977). The Puerto Rican woman. *La Luz,* 6.

McKenna, T., and Ortiz, F. I. (1988). *The broken web.* Encino, CA: Floricanto Press.

Muñoz, D., and Garcia-Bahne, B. (1978). *A study of the Chicana experience in higher education.* Final report for the Center for Minority Group Mental Health Programs, National Institute of Mental Health (No. NN24597–01). San Diego: University of California.

National Science Foundation (1988). *Women and minorities in science and engineering.* Washington, DC: National Science Foundation.

Nora, A., and Rendón, L. I. (1987). *A discriminant analysis of math and science students in southwest community colleges.* Paper presented to the American Educational Research Association, February.

Pantages, T. J., and Creedon, C. F. (1978). Studies of college attrition: 1950–1975. *Review of Educational Research,* 48 (1):49–102.

Rendón, L. I., Justiz, M., and Resta, P. (1988). *The transfer function in southwest border community colleges.* Columbia: University of South Carolina.

Rendón, L. I., and Nora, A. (1988). *Determinants of predisposition to transfer among community college students: A structural model.* Paper presented to the Association for the Study of Higher Education.

Successful Hispanic women claim high income, high job status. (1988). *Hispanic Times,* 9 (3):14.

U.S. Department of Commerce, Bureau of the Census (1987). *The Hispanic population in the U.S., March 1986 and 1987* (Advance Report Series P–20, No. 416). Washington, DC: U.S. Government Printing Office.

U.S. Department of Labor (1986). Weekly earnings of wage and salary workers: First quarter, 1986. *U.S. Department of Labor News.* Washington, DC: U.S. Government Printing Office.

Vasquez, M.J.T. (1978). Confronting barriers to the participation of Mexican American women in higher education. *Hispanic Journal of Behavioral Sciences,* 4 (2):147–165.

Wilson, R., and Melendez, S. (1987). *Minorities in higher education.* Washington, DC: American Council on Education.

9

Model Programs Prepare Women for the Skilled Trades

WENDY JOHNSON

PROBLEMS AND OPPORTUNITIES

Women's steady movement into the paid labor force over the past three decades, combined with complex social, economic, and political factors, has created dramatic changes in employment and poverty patterns across the United States. A vast new class has emerged of poor and working-poor people whose faces are those of women and their dependent families. The explosive movement of women into the labor force has resulted in more than 5.4 million women working in jobs paying minimum wage or less; at the 1992 rate of $4.25 per hour, women face overwhelming obstacles as they work to fill the double role of wage earner and caregiver (National Commission on Working Women, 1987).

Eighty percent of all women in the labor force are still employed in office/clerical, manufacturing, and retail occupations, and in the growing service industries where pay is low and benefits are often nonexistent (U.S. Department of Labor, 1986). Black women are segregated even further into the more menial service jobs and machine operator categories, jobs that represent the dregs of an already low pay scale. The National Commission on Working Women (NCWW) reports that "half of all Black and Hispanic women workers were in clerical and service occupations in 1987" (NCWW, 1988b).

While white women earn 36 cents less on every dollar earned by white men, women of color fall 8 to 11 percent behind their white counterparts. More specifically, black and Hispanic women working full time year round earn 56 cents and 53 cents respectively, when compared to the $1.00 earned by white males (NCWW, 1988b). With racism *and* sexism at work, women of color have little hope of shedding the shackles of occupational segregation without significant changes in educational, training, and employment opportunities.

Even more striking is the fact that "between 1970 and 1980 the number of female-headed households with children under the age of 18 increased by 82 percent in all families and by 92 percent in Black families" (Reder, Arrindell, and Middleton, 1984). At the same time the number of women in the paid labor force reached an all time high at 45 percent. These trends have galvanized our attention to women, children, and work and the chilling reality that poverty knocks at the door of a disproportionate number of women and their children. In a society where working outside the home is no longer a choice but a necessity for most women, women's breadth of opportunity remains limited.

An assessment of women's status in today's economy must include an understanding of the roles schools have played in shaping the occupational outlook and attitudes of boys and girls and the impact that education has had upon women's occupational choice, access, and opportunity. During the early 1970s Nancy Frazier and Myra Sadker observed that:

> During the high school years, all students make some crucial decisions. It is at this time that schools of higher education and careers are chosen, as are marriage partners and life styles. As a young woman attempts to make these choices, she looks to the school environment for help. A good or bad report card, a friend's advice, a session with the guidance counselor, a teacher's casual comment, a compelling biography—these are the stuff decisions are made of, and often there is little in the school environment that nourishes and inspires women and a great deal that discourages, inhibits, and sets a hard low ceiling on their aspirations (Frazier and Sadker, 1973).

We have long known that girls and boys are taught to adopt certain behaviors and attitudes and encouraged to aim for certain goals as they begin to ready themselves for their rightful and "acceptable" places in society; girls were to be respectable, submissive, helpful, and nurturing, heading toward wifely duties; boys, on the other hand, were to be strong, competitive, aggressive, and in control, heading toward breadwinner duties. Substantial research has concluded that while boys and girls are being taught reading, writing, and arithmetic, they also are learning a more insidious lesson: sex-role stereotyping (see Sadker and Sadker, Chapter 5).

Researchers and others have observed that the academic curriculum is accompanied by a "second curriculum," a gender-role curriculum that teaches children the traditional role behavior for their sex (Best, 1983). Best further observed that in her school setting, "career choices offered

Table 9.1 Median Annual Earnings, 1987

Education Completed	Women	Men
8 years or less	$10,251	$15,703
1–3 years of high school	12,396	19,287
4 years of high school	15,341	23,119
1–3 years of college	17,872	26,211
4 years of college	22,032	30,942
5 years of college	24,034	33,242
5 or more years of college	26,631	37,000

Source: Bureau of Labor Statistics (1988). Unpublished data.

to boys were limitless" while girls' choices were "narrow and restricted." Career options as outlined by career education booklets, for example, put forward more than eighty career options for boys while girls were offered a field of eighteen acceptable choices (Best, 1983). As a result, women have been steered to career choices and aspirations that severely limit their wage earning capacity and often destine them to a life of poverty.

Largely as a result of such educational tracking and the continuing low pay for "women's work" in the sex-segregated work place, women's wages continue to lag behind men's. In 1979, "women with three years of college earned less than a male with an eighth grade education" (NCWW, 1980). More recent data comparisons indicate that the earnings gap between women and men remains stark (see Table 9.1).

Although the dream of upward mobility tells us that education is the primary way to a better life and economic self-sufficiency, education does not necessarily help women economically. According to the Census Bureau,

much of the wage gap cannot be explained by differences in the qualifications of men and women workers . . . for non-high school graduates, differences in skill and experience between men and women account for only 27 percent of the wage gap. Among high school graduates the proportion of the gap accounted for is 23 percent. Among college graduates, the proportion of the gap accounted for rises to 47 percent. But even among college graduates, fully one-third of the earnings gap between men and women cannot be accounted for by factors reasonably believed to be associated with productivity differences. Such large unexplained differences suggest that discrimination is still an important factor in the labor market. Improving women's education, training, and experiences is important, but wage differences would likely remain unless discrimination is also eliminated (U.S. Department of Commerce, 1987).

Laws and regulations prohibiting sex discrimination have been in place since the 1960s, but statistics indicate that women have not secured a significant share of "nontraditional" jobs in formerly male-dominated industries. In the construction industry, for example, women are only two percent of the 5.1 million skilled craft workers; and they have met hazards along the way (U.S. Department of Labor, 1988c). Obstructions limiting women's access to the skilled trades include discrimination and sexual harassment, nonenforcement of laws and regulations, insufficient job training, and societal attitudes regarding appropriate roles for men and women.

Many women have taken their cases of alleged discrimination to the courts and some have won. Jane Catlett and three other women applied for maintenance positions with the Missouri Highway and Transportation Commission; these entry-level positions required an eighth grade education and the ability to operate a lightweight truck. Although the women met the criteria, they were denied employment. During the same period, however, eighty-nine men were hired in similar positions. In a lawsuit that evolved over more than ten years, the courts found that Missouri had engaged in an intentional pattern and practice of discrimination based on the sex of the applicants. A $1.2 million settlement was paid to the original four women and the class of some 150 additional women who had applied for maintenance positions with the state between January 1, 1975, and May 31, 1980 (*Catlett v. Missouri Highway and Transportation Commission,* 1987).

Women's struggle for equality in the nontraditional workplace is primarily reinforced by economic necessity, but many are seeking jobs that will give them significant and marketable skills to secure their futures. For example, while a secretary's average annual income is around $15,000, plumbers will easily earn $30,000. While an electrician's median income is over $470 per week, the average weekly paycheck for a female salesclerk is under $200 per week (U.S. Department of Labor, 1988c). Others simply like outdoor work, the challenge of physical work, and working with their hands (Scheider and Johnson, 1986).

ADVOCACY FOR CHANGE: MODEL PROGRAMS

Since the eary 1970s, women's advocacy and training groups across the country have been engaged in providing education and training opportunities that will allow women to compete for high-paying jobs within the skilled trades. The construction industry is one of the few well-paying growth industries of the future. The Surface Transportation and Uniform Relocation Assistance Act of 1987 (P.L. 100–17) allocates $87.5 billion for highway construction alone over the next five years. This allocation to the fifty states will generate approximately 400,000 jobs during that period.

Presently, construction officials are grappling with how to meet the future demands of the industry. There is general agreement that training programs must emanate from the community or grassroots level; therefore, existing training programs, such as Jobs Training Partnership Act (JTPA) and vocational education programs, and union apprenticeships are excellent vehicles for planning and shaping community-based programs that effectively recruit and train applicants for these jobs of the future (Kraker, Bradford, and Lawson, 1988). These localized efforts also can pay special attention to attracting and retaining women, especially women of color, to the skilled trades.

Today it is also clear that skilled women will be needed to fill the increasing number of construction jobs in the coming decade. The U.S. Department of Labor predicts that between 1986 and 2000 the number of construction craft jobs will rise by 823,000 (Kraker, Bradford, and Lawson, 1988). And the emerging work force over the next decade will be increasingly female: "two-thirds of the new entrants into the work force between now and the year 2000 will be women, and 61 percent of all women of working age are expected to have jobs by the year 2000" (Johnston, 1986). This can present new opportunities for elimination of barriers to women's full participation in the skilled trades in construction; further, with the anticipated shortage of construction workers, more than 200,000 new craft employees will have to be trained yearly for the next decade (Kraker, Bradford, and Lawson, 1988). If these predictions are correct, training opportunities for women should increase.

Various approaches have been used to prepare women for construction work. Historically, apprenticeship programs have been and continue to be the primary route for gaining trade skills (Shanahan, 1983). Priscilla Golding, director of Women in the Building Trades (WIBT), believes that for women the "best way to go is through the union because the organized labor sector of construction provides jobs with excellent benefits, grievance procedures, and opportunities for long-term work" (Golding, in conversation, 1988). These structured training programs may be sponsored by an employer, a group of employers, or a union. A common practice involves employers and unions forming Joint Apprenticeship Committees (JAC) (Shanahan, 1983) that determine industry skill needs and the kind of training required and then establish standards for acceptance into the programs. For example, the operating engineers apprenticeship program in Kentucky is sponsored by the Construction Employers Association of Central Kentucky, Inc., Tri-State Contractors Associations, and Local 181 of the International Union of Operating Engineers. Operating engineers operate heavy equipment such as cranes, dozers, scrapers, and rollers used on buildings and highways. This joint program teaches the skills required to operate this heavy equipment, ensuring the quality of performance required by Local 181, and is registered with the Bureau of Apprenticeship and Training of the U.S. Department of Labor. The program sets out a very structured course of classroom study and training plus on-the-job training; women and men entering this program are expected to successfully complete 432 hours of classroom training and 6,000 hours of on-the-job training paying apprentice wages. Apprentices typically receive 50 percent of a journeyman wage to start and progress to 90 percent near the end of the program (Josephs, Latack, Roach, and Levine, 1988).

The basic requirements for selection in all apprenticeship programs include: meeting the minimum age requirement; necessary physical ability; passing an aptitude test; and completing a written application process (Shanahan, 1983). Joint Apprenticeship Committees are bound by state and federal laws to develop and implement selection processes that will ensure equal access and opportunity for women and other underrepresented groups. One such policy states that: "The recruitment, selection, employment and training of apprentices during their apprenticeship shall be without discrimination because of race, color, religion, national origin or sex. The sponsor will take affirmative action to provide equal opportunity in apprenticeship and will operate the apprenticeship program as required under Title 29 of the Code of Federal Regulations (CFR) as amended" (Shanahan, 1983).

Despite these provisions, women are still significantly absent from the ranks of skilled workers. Data from the Bureau of Apprenticeship and Training (BAT) show women with a dismal share of apprenticeship slots; as of June 1988, with 70 percent of the data in, women represented 2 percent of all registered apprentices in sixteen construction classifications (Kraker, Bradford, and Lawson, 1988).

Women, particularly women of color, still face barriers to their efforts to become skilled craft workers: The apprentice applicant confronts a selection process that is often arbitrary and possibly discriminatory. Many of the aptitude tests that are commonly used, for example, have been shown to have adverse impacts upon women and people of color (Strenio, 1981). Most skilled craft jobs are physically demanding and tests measuring physical strength often put women at a disadvantage, especially if significant upper body strength is required. Thus, comprehensive preapprenticeship training programs for women will include components that focus on fitness training and prepare women for the specific physical demands of their chosen trade. Indeed, many women have proven time and again that enhancing physical strength and endurance can be easily achieved through structured fitness programs.

If a woman succeeds in these two areas she must then go through the personal interview which, according to Mary Ellen Boyd of the New

York-based Nontraditional Employment for Women (NEW) program, "is the most subjective part." Women have reported to NEW that they are asked such questions as "who will mind their children, what do their husbands think of their working in construction, how will they handle harassment, and why do such pretty and feminine women want to do this work, and couldn't they find something else to keep them busy?" (Boyd, 1988).

If women make it to the other side of the barrier, on the job site "the thing that's most important is perseverance—a willingness to sometimes work in harsh conditions" (Ricci, 1981). With women composing only 107,000 of the 5.1 million skilled craft workers across the country, isolation on a work site is more the rule than the exception (U.S. Department of Labor, 1988c). Women working alone or even in pairs often find themselves treated as unwelcome intruders in a "man's world." Women have reported a range of incidents involving sexual harassment (both verbal and physical), deliberate embarrassment, and physical endangerment that supervisors and co-workers allowed to happen because they did not want women on "their" work site. Other women apprentices in their crafts complained of being given only trivial assignments or being refused work that would qualify them for journey-level positions, while men with the same or less experience and time in training received more and better assignments (Scheider and Johnson, 1986). And while white women are contending with sex discrimination, women of color must also deal with the added element of racism on the white-male-dominated work site. Women of color "often can't tell if they are objects of harassment because of race, gender, or status as apprentices" (Martin, 1988).

Women facing the challenge of trading in a malnourished paycheck for the more healthy wages of a skilled craft worker will have one thing in common—an even healthier dose of confidence. As one aspiring craft worker stated: "Having handled all sorts of prejudices, I feel [dealing with] sexual prejudice is just another stepping stone; hopefully my ability to work with my hands, my ambitious, hard-working attitude, and my determination will help me overcome any obstacles working in a nontraditional job for women" (Scheider and Johnson, 1986).

New partnerships are forming that involve the broader community. In the city of Boston, a unique training and placement initiative has emerged that includes participation from the public school system, local government, and building trade unions. This "Boston Compact Agreement with Labor" has as its goal attracting increased numbers of women and people of color to apprenticeship programs with trade unions. The school's role, according to Sharon M. Jones, the Compact's coordinator, is to "improve the preparation of students for graduation and to increase their aspiration and motivation, while the trade unions agree to expand their assistance to the schools" (Jones, 1988). Local government infuses the program with necessary funds for activity and program development.

While high school male students, especially black, Hispanic, and Asian American students, have benefited through placement with union apprenticeship training programs, high school women have not been significant beneficiaries of the Compact program. Only one woman, out of fifty program participants, was placed in an apprenticeship slot; and within three months she left the position. Jones attributed the poor participation of young women to their own lack of foresight about the future reality of women and work: "Although there is overwhelming evidence that today's young women will grow up and have to work to support themselves and their families, they continue to cling to Cinderella's dream of marrying Prince Charming and living happily ever after" (Jones, 1988). Neither schools nor media portrayals sufficiently encourage young women to consider these facts and prepare for work in nontraditional fields. Some research on women in nontraditional work suggests that the women most likely to enter nontraditional trades are somewhat older (in their late twenties and early thirties) and already have worked in low-paying, dead-end, traditional female jobs (O'Farrell, 1987; Martin, 1988; Golding, in conversation, 1988).

An advocacy model that brought about significant policy change and training opportunities for women was implemented by Southeast Women's Employment Coalition (SWEC), a regional coalition of women leaders working to improve the quality of life for women and children in the Southeast by challenging systemic race and sex discrimination in employment. A SWEC program, Women's Opportunity in Road Construction (WORC), focused on increasing employment and training opportunities for women wanting to work in the highway construction industry through strategies of legal action, public pressure, and grassroots organizing. From 1984 to 1986, SWEC waged a multistrategy statewide campaign in Ohio to open up highway jobs for women.

Several elements were key to the success of this project: a high level of organization and communication among women's groups across the state and locally; the existence of three tradeswomen's groups, one well established and two fledgling; a swelling momentum to improve women's access to nontraditional jobs; and the formation of a statewide coalition that included tradeswomen as well as state and local leaders who wanted to focus on developing strategies to move women into nontraditional jobs. The latter element was fueled by the fact that Ohio was receiving a massive amount of federal money for highway construction (with projected expenditures for 1985 at $695 million) and was one of the largest employers in the state, with more than 6,000 employees. Further, major contractors had poor affirmative action programs and the vast majority had not met the U.S. Department of Labor's 6.9 percent hiring level for women since its implementation in 1978 (Scheider and Johnson, 1986).

The SWEC project began with an extensive research period, which revealed an array of roadblocks to women within the Ohio Department of Transportation, including two critical areas: limited entry-level training opportunities for women and a poor enforcement record. A series of strategies were then pursued to achieve real gains in these two areas.

On the training front, the SWEC Ohio coalition gained support from the Building Trades Council, union representatives, and a jobs training specialist, and advocated a jobs training program specifically for women who wanted to work in nontraditional occupations through the Jobs Training Partnership Act (JTPA). The training plan included recruitment, training, and placement of women in highway construction jobs. In December of 1984, the Private Industry Council (the government-appointed panel that reviews and approves state training plans) allocated $629,000 for metro-area programs in three cities—Dayton, Columbus, and Toledo. At that time, this was the largest amount ever allocated to women's nontraditional training (Scheider and Johnson, 1986). Preparation Recruitment Employment Training, Inc. (PREP), a nonprofit organization with a twenty-year history of developing and administering training programs for women and people of color, administers the JTPA program; since its first year, it has continued to exceed its training and placement goals for women.

In the policy arena, an executive order from Governor Richard Celeste's office proposed establishing state hiring goals for women and people of color that would mirror the U.S. Department of Labor's hiring levels of 6.9 percent for women and 11 percent for people of color. A protracted debate was waged over several months between women's advocates and private contractors and other opponents. Two public hearings were held, for which SWEC coordinated the participation of tradeswomen and advocates. Finally, Governor Celeste signed Executive Order 84–9 in January of 1985.

Priscilla Golding, director of the Boston-based Women in the Building Trades, credits the high participation of women of color in the WIBT program to their program's very visible presence in the black community; WIBT operates its program out of Roxbury Community College, a historically black institution that also provides an array of adult education programs. Of the more than 140 women who have gone through WIBT's program since 1986, fifty are enrolled in union apprenticeships and approximately one-half are women of color. WIBT has placed women in carpenters, plumbers, ironworkers, painters, electricians, and operating engineers unions.

Golding states very firmly that women of color must be "specifically recruited." Outreach efforts must speak directly to these women so that they know they are welcome to explore new employment opportunities. An example of this attitude is the flyer that advertises the WIBT program and features the picture of a black woman performing carpentry duties. WIBT's recruitment for potential candidates includes: placing advertisements in local newspapers; developing flyers and distributing them to employment offices, social service agencies, and union networks; and creating public service announcements for radio and television and the women's community. Introductory workshops for interested women are held, often sponsored by community-based agencies. These free workshops provide women the opportunity to take a deeper look at what the construction industry is all about, to gain knowledge about apprenticeship opportunities and how to apply, and to talk with experienced tradeswomen. Women attending the workshop can also apply to WIBT's ten-week preapprenticeship program.

Preapprenticeship training cycles can vary in length from three to ten weeks, but all effective programs contain components of orientation and assessment, work orientation, skills development, placement, and on-going support. The orientation phase involves individualized assessment of participants' needs and interests and is quite comprehensive; it includes an inventory of present skills, educational attainment, physical fitness, and support services needed. The applicant engages in self-assessment, evaluation of emotional make-up, attitude and confidence level, and job readiness skills (such as resume preparation). "This orientation period turns many women on to nontraditional work—but equally important, sometimes it convinces them they aren't cut out for it" (Ricci, 1981).

In most, if not all, cases, women need assistance with child care and transportation. Some programs, PREP, Inc. for example, incorporate support services throughout the training process and provide the necessary services or refer the participant to appropriate community resources. Training programs and employers must demonstrate a strong commitment and responsibility to providing these essential services to potential applicants and employees throughout the training process. PREP, Inc. provides these services to all participants who indicate a need for them during the recruitment, intake, and assessment process. Having these pressures removed allows women to give full concentration to their training and results in a decreased rate of absenteeism.

Child care is a critical issue for all working women with children, but especially for blue-collar women who need to be on the work site as early as 6:00 in the morning; they must find the rare child-care arrangements that will take their children as early as 5:00 a.m. The training program can assist with child care arrangements by providing individualized planning, identifying existing child-care facilities, or forming community day-care centers in targeted areas. The WIBT program offers one example of how child care needs were met for women in nontraditional jobs. When a preapprentice plumber had completed her training program, she was not immediately accepted into the union apprentice program because only a limited number of slots was available; she therefore was placed on a waiting list for the next available opening. With children of her own she knew how critical it is to find child care services with early drop-off. In response to this need, she and her mother opened a licensed day-care center that caters to the schedules of women working in nontraditional trades.

Orientation to the work site environment is also a critical element in the training design and should include visits to apprenticeship schools and construction work sites where women can observe the work and tools of various trades. WIBT utilizes apprentice directors from various unions (electricians, carpenters, plumbers) to provide firsthand information regarding their respective programs. Journeywomen and female apprentices give personal accounts of their experiences as well and serve as role models for the aspiring tradeswomen. These site visits also inform women of the potential hazards a particular trade may present (Pugh and Himes, 1979). For example, ironworkers have several categories of work that are particularly hazardous: "working rods" requires handling iron rods 60 feet long and weighing 350 pounds and is described by ironworker Fran Krauss as "the most hazardous job, in terms of wear and tear on your body." She also identifies structural work as having "the highest number of fatal accidents" because the workers handle large sheets of corrugated iron on narrow metal beams, at very high heights (Martin, 1988). The visit should also provide a general overview of tools and equipment used in specific trades. A more detailed lesson on tool identification and use should follow soon after in the classroom, where women actually are instructed on the proper identification and use of tools.

Work site orientation could also be the point where the issue of assertiveness training is raised and women are taught strategies to deal with harassment, sexual and otherwise. Although barriers have been lifted somewhat, a woman entering a historically all-male environment most often will be met with hostility by her new male coworkers. Developing effective coping and communication skills will maximize her chance for success on the work site. Many women develop their own ways of coping and surviving on the work site—becoming impervious to the hateful and snide remarks leveled at them by their male coworkers by developing a "thick skin." Other women believe that direct confrontation is necessary, believing if they do not speak up things will only get worse (Martin, 1988).

WIBT's skill development program comprises 30 percent of the ten-week training session and involves basic math review, blueprint reading, mechanical principles, recognition and use of tools, measurement and application, and interviewing skills. Individualized math and reading remediation is also provided for those women needing to bolster skills in these areas. Physical conditioning is especially important, as most skilled trades require long hours of repeated motions by various body parts. This course should provide a broad range of information from how to strengthen specific body parts through individualized conditioning to how to lift, push, or move heavy objects so that back problems are less likely to occur (Pugh and Himes, 1979). Finally, the women in the class are ready to choose a trade. This should involve scheduled times with an employment counselor who will help identify resources and existing training or apprenticeship opportunities and coordinate actual placement.

For more than two decades, women have tried to transcend prescribed gender roles to change the face of employment statistics. Maids have become carpenters. Secretaries have turned in their typewriters to become card-carrying teamsters. Waitresses have put down their trays and donned electricians' belts. Yet, if women are to participate fully and equally in this economy, in addition to training they must also know that their rights will be protected. The federal government must enforce antidiscrimination laws and regulations, to ensure that training opportunities translate into employment opportunities that pay a living wage. As we journey to the year 2000 and prepare the nation's work force for skilled craft jobs, women must be guaranteed the right to ride in the seat of opportunity.

REFERENCES

Best, R. (1983). *We've all got scars: What boys and girls learn in elementary school.* Bloomington: Indiana University Press.

Boyd, M. E. (1988). Testimony before the U.S. House of Representatives Committee on the Judiciary, Subcommittee on Civil and Constitutional Rights. Washington, DC.

Catlett v. Missouri Highway and Transportation Commission. (1987). *Federal Reporter,* 2d. Series, 828 F. 2d, (8th Circuit), 1261–1272.

Chafe, W. H. (1977). *Women and equality: Changing patterns in American culture.* New York, NY: New York University Press.

Frazier, N., and Sadker, M. (1973). *Sexism in school and society.* New York, NY: Harper and Row.

152   *Wendy Johnson*

Johnston, W. B. (1986). *Demographics as destiny: The U.S. workforce in the year 2000*. Indianapolis, IN: Hudson Institute.

Jones, S. (1988). Unpublished testimony before the U.S. House of Representatives, Committee on the Judiciary, Subcommittee on Civil and Constitutional Rights. Washington, DC.

Josephs, S., Latack, J. C., Roach, B. L., and Levine, M. (1988). The union as help or hindrance: Experiences of women apprentices in the construction trades. *Labor Studies Journal*, Spring, 3–18.

Kraker, J., Bradford, H., and Lawson, M. (1988). Industry is divided over whether craft shortages will be wrenching. *Engineering News Record*, October.

Martin, M. (ed.) (1988). *Hard-hatted women: Stories of struggle and success in trades*. Seattle, WA: Seal Press.

National Commission on Working Women of Wider Opportunities for Women (1988a). *An overview of women in the workforce*. Washington, DC: NCWW.

———— (1988b). *An overview of women of color in the workforce*. Washington, DC: NCWW.

———— (1987). *Women, work and poverty*. Washington, DC: NCWW.

———— (1980). *An overview of women in the workforce*. Washington, DC: NCWW.

O'Farrell, B. (1987). Women in nontraditional jobs. Unpublished testimony before U.S. Senate, Subcommittee on Labor, Senate Committee on Labor and Human Resources. Washington, DC.

Pugh, M., and Himes, J. (1979). *Opening trade barriers: A training blueprint*. Fort Wayne, IN: Fort Wayne Women's Bureau.

Reder, N., Arrindell, D., and Middleton, M. (1984). *Meeting the employment needs of women: A path out of poverty?* Washington, DC: League of Women Voters, 359.

Ricci, L. J. (1981). *High-paying blue collar jobs for women*. New York, NY: Ballantine Press.

Scheider, S., and Johnson, W. (1986). *Job development in highway construction: A road map for women and advocates*. Lexington, KY: SWEC.

Shanahan, W. F. (1983). *Guide to apprenticeship programs*. New York, NY: Arco Publishing.

Strenio, A. J., Jr. (1981). *The testing trap: How it can make or break your career and your children's future*. New York, NY: Rawson Wade Publishing, Inc.

U.S. Department of Commerce, Bureau of the Census (1987). Male-female difference in work experience, occupation and earnings, 1984. *Current Population Survey* (P–70). Washington, DC: U.S. Government Printing Office.

U.S. Department of Labor (1988a). *Females and veterans by selected groupings*. Unpublished data, Washington, DC: Bureau of Apprenticeship and Training.

———— (1988b). *Occupational outlook handbook*. Washington, DC: Bureau of Labor Statistics.

———— (1988c). Earnings for 1987. *Current Population Survey*. Unpublished data. Bureau of Labor Statistics.

———— (1986). *20 facts on women workers*. Washington, DC: Office of the Secretary, Women's Bureau.

PART FOUR

From Poverty to Self-Sufficiency:
The Role of Higher Education
for Women

10

Higher Education as the Route to Self-Sufficiency for Low-Income Women and Women on Welfare

SAUNDRA MURRAY NETTLES

"Dependency" has become a buzzword for undesirable conditions ranging from substance abuse to a family's continued need for welfare. But dependency is an alterable condition—drug treatment programs can help users reduce and ultimately eliminate addiction to drugs and various programs can help the welfare family "off the rolls." When drug users are successfully treated, they become "drug free," and when families support themselves through earnings, they become "self-sufficient." Like most buzzwords, "dependency" and "self-sufficiency" convey only hints of the realities they denote. Dependency—on drugs, welfare, or parents— is the result of a host of psychological, economic, and social factors. "Self-sufficiency" as a label likewise obscures the hardships of families headed by women whose jobs pay low wages, provide no benefits, and offer few possibilities for advancement.

This chapter examines the prospects for women on welfare to become self-sufficient and for low-income women to increase their incomes to reduce the likelihood that they will need welfare. Two routes to self-sufficiency are the focus: higher education and, for comparison, job training. Job training is one of the favored mechanisms to move persons who receive Aid to Families with Dependent Children (AFDC); it has its origins in the antipoverty efforts of the late 1960s and 1970s. Higher education, however, has been defined as an approach to welfare reform only since the mid-1980s and is not yet a standard option in self-sufficiency programs.

The condition and experiences of African American women will be used to examine the pursuit of self-sufficiency and upward mobility. African American women and their families figure disproportionately among the ranks of the poor: Among black families with 1985 income below the poverty level and with children under 18, 58.9 percent were headed solely by women (Children's Defense Fund [CDF], 1988), and in 1986, approximately 41 percent of AFDC families were non-Hispanic Blacks (Center for Law and Social Policy, 1989). African American women have played significant roles in other aspects of the U.S. welfare system: as leaders in the welfare rights movement of the 1960s; as social workers and in other positions in welfare offices; and as scholars documenting and analyzing the consequences of receiving welfare as income.

HIGHER EDUCATION

Higher education as a route to self-sufficiency is promising, but it is also problematic. For example, until 1986, when an amendment offered by Representative Steve Gundersen (R–WI) became law (as Section 479A of Public Law 99–498, the Higher Education Amendments of 1986), federal student aid was considered income for AFDC clients, and their benefits were reduced accordingly, thus making higher education economically impossible for most. The new law stipulated that no federal student aid provided for educational expenses (tuition, books, supplies, fees, transportation) could be considered as income in determining eligibility for any public assistance program that receives federal funding (Wolanin, 1988). This was a significant development in that the threatened reduction of welfare benefits often discouraged many would-be applicants to college (College Entrance Examination Board, 1984; Wolanin, 1988). However, AFDC clients must report student aid from state, local, and private sources to welfare agencies, which consider the aid in determining eligibility for AFDC funding.

Women have faced a range of other problems in their efforts to use higher education as a route to self-sufficiency. For example, AFDC policies often encourage clients to obtain jobs as quickly as possible, rather than to seek postsecondary education or job training. Further, limits are placed on the number of years of postsecondary education that can be pursued. There is generally a lack of information available to AFDC clients about their options concerning postsecondary education and financial aid. Few self-sufficiency programs bill postsecondary education as the central feature and higher education is not an option at all in many programs (Nettles, 1988). Finally, student financial aid is not sufficient to cover the expenses of schooling. The maximum Pell Grants in fiscal year 1987, for example, were only 20 percent more than they were in 1980, although tuition costs in postsecondary institutions rose 75 percent during that period (Children's Defense Fund [CDF], 1988).

Would higher education enable an African American AFDC client to earn enough to get out of poverty? Data on the labor market experiences of black women suggest that higher education might produce the desired outcomes, but there are no guarantees. Farley and Allen (1987), for example, presented data from the 1980 census that showed a relationship between educational attainment and employment. Among the population of younger (ages 16 to 24) African American women at work in 1980 and not currently enrolled in school, only 26 percent who had completed less than twelve years of school had jobs, compared to 51 percent of women who had completed high school, 66 percent of women who had completed one to three years of college, and 81 percent of women who were college graduates. Among unemployed younger women not in school, 36 percent who had completed less than twelve years of schooling were not working, compared to 20 percent of women who completed high school, 13 percent who had completed one to three years of college and 8 percent who were college graduates.

Among older women, ages 25 to 54, the advantages of education for employment were comparable to those of younger women. For example, 87 percent of black women with four years of college were at work, compared to 43 percent with elementary schooling and 66 percent with four years of high school. The unemployment rate for women with elementary schooling was 11 percent, whereas the rates were 9 percent and 3 percent for women with four years of high school and four years of college, respectively.

Educational attainment also paid off in purchasing power for African American women. Median incomes in 1984 were $18,400 for college graduates; $11,600 for African American women with one to three years of college; $8,400 for high school graduates; $5,000 for those with one to three years of high school and 8 years of elementary school, and $4,000 for women with less than eight years of elementary school (Farley and Allen, 1987).

However, African American women often fail to reach educational attainment levels that would make a difference in their ability to support themselves and their families. Sizeable proportions of African American women at every age but the very youngest are high school dropouts, as shown in Table 10.1 with equivalent data for white women.

Even for women who attain high levels of education, poverty is a possibility. According to the National Commission on Working Women (1985–1987), more than 20 percent of women of color with some college education live in poverty. The rate for men of similar educational background is only 3 percent. For women with few academic skills (three-fifths of adults on AFDC have not completed high school) (CDF, 1988), higher education as a pathway to self-sufficiency may be an

Table 10.1 Percentage of Women Dropouts, October 1983, by Age and Race

Age	Percentage of Dropouts	
	Black Women	White Women
14 and 15	2.9	1.6
16 and 17	6.0	6.9
18 and 19	15.6	11.8
20 and 21	19.6	14.2
22 to 24	21.6	12.7
25 to 29	19.9	12.8
30 to 34	17.7	11.6

Source: Office of Educational Research and Improvement (1986). *Digest of educational statistics.* Washington, DC: U.S. Department of Education.

ultimate goal, but some form of training may be the most realistic option in the short run.

JOB TRAINING

Job training is one of the favored mechanisms to help women on welfare to become independent. It can take many forms, including instruction in nontraditional jobs, vocational education at community colleges, training provided through proprietary schools or specialized organizations, and courses designed and implemented by partnerships among business, local education agencies, social service agencies, and community action agencies. Many programs also provide essential support services such as child care and transportation. The program may pay for the AFDC client's training expenses and offer workshops in life skills—such as searching for a job, budgeting, and parenting. During the 1980s, states and cities experimented with a variety of program designs using provisions under the WIN Demonstration Program, antipoverty funds provided under the Community Services Block Grant, and local funding (Danziger and Weinberg, 1986; Nettles, 1988).

Through a series of feature articles in the *Washington Post* (Spolar, 1987, 1988a, 1988b), residents of the metropolitan Washington, D.C., area examined one program from the perspective of a 24-year-old African American woman. The program is in Montgomery County, Maryland, an affluent suburb to the north of the city and is called the Family Independence Project. It is locally funded at a cost of $397,000 and began in 1986. No direct services are provided, but clients are referred to job training and educational opportunities and receive assistance in arranging child care and transportation. As of August 1988, of 120 women who had completed the initial phases of the project, 38 percent had dropped out, 49 percent were in jobs or job training but still receiving AFDC, and 13 percent were working and no longer on welfare.

The young woman who was featured in the series was enrolled in business classes but had not yet been working in a paying job because she enrolled in the project late in 1987. In fact, her $4,260 business training (paid for by a Jobs Training Partnership Act grant and a Pell Grant) was obtained only after she failed (although she was a high school graduate) and subsequently passed an adult basic skills test. She received $321 a month to support her two young daughters, ages 4 and 7.

The chances that this woman and her peers will become self-supporting depend on several factors: their willingness to participate in a long period of skills development, training, and job search; the availability of support from family and local government; the availability of job opportunities requiring the skills they have learned and the willingness of employers to hire them. Against that background, there is also the long period when many African American families remain poor while they are trying to move up the socioeconomic ladder. As McAdoo (1981) noted in her study of upward mobility in black families, "the mobility patterns revealed, surprisingly, that no one was able to move from abject poverty into middle-income status in just one generation" (page 163).

Although job training is used extensively as a means to economic independence, this route has several drawbacks. One important factor is a changing economy that necessitates retraining for the bulk of American workers. The American Society for Training and Development estimated that by the year 2000, 75 percent of currently employed workers will need to be retrained for jobs in the service and information industries ("Retraining America's Workers," 1987). Moreover, persons unemployed due to permanent separations must be retrained because their jobs (typically, in the declining manufacturing industries) no longer exist.

The retraining issue is a complex one. It involves questions about how retraining should be accomplished for the populations (for example, youth and dislocated workers) that need services. There are questions about the federal role in stimulating the creation of new jobs that pay decent wages and contribute to economic productivity and questions about the nature of the jobs that will be available for newly qualified workers. According to Duggan (1984), an important set of issues pertains to the structure of training. Currently, training takes place in many settings, including public schools, private vendors, and companies. These structures are "ill-fitted to one another in terms of their financial arrangements, their locus of decision-making, and their quality control mechanisms" (page 21).

This state of affairs presents special impediments to the welfare recipient who is seeking self-sufficiency through job training. She is likely to be restricted to a narrow range of training programs designed specifically for AFDC recipients or persons with tenuous ties to the labor market. The programs to which she has access are unlikely to be of the caliber of programs offered by corporations for their employees. Moreover, she must compete for training services with persons from other populations of the unemployed.

Even if she finds a job, self-sufficiency may not be the outcome for the African American woman who makes the choice. As the data presented above indicate, high school graduates in 1984 had median earnings of $8,400. Not only was that income insufficient to support a family, it was far less than the median earnings for African American men (who earned $12,900) and white men (who earned $19,600) with comparable schooling (Farley and Allen, 1987). These income disparities are not surprising, given that wages are the largest component of income and, at virtually all levels of educational attainment, occupation, and age, African American women's wages are lower than those of black men. However, according to the Farley and Allen analysis, there is evidence of declining race differences *among women:* Black women's wages were comparable to or higher than those of white women.

Black women's low wages can be attributed to a variety of factors. One set pertains to race, sex, and class bias in education. The results of such bias may be manifested in African American women's entrance into traditionally female (and low-paying) jobs and careers, high dropout rates, and poor academic performance. Moreover, the inequitable treatment that contributes to these outcomes often is subtle. For example, African American girls are reinforced in school for stereotypic behavior associated with African American women's roles. Grant (1984) found that teachers of African American first-grade girls in desegregated classrooms viewed these students as being socially but not cognitively mature and called upon them to help peers in nonacademic situations. In contrast, teachers tended to enlist white girls to carry out academic tasks. Other biases that African American girls face involve negative stereotyping, invisibility in curricula and materials, and low levels of interaction with teachers (Butler and McNeeley, 1987; Nettles and Scott-Jones, in press; Lewis et al., 1985).

The poor, black teenage mother exemplifies most visibly the convergent effects of racism, classism, and sexism and the failure of schools and other institutions to develop effective strategies for addressing the needs of students who must surmount multiple impediments to success. She tends to be single, a school dropout, on welfare, and lacking in basic academic skills. She may be in poor health. Her educational experience has been in schools abandoned by whites and upwardly mobile Blacks and characterized by the lowest scores on standardized tests, low teacher morale, low resource levels, and high rates of pregnancy and delinquency. Unfortunately, her counterparts who persist in these and other schools may graduate with poor basic and other academic skills. For example, African American students score lower in the SAT than other populations. In 1988, the average verbal score for African American students was 353, compared to 445 for whites, 408 for Asian Americans, and 382 for Mexican Americans. Scores on the mathematics section were 384 for African Americans, 490 for whites, 522 for Asian Americans, and 428 for Mexican Americans (Evangelauf, 1988).

A second set of factors that contribute to African American women's low wages pertains to experiences in the labor market. Black women remain segregated in low-paying service and clerical occupations. This may stem from factors such as sex inequity in education, sex-role socialization in the home and within society, unequal access to training and employment opportunities in higher-paying occupations, and the need to pursue jobs that will have the least impact on familial obligations. Moreover, as Braddock and McPartland (1987) point out, African American workers are still subject to racial discrimination. For example, qualified Blacks are often screened out of desirable entry-level jobs that require basic and advanced skills in math and reading, interpersonal and leadership skills, or decision-making skills. These are jobs that often offer advancement and training opportunities that might eventually lead to self-sufficiency.

SOCIAL SUPPORT

Support networks of kin and friends have been widely viewed as important buffers for stress in the lives of upwardly mobile African American women (Allen and Britt, 1984; McAdoo, 1981) and as sources of services and money among poor black women (Stack, 1974). Particularly in low-income black neighborhoods, the networks are characterized by high levels of mutual obligation and interdependent, face-to-face relationships among the various participants. The networks can be indispensable to persons who lack the resources that more affluent persons take for granted.

Although the exchange of resources that constitutes social support may be beneficial to participants, negative outcomes may also occur (Shumaker and Brownell, 1984). Weis (1985) cites such outcomes in her explanation of the difficulties women on welfare have in attending class, persisting in college, and graduating. One outcome is dependency on the network and its resources. Without money, there is no other way to obtain needed services and aid, but success in school may require that one break away from this network. The student is not to skip class to fulfill obligations (such as child care or taking someone to a doctor's appointment) or use transportation money to pay a debt. As Weis commented:

> Under these conditions, social mobility, as represented by schooling, involves a precarious risk. One's day-to-day survival, in a sense, demanded its sacrifice. To be upwardly mobile means that one has to amass a certain amount of capital—capital that could otherwise be distributed through the kin network. The poor harbor no illusions. They know they must depend on each other, and an attempt to break out of the kin network is made only after a careful appraisal of one's chances. The kin network is especially important to women in that child care arrangements are generally made within it. It is a paradox that poor women are dependent on these collective networks at one and the same time that they are attempting to break away from them by dreaming of upward mobility through school (page 253).

The dynamics of the break from kin and friends were explored by Fordham (1988), who presented evidence that high-achieving African American adolescent girls attempted to become "raceless" in order to meet the requirements for academic success in a low-income school. They tried not to engage in behavior similar to that of their less achievement-oriented classmates (for example, listening to radio stations that played "black" music) and played down or hid their academic pursuits and triumphs. Fordham suggested that the school demands the "raceless" persona, which ultimately puts social distance between the adolescent and her family community: "These students appear to understand that the school and their teachers expect them to distance themselves from the "black" aspects of their home, peers, and immediate community in ways that suggest an individualistic orientation toward success and social mobility" (page 74). I have observed firsthand how similar dynamics work to reduce AFDC clients' chances of completing job training programs. The following is one woman's comment about family reaction to her participation in a program sponsored by a community-based organization: "If James tries to help himself fine, then we can go on together. But if he wants to sit there and smoke his pipe fine . . . because I'm going to go ahead because I've been down too long; this program has really helped me. And my cousin, she says I don't know why you are going, you ain't going to be about nothing. And I said, well you know what, after all that I have achieved in this program if I still continue to do the things that I've been doing then it is not meant for me to have anything. Because I said I might not get the big executive's position but I can bet you I will be right up under the supervisor. I will have something; I'm striving for me, Beverly, now." This comment alludes to the cousin's criticism about Beverly's efforts, to Beverly's sense that she will make it no matter what others say or do, and to the individualistic orientation that Fordham (1988) says is part of the process of upward mobility for the poor girl who wants to be successful.

ACCESS TO PROGRAMS AND INFORMATION

Women on AFDC have had access to training and postsecondary opportunities through the Work Incentive Program (WIN), which required all able-bodied adults on AFDC to register for employment and training services, through the WIN Demonstration Program, a program that permitted state welfare agencies maximum flexibility in local program design and implementation, and programs such as the widely acclaimed Employment and Training (ET) Choices Program in Massachusetts. This program permitted AFDC clients to choose higher education or educational programs at other levels, depending on need and job training.

Low-income women who are not on welfare often must seek, on their own, resources available to the working poor. Community action agencies provide referral services to any persons whose family incomes fall below the poverty level, and many of these agencies offer self-sufficiency programs through Head Start, the Community Services Block Grant, or local funds (Nettles, 1988). For example, the National Association of Community Action Agencies (1987) cited such programs as the Family Development Approach in Michigan and Connecticut's Community-Neighborhood Services as examples of new forms of family support. Each program includes assessment of family needs, development of a plan for family members to follow toward self-sufficiency, and provision of counseling, financial, and other services while the plan is being carried out. The agencies seek to link families with existing resources such as the federally funded Educational Opportunity Centers that provide a variety of services to assist individuals pursuing postsecondary credentials. Unfortunately, there are virtually no evaluations of the extent to which these programs help participants to achieve self-sufficiency. One reason for the lack of assessment is that funding for community action agencies is sparse (the major source, the Community Services Block Grant, was under $400 million in fiscal year 1988); therefore agencies tend to use the funds for direct services rather than evaluation.

African American women themselves sponsor projects through national sororities and other organizations. For example, Delta Sigma Theta Sorority sponsored "Summit II: A Call to Action in Support of Black Mothers" in May and June of 1984. Summit II was a series of conferences, convened in thirty-eight cities throughout the United States, to identify solutions to the problems of single mothers who are either on welfare or self-supporting. The proceedings of the conferences included descriptions of existing Delta programs for single mothers, recommendations for local action, and rosters of service agencies represented at the conferences (Delta Sigma Theta, Inc., 1984). In 1987, the sorority and the Delta Research and Educational Foundation cosponsored an international conference whose theme was "Woman to Woman: Single Parenting from a Global Perspective."

In addition, poor women are among those who have initiated projects; these projects are often more accessible to low-income women than other efforts because they are located in the community and may be staffed by persons familiar with the women's needs. For example, the Kenilworth-Parkside Resident Management Corporation in Washington, D.C., had its origins in the 1970s as an effort, sponsored by mothers in the Kenilworth-Parkside housing project, to assist youngsters living in the project to prepare for college and persist until graduation. Under the leadership of Kimi Gray, the corporation now owns the project and provides social services, medical services, and job training on site. Indeed, the corporation is an exemplar of community development as a strategy to foster self-sufficiency.

Another project, "Strategies for Improving the Academic Performance and Persistence Rate of Black Females in K–12 Education Settings," recently published a directory of programs (Butler and McNeeley, 1987). The entries include projects and curriculum resources that have been developed to encourage young African American women to explore careers and majors in nontraditional careers and to continue with schooling if they become pregnant or have a child. The latter projects are of particular importance because young, single black mothers often must rely on welfare and may remain there for many years. Moreover, intervention can make a real difference in their long-term prospects. In an analysis of data collected over a two-year period, Polit and Kahn (1987) examined the school-related experiences of a group of extremely disadvantaged teenage mothers. Nearly half of the women in the sample were African American and approximately 65 percent lived in AFDC households. Staying in school despite pregnancy or childbirth made differences in these adolescents' prospects; girls who were enrolled in school when the data were collected initially (at "baseline") had, after two years, either completed an educational program or were enrolled in one. In contrast, only 28 percent of girls who had dropped out at baseline were in an educational program. Girls who reported that they had had educational counseling during the second year of data collection were more likely than the other girls to have completed or be enrolled in an educational program (Polit and Kahn, 1987).

CONCLUSION

The foregoing suggests that higher education and job training will have only a small impact on increasing self-sufficiency and upward mobility for low-income black women. The effects of sex and race discrimination are still evident in salary and hiring practices, and many African American women do not have the educational backgrounds required for admission to postsecondary programs or they may be perceived by employers as lacking in the skills needed for the "best" entry-level jobs. Moreover, the conflict between individual goals for economic independence and collective goals requiring mutual support may hinder low-income women's progress through training and postsecondary programs.

Higher education and job training might, however, make a difference if other existing mechanisms are vigorously used. Among the approaches are: affirmative action, to offset the sex and race discrimination apparent in salaries and selection practices of employers; job creation, through strategies such as diversion of AFDC funds for self-employment opportunities and subsidies to employers who will hire AFDC clients; improvement of urban schools to upgrade academic performance and persistence; implementation of sex equity programs for African American girls that provide information, counseling, and experiences in nontraditional careers.

There might be benefits in rethinking the issue of self-sufficiency so that new strategies can be identified. For example, we know virtually nothing about how the concentration of black low-income women in deteriorating urban centers affects their movement upward or out of poverty, nor do we know how urban versus suburban residence makes a difference.

Another possibility is the establishment of a national advocacy project, where women would monitor the conditions of low-income women and the federal and private efforts to upgrade their status; compile and disseminate information on promising policies and practices; and conduct special studies and projects. In such a project, low-income women would compose the leadership, drawing on their legacy as key figures in the movements for civil rights, women's rights, welfare rights, parental involvement, and community control of schools. As Sacks (1988) noted: "The women's movement owes its critique of public policy to the women of the National Welfare Rights Organization, who made some of the earliest demands for economic independence for women, but who are too often ignored in white feminist movement genealogics" (page 24). We cannot afford similarly to ignore talented, but poor, African American women who lack formal credentials. Their ideas and understanding of the realities of being poor, Black, and female may provide the impetus for restructuring systems to support families in the United States.

REFERENCES

Allen, L., and Britt, D. W. (1984). Black women in American society: A resource development perspective. In A. U. Rickel, M. Gerrard, and I. Iscoe (eds.), *Social and psychological problems of women: Prevention and crisis intervention,* pp. 61–79.

Braddock, J. H. & McPartland, J. M. (1987). How minorities continue to be excluded from equal employment opportunities: Research on labor market and institutional barriers. *Journal of Social Issues* 43:5–39.

Butler, A. S., and McNeeley, P. V. (1987). *Black girls and schooling: A directory of strategies and programs for furthering the academic and persistence rate of Black females K–12.* Manhattan, KS: Kansas State University.

Center for Law and Social Policy (1989). AFDC data. *The Partnership* 2, 4.

Children's Defense Fund (1988). *A children's defense budget: An analysis of our nation's investment in children.* Washington, DC: CDF.

College Entrance Examination Board (1984). *College opportunity and public assistance programs: Ideas for resolving conflicts.* Washington, DC: College Board.

Danziger, S. H., and Weinberg, D. H. (1986). *Fighting poverty: What works and what doesn't.* Cambridge, MA: Harvard University Press.

Delta Sigma Theta Sorority, Inc. (1984). *Summit II: A call to action in support of Black single mothers.* Washington, DC: Delta Sigma Theta.

———— (n.d.). *International women's conference, "Woman to woman: Single parenting from a global perspective."* Washington, DC: Delta Sigma Theta.

Duggan, P. (1984). *Shaping the work force of the future: An agenda for change.* Washington, DC: Northeast-Midwest Institute.

Evangelauf, J. (1988). Minority groups continue gains on admissions tests. *The Chronicle of Higher Education* 35 (1):132.

Farley, R., and Allen, W. R. (1987). *The color line and the quality of life in America.* New York, NY: Russell Sage Foundation.

Fordham, S. (1988). Racelessness as a factor in Black students' school success: Pragmatic strategy or pyrrhic victory? *Harvard Educational Review* 58:54–84.

Grant, L. (1984). Black females' "place" in desegregated classrooms. *Sociology of Education* 57:98–111.

Lewis, S. et al. (1985). Achieving sex equity for minority women. In S. Klein (ed.), *Handbook for achieving sex equity through education.* Baltimore, MD: Johns Hopkins University Press.

McAdoo, H. P. (1981). Patterns of upward mobility in black families. In H. P. McAdoo (ed.), *Black families.* Beverly Hills, CA: Sage Publications.

———— (1980). Black mothers and the extended family support network. In L. F. Rodgers-Rose (ed.), *The black woman.* Beverly Hills, CA: Sage Publications.

National Association of Community Action Agencies (1987). *Total family support/ total community mobilization.* Washington, DC: NACAA.

National Commission on Working Women (1985–1987). *Fact sheet series.* Washington, DC: NCWW.

Nettles, S. M. (1988). Fostering self-support: Programs in the states and cities. In M. Ackelsberg, R. Bartlett, and R. Buchele (eds.), *Women, welfare and higher education: Toward comprehensive policies.* Northampton, MA: Smith College.

Nettles, S. M., and Scott-Jones, D. (in press). The race of sexuality and sex equity in the education of minority adolescents. *Peabody Journal of Education.*

Office of Educational Research and Improvement (1986). *Digest of educational statistics, 1985–86.* Washington, DC: U.S. Department of Education.

Polit, D. F., and Kahn, J. R. (1987). Teenage pregnancy and the role of the schools. *Urban Education* 22:131–153.

Retraining America's workers. (1987). *The Futurist* 21.

Sacks, K. B. (1988). Out of the frying pan, into the fire: Macroeconomic trends and women's life chances. In M. Ackelsberg, R. Bartlett, & R. Buchele (eds.).

Shumaker, S. A., and Brownell, A. (1984). Toward a theory of social support: Closing conceptual gaps. *Journal of Social Issues* 40:11–36.

Spolar, C. (1988a). Program maps Maryland welfare mother's road to change. *Washington Post* March 14, D1.

—— (1988b). Unlearning dependence. *Washington Post* August 31, A1.

—— (1987). One woman's efforts to break off welfare. *Washington Post* December 22, B1.

Stack, C. B. (1974). *All our kin.* New York, NY: Harper and Row.

Weis, L. (1985). Without dependence on welfare for life: Black women in the community college. *Urban Review* 17:233–255.

Wolanin, T. R. (1988). Why don't the federal student aid programs make sense for many potential students receiving public assistance? In M. Ackelsberg, R. Bartlett & R. Buchele (eds.).

11

Women on Welfare:
Education and Work

MARILYN GITTELL

EDUCATION, EMPLOYMENT, AND POVERTY

In spite of the fact that the number of women working in the labor market has increased in the last decade, more women are living below the poverty level. The average single mother in poverty, according to a 1984 Department of Labor study on women workers, supports a family of 3.4 persons and is a high school graduate aged 33.4 years (U.S. Department of Labor, 1984). The jobs available to her, however, are unlikely to change her economic status. The highest rates of poverty for working *women* are in the "traditional" occupations—service sector jobs, private household work, operative work, and sales. The lowest poverty rates for working women are for professional, technical, managerial, and administrative employees. A study of occupations and incomes of college graduates in 1982 found that 84 percent of graduates were employed in the higher-paying professional, technical, and managerial areas (U.S. Department of Labor, Women's Bureau, 1983) and that women college graduates surpassed the average earnings of their cohorts with high school educations within two years of graduating from college (Henderson and Ottinger, 1985). To get these jobs, women need postsecondary education. Although women as a share of the workforce are increasing, the increase is, for the most part, in low-paying service sector jobs (see Table 11.1). Sex stereotyping in education contributes to directing women to these lower-prestige, lower-paying occupations. This problem is felt most intensely by poor women, particularly women of color, who historically have received lower-quality educations in inferior schools, with little or no support for school completion, and sharply limited opportunities to pursue a postsecondary education.

Table 11.1 Number of New Jobs, Average Pay, and Female Share of Work Force in Various Occupations, 1986

Occupation	Number of New Jobs	Percent Female[a]	Average Pay ($)[b]
Registered Nurse	612,000	93	11.79
U.S. Average Male Wage			11.24
U.S. Average Wage			9.60
Truck Driver	525,000	3	8.72
Office Clerk	62,000	80	8.11
U.S. Average Female Wage			7.80
Janitor/Maid	604,000	28	6.76
Nursing Aide	433,000	88	6.05
Cashier	575,000	80	5.37
Waiter/Waitress	752,000	79	5.05
Retail Sales	1,200,000	69	4.82
Food-Counter Worker	449,000	79	3.80
General Manager	582,000	NA	NA

[a]Women as a share of all workers in 1986
[b]Hourly earning in 1986
NA Not available
Source: Bureau of Labor Statistics, Census Bureau, 1988. BW EST.

WOMEN ON AFDC WANT
GOOD JOBS AND INDEPENDENCE

In a 1986 study on Aid to Families with Dependent Children (AFDC) recipients and education, Gittell and Moore (1987) found that many AFDC women have both the qualifications and the inclination to attend college but that social and institutional barriers make it difficult, if not impossible, for them to do so.

Although their reasons varied, almost all of the eighty-five AFDC women interviewed in three different cities and states for this study described full-time employment as their strongest personal goal. One of their reasons most strongly articulated for wanting full-time employment outside the home was to be financially independent and to have control over their lives. AFDC as a means of support was seen as imposing, demeaning, and unreliable. Women commented frequently on the loss of privacy they suffered under AFDC; others cited the "indignities of welfare," while still others talked about the low self-esteem they developed "waiting for checks." Many women had been randomly removed from AFDC without warning, and even though they were later reinstated with reimbursement for the loss, it did not erase the hardship they and their families had endured when they were suddenly left without an income.

Although the women placed full-time employment at the top of their priorities, they did not mean just any employment. Many had been full-time homemakers for different lengths of time, but almost all had some history of employment outside the home. Of the work experiences they described, the women mentioned part-time jobs most often; other unskilled, nonunion factory jobs were common, as were fast-food and nursing assistant jobs. Women spoke of jobs that paid minimum wage or just above—where they encountered racial and sexual discrimination and harassment, where hours were incompatible with family responsibilities, locations were difficult and expensive to reach, and benefits, especially medical coverage, were nonexistent.

These women's descriptions of their problems in finding secure employment with reasonable benefits are a realistic appraisal of the conditions they face in the labor market without an adequate education. Yet, many state "workfare" employment programs for AFDC women reinforce occupational segregation and pay inequities. These job placement programs place most women in low-wage, low-skill, and low-prestige jobs with few opportunities for advancement—jobs where women have traditionally been concentrated.

AFDC recipients are more realistic about what they need; in their interviews Gittell and Moore (1987) asked women who set employment as their goal what barriers prevented them from achieving this goal. The most frequently mentioned impediment to success was the lack of an adequate education, although their self-defined education needs varied according to each woman's specific background. For many AFDC women, basic skills or a GED would provide short-term qualifications for employment. Most women noted, however, that once they finished high school or a GED program, they were still not ready for a job. For many jobs they needed college credentials, and in some cases, jobs they had previously held required stronger credentials when they returned. For example, women in Baltimore, Maryland, who had worked for years as nursing assistants found it impossible to return to equivalent jobs after they had spent several years at home with their young children. Legislation passed in the intervening years required certification and a college degree to be a nursing assistant; that meant completing a community college certificate program. Further, despite the increased requirements, many women found that the pay for nursing assistant jobs was insufficient to support a family. For many of these women, applying to a four-year nursing program would have been the best solution; unfortunately, the cost of obtaining a four-year college education was prohibitively expensive.

BARRIERS TO EDUCATION

When women who set education as their goal were asked what prevented them from achieving their goal, most stated that the major barrier is an uncooperative and often difficult welfare agency. In several state workfare programs, including Employment Training in Massachusetts, women are not informed of the option to choose an education program; it is then very difficult to transfer into the education program once they find out it is an option. In most state programs, however, education is not an option.

Covering tuition expenses is another major obstacle. Some women lack information about how to cover tuition and school expenses. Others fear that applying for a tuition loan or grant will lead to the loss of their welfare benefits. In fact, fear of losing welfare benefits discourages many women from seeking education financial aid that they have a right to claim under federal legislation.

In addition to these obstacles, the lack of adequate basic skills in education is a pervasive problem that requires special college attention. Fear of test-taking was another obstacle mentioned by many women, making the college experience even more daunting.

Because of the diversity of the AFDC population, there is no simple formula for removing these barriers. A look at the demographics of the AFDC population indicates that women on AFDC vary substantially by age, level of education, amount of prior work experience, and number and age of children. While the largest proportion of AFDC women are 21–29 years of age (44.9 percent), 31 percent are 30–39 years old, and 14 percent are 40 years and older. Sixty percent of the AFDC families have children under six years, and over 42 percent have children 7–13 years of age (Stein, 1985).

AFDC women's level of educational attainment is also varied. National data show that 37.2 percent of adults on AFDC in 1975 had completed at least a twelfth grade education (Hollister and Maynard, 1984). The largest percentage of women who graduated from high school were in the youngest age group, 15–24 years. In each of the cities studied by Gittell and Moore (1987), more than 40 percent of the women interviewed had graduated from high school and almost 10 percent had some college education. Only in Boston did the women in the 25–64 years age group have a larger percentage of high school graduates (50.9 percent). In the latest year for which data is available (1979) women in the 15–24 years age group made up some 20 percent of the total population of women below the poverty level who were heads of household in each of the cities—and that number is increasing (U.S. Department of Commerce, 1980).

These data point to a variety of program needs and related services such as child care and health care. Differences in the early work experience and employment skills of AFDC recipients suggest that still more adjustments are required to address their needs. Yet, many college programs fail to tailor their offerings to these special and varied needs. They neither encourage nor support the efforts of low-income women who make great sacrifices to acquire a postsecondary education.

Higher education is an important option for women on AFDC, and many *want* to go to college, to develop more advanced skills, and be prepared for more stable, long-term employment. The diverse backgrounds, educational preparation, and status of these women require diverse options for education and support programs. This is seldom recognized, however, and policies aimed at low-income women continue to conveniently address a stereotyped population with programs narrow in scope and goals.

INVESTING IN HUMAN CAPITAL

The narrowness of welfare policies and their general refusal to offer higher education as an option is harmful to AFDC women, but it is harmful to society as well. According to Henry Levin, the failure of U.S. policymakers to invest in the education of citizens living below the poverty line could lead to a deterioration of the labor force and a continuing decline in the competitiveness of U.S. labor (Levin, 1985). Recent economic developments support this view and the need for investment in a highly skilled labor supply to respond to a changing deindustrialized economy (Beck, 1985).

Mark Blaug argues that the labor force benefit is only a secondary one, that the primary benefit to be derived from a postsecondary education is socialization (Blaug, 1985). University graduates will be those prepared for the upper-level jobs, having learned the necessary traits of self-esteem, self-reliance, versatility, and leadership. The university experience prepares those workers privileged to enter the primary labor market. Unless a postsecondary education is available to economically disadvantaged people, persons of color, and women, the same educational system will act as a "screen" denying their access to the primary labor market. In a society that boasts of equal opportunity, this is unacceptable.

Gary Becker, in his work *Human Capital,* shows that any activity that raises future productivity as a result of direct or indirect opportunity costs is part of a society's investment in human capital (Becker, 1964). In general, U.S. economic, education, and employment policies seek immediate cost benefits. These social policies that eschew long-term investment in human capital are shortsighted and often counterproductive, perpetuating the discriminatory practices that exclude women from the education they need in order to hold stable, rewarding jobs and to escape welfare dependency. The dearth of state welfare/work programs that consider college education as a viable and positive option for AFDC women is evidence of this shortsightedness.

Workfare requirements under the 1981 Budget Reconciliation Act stressed immediate job placement, overlooking the demonstrated value of education combined with work experience in preparing lower-income populations for employment (Auletta, 1983). This reflects the general lack of interest in the development of federal and state policies that will provide the most effective long-term preparation of low-income populations for productive work experiences.

THE STATE'S ROLE: EDUCATION AS AN OPTION

From its inception in the 1930s, the AFDC program was maintained as a state program, allowing the states to determine eligibility and income standards even as federal funding grew and federal regulations increased. The fact of the predominant role of states in the formulation and implementation of welfare policies means that states vary in their inter-pretation of federal regulations and their implementation. In states that decentralize the administration of welfare programs to the county and city levels, differences can even be observed within states (Derthick, 1970).

While state discretionary power under the ambiguous federal and state rulings benefits AFDC recipients who want to pursue an education in liberal states, there are many more conservative states that narrowly interpret the regulations and *prohibit* college attendance as an option. Local welfare agencies and caseworkers tend to be even more restrictive in the interpretation of the regulations if there is no specific commitment or policy directive from higher-level officials to allow, never mind en-courage, education as an option under work regulations.

An important problem facing AFDC recipients who aspire to a college education is funding. The lack of coordination between state education policy on student aid and welfare policy on student income and cost of living calculations results in conflicting state policies on financial aid which are insensitive to the needs of recipients. In many states, ambiguous state regulations regarding the relationship between student financial aid and welfare leave considerable discretion to caseworkers in calculating costs and income. And, as mentioned above, AFDC recipients in college perceive that caseworkers are generally not supportive of their college attendance and are inclined to interpret regulations narrowly.

Federal Public Welfare Title 45 (Section 233.20), adopted in November 1988, draws specific restrictions around what monies an AFDC recipient may keep without having them included as income and deducted from benefits. Food stamp programs pose a more restrictive and more difficult problem. Section 233.20 of Title 45 excludes from income "loans and grants, such as scholarships, obtained and used under conditions that

preclude their use for current living costs." There is also an exclusion
for income from Jobs Training Partnership Act (JTPA) participation, and
"any grant or loan to any undergraduate student for education purposes
made or insured under any programs administered by the Commissioner
of Education" (U.S. Code of Federal Regulations, 1984). This includes
student aid grants and federal student loans, but whether it includes
College Work Study is an issue interpreted differently by different state
courts. Yet, federal law makes it illegal for state welfare departments to
count certain federal school grants as income or to deduct the amount
of such aid to reduce AFDC payments. Clearly, in this new legislation
Congress intended to support and encourage AFDC women who choose
to go to college.

Even now, states can be supportive of students or provide disincentives
by the process they use to calculate aid. There is a tendency in some
states to discourage a college option since states would have to bear
additional costs. Presently, in most states the cost of living standard is
calculated at a lower level by welfare offices than by student financial
aid formulae.

For a single AFDC mother, taking time and scarce family resources
to pursue an education is prohibitively costly unless clear options are
presented. State and local welfare departments, however, do not advertise
higher education options and prefer fast-track training programs, for
dramatic short-term reduction of the welfare rolls. But, if they expect
AFDC women to think in the long term about their career development
and financial stability, state and local welfare departments must think
in the long term as well, providing real options and advertising them,
giving long-term substantive change priority over the quick fix.

Welfare reform legislation adopted by Congress in 1988 requires states
to create and operate welfare including education, training, and employment programs within three years. States must provide a broad range
of activities, including: high school or equivalent education; remedial,
basic literacy; postsecondary education, as appropriate; skills training;
community work experience; job search assistance; job development and
job placement; and other activities, as determined by the Department of
Health and Human Services. The law permits four-year college enrollment
as a training option. It requires states to consult with the private sector
in the development of the program and to coordinate with other work-
related programs, such as the Jobs Training Partnership Act, which will
continue to emphasize immediate job placement.

All nonexempt AFDC recipients are required under the new legislation
to participate in JOBS (Job Opportunities and Basic Skills); exemption
is allowed for parents of children under 6, or under 3, if day care is
available. States are required to target resources to long-term recipients,

or those who are at risk of being long-term recipients. They must also provide case management. States are required to reevaluate need and payment standards of recipients at least once every five years. Some transitional support has been granted as well; former recipients who are now employed may receive nine months of child care, with sliding-scale fees. Four months' health coverage is provided, and the state has the option to extend coverage for an additional five months, with co-payment. If these benefits are applied to those choosing education as an option, they may need to be extended in time.

The new federal legislation still permits wide state discretion in the structuring of education and work programs for AFDC recipients. The extent to which education is emphasized, particularly college education as preparation for work, will be a matter of state policy. But, more incentives are available to states for success in immediate job placement or short-term training programs; the costs are less and the immediate political payoffs are greater. The education establishment in each state must offer more effort and encouragement to convince state welfare policymakers that a long-term investment in human capital—a college education—will provide deeper and longer-lasting individual and social rewards. Leadership for changing the thrust of state welfare programs must come from governors.

The new federal approval of education options for welfare recipients also involves some dangers. Trade and proprietary schools, which are loosely regulated in most states and not at all by the federal government, will be promoting their short-term, vocationally oriented training programs for this new welfare clientele. In 1987 and 1988 students at for-profit trade schools received more than $1 billion in Pell Grants. Requirements for job training in the new federal welfare legislation will bring even greater numbers of AFDC recipients into proprietary schools. Critics fear that these schools' "unscrupulous owners will take advantage of the huge influx of welfare recipients" (Wilson, 1989). State education agencies will have to be more sensitive to these issues than they have been in the past and adopt stricter regulatory policies. To counter the appeal of proprietary schools, public colleges will have to take greater initiatives in developing programs to serve this population.

COLLEGE PROGRAMS: PROBLEMS AND CONCERNS

Gittell and Moore's review of college programs for AFDC women in the three cities studied (Baltimore, Boston, and Philadelphia) found a lack of concern for students on welfare and a dearth of programs and support services for them in traditional colleges. Programs in three community colleges with relatively large populations of AFDC women offered comparatively low-cost vocational training, basic skills, and GED programs. AFDC women were confronted with several problems, however, in attending these traditional community colleges. First, lower-income women were not generally addressed as a population with specific needs. Second, no "precurriculum" programs were in place to first provide basic skills instruction. And third, sex stereotypes for both education and employment were reinforced, encouraging women to enter low-paying jobs in traditionally female fields. Emphasis was on preparation for nursing aide and service-sector jobs.

Most important, though, community colleges, in spite of the fact that they enrolled large numbers of AFDC students, did not differentiate services and programs to respond to their special needs. Traditional educational institutions often did not keep records on how many of the students were AFDC or low-income or how many were single parents. Few did any follow-up, especially of first-time college students who were low-income women with children; this information would have been valuable in identifying those programs and other efforts that keep students in school, the barriers that make school impossible, and the opportunities that are available to AFDC students upon completion of programs. Those programs that did tailor their courses and support services to women and either targeted AFDC women or offered them extensive services, tended to be community-based and nontraditional education programs. Particularly noteworthy were the efforts of the Women's College in Philadelphia and Sojourner Douglass College in Baltimore. In both schools, day care was provided on site, classes were scheduled at later hours, and special basic skills components were available for students based on level of performance.

The more traditional higher education institutions reviewed also failed to translate research findings into educational practice. Although a variety of comprehensive studies have identified cooperative education—part-time work and part-time study—as a constructive educational approach to lower-income populations (Heerman, 1977), no cooperative education programs were available in the community colleges studied. Much greater effort must be exerted by state education and welfare officials to encourage public colleges and universities to develop more appropriate curricula, programs, and support systems for AFDC recipients who elect to go to college.

CONCLUSION

Acceptance of the principle that education and/or career training is a desirable option for AFDC women requires that several issues be addressed: (1) state policy barriers to the achievement of the goal must be eliminated, (2) incentives must be provided under new workfare programs to encourage AFDC recipients to elect an education or training option, and (3) education and career training programs that best respond to the special needs of this diverse population must be developed and implemented.

In their exploration of state policies and practices in several policy areas—education, employment, and economic development—Gittell and Moore (1987) were constantly struck by the extent of separation, and even conflict, in these areas of policy at the state and local levels and by the absence of long-range goals for education and employment of AFDC recipients. Separate departments and agencies administered programs in each of the policy areas and each agency made plans without consideration for, or knowledge of, related activities in the other agencies. The most compelling finding was that agencies were more dedicated to protecting their own programs than to developing cooperative programs with related agencies to meet the needs of AFDC women.

The National Governors' Association supported mandatory work programs for AFDC recipients, if they were developed as part of an overall training and employment policy, and their efforts are reflected in the 1988 legislation. Some of the states have begun to move in this direction, but progress is slow and incentives are limited. The 1988 federal legislation may provide these much-needed incentives; for the first time, federal welfare law provides for education as an option to immediate job placement. The states now can develop more substantial education programs and options under these federal guidelines. But coordinated state planning and integration of policymaking in welfare, employment training, and higher education is essential if states propose to fully address the needs and education and employment goals of the AFDC population. Commonly agreed-upon goals can be established and implemented by the appropriate state agencies, sharing resources and avoiding conflict, competition, and/ or duplication of services. The special training and education needs of AFDC women are also more likely to be re-evaluated in an integrated planning process at the state and local levels.

There is general agreement among policymakers, the public at large, and AFDC women that economic independence is preferable to welfare. What is lacking is agreement that education is a reasonable alternative to immediate employment because it offers greater opportunity for economic independence in the future. Policymakers and the public assume that any job is better than welfare; AFDC women know that is not the case. A good number of them, while anxious to be free of the welfare system, recognize that they need to develop the skills, the experience, and the self-confidence to secure employment that is more stable and offers opportunity for advancement. Their efforts to obtain job training and more education have been met with frustration because they are considered high-risk candidates, in spite of the fact that program assessments indicate a high degree of success by AFDC women in retention and program completion (Hollister and Maynard, 1984). They also suffer from special limitations because of their responsibilities for child care and their limited preparation for work. There are AFDC women who participate in career training programs and attend college, some at great sacrifice to themselves and their children and often without the knowledge or support of education and welfare agencies. An even larger number are college-ready and would choose to attend college if there were reasonable incentives to do so or if the many barriers that presently exist were eliminated.

Discretion for changing policies that will provide encouragement and support for AFDC students resides with the states. As in all policy areas, states will differ in their responses; many, for example, are concerned that a longer-term investment in education will add to already overburdened state budgets. Historically, several innovative states have been the source of new ideas and programs that are later adopted in other states and ultimately even adopted as national policy. For this reason, every effort should be made to encourage key states to experiment with changes in the options for education for AFDC women and to provide incentives for more responsive college programs and financial support for women willing and able to undertake a four-year college program. It is astounding that there is a dearth of research on women who completed college while on welfare and the impact college education has had on their employment, their families, and their own life experiences.[1]

As a society we sometimes blame poor people for their condition, denying that government policies are determinants of dependency; but government policies can also foster *independence*. For the AFDC population, government policies that expand their education and employment options, giving them a *real* opportunity to join the primary labor market in more secure and higher-paying jobs, can be the mechanisms for promoting their independence.

NOTES

I would like to thank my graduate students at CUNY, Janice Moore and Margaret Schehl for their important contribution to this work.

1. This author, in collaboration with the New York State Education Department, is currently conducting a study of college students who entered college in 1980 in New York who were on welfare and graduated by 1986; the study will examine their employment and personal lives since graduation.

REFERENCES

Auletta, K. (1983). *The underclass.* New York, NY: Vintage Books.

Beck, N. (1985). Financial aid today: An economic perspective. *College Board Review* 137.

Becker, G. S. (1964). Human capital. *NBER, General series* 80. New York, NY: Columbia University Press.

Blaug, M. (1985). Where are we now in the economics of education? *Economics of Education Review* 1 (4).

Boeckman, M. (1984). *Study of barriers to employment for WIN mandatory welfare recipients.* Baltimore, MD: Maryland Department of Human Resources, Office of Welfare Employment Policy.

Center for National Policy Review (1985). *Jobs watch alert.* January 9:1. Washington, DC: CNPR.

College Entrance Examination Board (1984). *The college opportunity and public assistance programs.* Washington, DC: The College Board.

———— (1982). *Income maintenance programs and college oppportunity.* Washington, DC: The College Board.

Dalby, N. (1985). Women facing problems under JTPA. *Jobs watch alert.* January 9. Washington, DC: CNPR.

Derthick, M. (1970). *The influence of federal grants: Public assistance in Massachusetts.* Cambridge, MA: Harvard University Press.

Feldman, R. (1984). *Employment, training and support services for mother-only families.* Report to the Ford Foundation.

Ford Foundation (1985). *Women, children and poverty in America.* New York, NY: Ford Foundation.

Franklin, P. L. (1985). *Helping disadvantaged youth and adults enter college.* Washington, DC: The College Board.

Fuchs, V. R. (1983). *How we live: An economic perspective on Americans from birth to death.* Cambridge, MA: Harvard University Press.

Gittell, M., and Moore, J. (1987). *Women on welfare: Education and work.* New York, NY: Ford Foundation.

Grant, S., and Moore, D. (1985). *Legislative alert.* February 11. West Orange, NJ: National Association of Commissions on Women.

Grubb, W. N., and Lazerson, M. (1982). *Broken promises: How Americans fail their children.* New York, NY: Basic Books.

Hansen, J. S. (1985). *College opportunity and public assistance programs.* Testimony on reauthorization of the Higher Education Act to the Subcommittee on Postsecondary Education, Committee on Education and Labor, U.S. House of Representatives. July 9. Washington, DC.

Hayes, J. S. (1984). *Welfare to wages? Women in the WIN program.* Washington, DC: Wider Opportunities for Women.

Heermann, B. (1977). Experiential learning in the community college. *Topical Paper* 62.

Henderson, C., and Ottinger, C. (1985). College degrees . . . Still a ladder to success? *Journal of College Placement* Spring.

Hollister, R. G., and Maynard, R. A. (1984). The impacts of supported work on AFDC recipients. In R. Hollister, P. Kemper, R. Maynard (eds.), *The national supported work demonstration.* Madison, WI: University of Wisconsin Press.

Koshel, J. (1984). *Work programs for welfare recipients.* Washington, DC: Center for Policy Research, National Governers' Association.

Levin, H. M. (1985). *The educationally disadvantaged: A national crisis.* Report to the Stewart Mott Foundation.

Lloyd, C. B., and Niemi, B. T. (1979). *The economics of sex differentials.* New York, NY: Columbia University Press.

Long, J. P. et al. (1984). *Economic development and the community college.* Columbus, OH: National Center for Research in Vocational Education.

Marano, C. (1985). *The Carl Perkins Vocational Education Act: A sex equity analysis.* Washington, DC: Wider Opportunities for Women.

Maryland Department of Employment and Training (1985). *State plan and annual report.* Baltimore, MD: Department of Employment and Training.

Massachusetts Department of Public Welfare (1986). *Massachusetts employment and training choices program: Program plan and budget request, FY87.* Boston, MA: Executive Office of Human Services.

Mellor, E. F. (1984). Investigating the differences in weekly earnings of women and men. *Monthly Labor Review* June.

Palmer, E. (1985). Congress showing more than usual concern about the needs of non-traditional students. *Chronicle of Higher Education* July 3.

Stein, S. G. (1985). *Women, poverty and welfare: Breaking the cycle.* Paper presented at the conference, Women, welfare, and higher education: A policy conference. Northampton, MA: Smith College.

U.S. Code of Federal Regulations (1984) *Public Welfare Title 45* (Parts 200 to 499). October 1.

U.S. Department of Commerce, Bureau of the Census (1980). *Poverty status in 1979 of families and unrelated individuals by years of school completed.* Washington, DC: Census Bureau.

U.S. Department of Labor, Bureau of Labor Statistics (1984). *Employment in perspective: Working women* (Report 716) fourth quarter. Washington, DC: U.S. Dept. of Labor.

U.S. Department of Labor, Employment and Training Administration (1977). *The Work Incentive (WIN) program and related experiences: A review of research with policy implications.* (R & D Monograph 49). Washington, DC: U.S. Dept. of Labor.

U.S. Department of Labor, Women's Bureau (1983). *Time of Change: 1983 Handbook on Women Workers* 298. Washington, DC: U.S. Dept. of Labor.

U.S. Public Law 88–21. (1963). *Carl D. Perkins Vocational Education Act.* 98th Congress of U.S. 2nd session, January 23, 1984. H.R. 4164.

Wilson, R. (1989). Many states seek tougher regulation of for-profit schools. *Chronicle of Higher Education* 18 (1).

12

Transforming Rhetoric into Choice: Access to Higher Education for Low-Income Women

ERIKA KATES

If it came down to one thing I've learned it's now I have choices. An AFDC mother does not have many choices, at least she doesn't think so.
—Dora, a 38-year-old white woman, an AFDC recipient, mother of three teenage boys, and student at a four-year state university

With few exceptions, the current policy environment mitigates against access to higher education as a viable choice for AFDC recipients. Despite recent reforms in both higher education and public assistance, the future looks bleak for AFDC recipients and others concerned with improving access to higher education for low-income women. Thus, although the Family Support Act mandates completion of a high school education for youthful recipients, it remains ambiguous about higher education. The act states that if a caretaker "is attending an institution of higher education . . . consistent with the individual's employment goals . . . at a time he or she would commence participation in the program, such attendance may constitute satisfactory participation in the program (Family Support Act, 100–485PL). But it is not clear to what extent new program participants might be able to attend institutions of higher education or whether such an option will be actively encouraged. Responding to the act, a number of administrators in community colleges and vocational schools—institutions that are expected to participate in some of the recipient skill and need assessments for the new Job Opportunities and Basic Skills (JOBS) Program—expressed concern that states might be encouraged to use the least expensive, and often, least effective, options for program participants. They also expressed concern that states could

181

require welfare recipients to enroll in job training programs that might interfere with college. In addition, they observed that while some colleges welcome new opportunities to meet welfare recipients' needs, many are clearly unprepared for the new roles that may be thrust upon them. The executive director of the Center for Law and Social Policy commented: "Higher education has got to start talking to state welfare agencies and state legislators about colleges' role in this. If they don't they are going to find themselves dealing with a lot of wrong decisions" (Houseman, 1988).

This chapter looks at the development of working relationships between institutions of higher education and public welfare and defines a specific role for low-income women in the shaping of these policies.[1] Access to higher education is a critical policy issue for AFDC recipients and other low-income women with dependent children; further, this issue has significance for a much larger proportion of women living in poverty than is currently recognized. In order to be effective, policies to improve access to higher education must be informed by the experiences of low-income women in higher education.[2] This study draws attention to the systems of support and types of activism that low-income women have developed and suggests ways in which future policy developments could include, support, and extend these efforts. The primary sources of information were in-depth interviews with twelve AFDC recipients attending college in Massachusetts and conversations with an on-going group of low-income women students.[3]

THE RATIONALE FOR ACCESS
TO HIGHER EDUCATION

Poverty Among Female Single Parents

One of the most dramatic sociodemographic trends in the United States during the past twenty years has been a very rapid increase in the proportion of female-headed households with dependent children. Overall, this proportion grew from 11 percent of all households in 1970 to 16 percent in 1985, according to Census Bureau data; but for women of color the proportion is much greater—42 percent of African American women and 23 percent of Hispanic women, for example, compared to 13 percent of white women, are sole heads of household (Rix, 1987:296). A large number of these women and their children live in poverty. Currently, 34 percent of all female-headed households are poor, and for African American and Hispanic women the proportion is much higher (51 percent and 53 percent respectively) (Rix, 1987:319). While some of these families became poor as a result of marital dissolution, others were poor previously (Bane, 1986).

Failure of Existing Policies

Public policies ostensibly designed to alleviate the worst effects of poverty have not provided substantial help to these women and their children. A review of the effects of the Omnibus Budget Reconciliation Act, a succession of workfare, WIN, and similar programs, and an examination of various states' AFDC payments and income levels of women in the labor force show that now, more than ever, women are struggling to feed, clothe, and house their families (Zinn and Saari, 1984; Gueron and Nathan, 1985; Kluver, 1985). Nationwide, current AFDC benefits do not bring women up to the austere poverty levels established by the federal government. In Massachusetts, for example, cash benefits for a family of three amounted to $5,700 in 1986, leaving women to support their children at about 40 percent below the poverty level of $9,100, and well below the state's estimated low standard of living of $11,000. Even the much-acclaimed Massachusetts Employment and Training Choices (ET) Program does not dramatically increase the standard of living for women and children once taxes, health care benefits, loss of housing subsidies, and employment-related expenses are taken into account (Kluver, 1985). Further, labor force participation does not necessarily alleviate poverty; a substantial number of women with dependent children who *are* employed full-time receive a median wage of just over $7,000, and live at, or below, the poverty level (National Commission on Working Women [NCWW], 1987).

Higher Education as an Option

One factor that makes a difference in raising women's income levels is higher education. The median income of a woman with a college education in 1984 was $16,322 (compared to $16,938 for a man with one to three years of high school) (U.S. Department of Labor, 1984). While pursuing a college degree in order to earn a decent income is obviously not a suitable strategy for all AFDC recipients—and is certainly not a panacea for gender-segregated labor markets and gender-based pay inequities—it is certainly a policy option worthy of further exploration. Apart from the obvious monetary benefits, the college experience is frequently empowering and intrinsically rewarding for low-income women. Moreover, an estimated one-third to one-half of AFDC recipients already have earned high school diplomas or a GED; thus, they are eligible, at least in educational terms, to consider higher education as an option.

In Massachusetts, 34 percent of AFDC recipients have completed high school and an additional 16 percent have some college education or are college graduates (Burke-Tatum, 1988). Nationwide, 47 percent of all women in poverty are high school graduates, as are 53.5 percent of women who are sole heads of household (NCWW, 1987).

Further, it might be assumed that the entry of low-income women into higher education would be facilitated by the dramatic increase in the number of women, especially older women, who are entering higher education. As early as 1961 it was reported that "the group increasing most rapidly in proportion to the total student population in American colleges and universities is women over the age of 30" (Wise, 1961). Currently, two-thirds of students aged 35 or older are women and the number, currently estimated at 1 million, is growing rapidly (American Association of University Women [AAUW], 1985). Some of these women are completing an interrupted education, while others are starting out afresh. This increase in enrollment of older students is occurring simultaneously with a decline in the number of "regular" college students. Thus, while women in general are contributing to a whole new style of postsecondary education, "it appears that this trend largely reflects the influx of older female students" (Moran, 1986).

An increasing number of public and private institutions of higher education, recognizing the achievements of older students and concerned with maintaining enrollment levels, have responded to the influx of older women by offering special programs or resources designed to facilitate their college entry and retention. These options range from providing informal meeting places and "women's centers," where women can meet and provide mutual support to each other, to specially designed programs providing academic, family, and personal assistance.[4] While it might be assumed that the development of such resources would be advantageous for low-income women, this is not necessarily the case. There are indications that college attendance for low-income women remains highly problematic.

OBSTACLES TO HIGHER EDUCATION

"It looks great on paper and everybody is for it. But when you go apply for this, this and this, you find out you are not eligible. And when you get to where you're going, you can't really afford to be there" (Stephanie, a 39-year-old white woman with three children, who has been divorced twice, attending a four-year liberal arts women's college).

Three major problems affect the distribution of resources to low-income, older women students. The first reflects policy conflicts between public assistance and financial aid; the second set of problems emanates from outright restrictions or ambiguities in policies regulating AFDC recipients' participation in higher education; and the third problem is the continuing "invisibility" of this group of women in the formulation, adoption, and implementation of current public welfare and educational policies.[5]

Conflicts Between Financial Aid and AFDC Benefits

"I know from long experience that everything they give you they take away with the other hand" (Joan, a 40-year-old white woman with three children, attending a community college).

The limitations on access to necessary resources revolves around some key questions. To what extent do federal, state, and local welfare policies facilitate college attendance for AFDC recipients? To what extent do institutions of higher education both recognize and support the needs and concerns of low-income students, especially if they have dependent children? And how do these sets of policies interact? The answers emerge from a highly complex policy system involving several discrete policy areas—all of which critically affect the distribution of resources necessary for college attendance. These resources include not only college tuition and related expenses, but also housing, utilities, food, medical expenses, clothing, transportation, and child care. They may also be provided by a variety of public and private agencies funded by federal, state, and local sources. Typically, education funding includes state and federal grants, scholarships, loans, and awards. Living expenses most commonly are covered by AFDC benefits, Medicaid, emergency assistance, fuel assistance, food stamps, subsidized day care or day care vouchers, public transportation tokens or automobile mileage expenses, and subsidized state, federal, or university housing units.

While women in general are at a disadvantage in the distribution of student financial aid, poor women are even more disadvantaged.[6] To the extent that any educational assistance is construed as increasing a household's disposable cash income, an AFDC recipient will experience corresponding losses in AFDC benefits or food stamps.

"Food stamps are the most frustrating thing to go through. Every time the federal government gave me money the food stamps would be cut. It was like, we're going to give you with this hand, but we're going to take with this hand" (Dora, a 38-year-old white woman, with three teenage sons, separated from her second husband, attending a state university).

In addition, since a family's disposable income—which may include children's earnings, gifts, and earnings from labor participation—fluctuates over a period of time, net income is often uncertain from one month to another. Although some attempts have been made to more clearly define the relationship among benefits, ambiguity, and conflicts persist.[7]

In addition to these financial concerns, lack of viable and affordable transportation and child care services often represent almost insurmountable obstacles for low-income women. And even when resources are nominally available, women may be denied access to them through restrictive practices by departments of public welfare and individual child care agencies. These problems occur even in Massachusetts, currently one of the most progressive states in this regard (Kates, 1988; Rosen, 1988). For example, Bertha, divorced with a four-year-old son, had transferred from a community college to a women's college in order to keep her child care slot: "I don't really want to go to summer school; I'm not even having the credits transferred, and I'm actually taking a course over. But you have to be there in July, and start paying, I guess, to reserve a place in September."

Pauline, an unmarried black woman with three daughters, attending a community college, lived in the same town in which her college was located. Although she owned a car, her local welfare agency would not reimburse her mileage expenses but would only provide her with bus tokens. As a result, she had to get up an hour earlier to take her children to school and the day care center: "My friends in [neighboring cities] get transportation but [my city] won't give me any. It's more complicated and it's a strain on me. I just parked my car and now I use the bus. I have to take my daughter to day care, so I use the bus pass and I drop her off. And I have to wait because the bus leaves. I didn't want to wait outside for a whole half-hour, so I asked if I could stay in the building [until the next bus came along]." Because of these numerous obstacles many women are discouraged from applying to college or drop out after enrollment. Nelly, 40 years old, twice divorced with four children, attending a state university, expressed her frustration with the welfare department: "I would say [caseworkers] are not helpful. They don't tell you anything. I've found out everything about welfare—what I can have, what I can get—from other people." In short, in order to attend college and meet her ordinary needs of daily living, each AFDC recipient must negotiate a complex web of policies. Even when she does so, she may also lose financially. Moreover, for many women already living below the poverty level, the additional *uncertainty* of income is particularly daunting.

The "Permissibility" of College Attendance

An additional factor affecting college attendance is the extent to which public assistance programs actively support that option. Very few states either overtly permit or encourage AFDC recipients to attend college. Massachusetts is one of the few states that does; through the Employment and Training Choices (ET) Program, women can enroll in college; they are aided by a tuition waiver arrangement with state colleges that allows free attendance for two semesters. A woman then must apply for her own financial aid. Registration for the ET Program is mandatory for women whose children are over 6 years of age; but if her caseworker concedes that a college education would be a valid "work plan" option, she may apply to ET only for that portion of the program providing assistance with child care and transportation expenses. However, even within a state that is comparatively open to considering higher education as an option for AFDC recipients, women confronted negative attitudes from their caseworkers. As Pauline stated: "But you can't tell them anything because they know everything. [They think] I'm stupid and I can't know what they know. They already have their degree and I'm trying to get it. They can't see any intelligence in me, and so I can't argue with them." Ann, 20 years old, white, never married, with a 5-year-old daughter, attended a state university. She discussed the nature of discouragement in these terms: "It's just weird the kind of stuff that comes up between women [the caseworker and the AFDC recipient] and shouldn't be there, but it is. It is kind of like she feels she has power or something. All she wants to know is 'how am I ripping off the system?'"

Individual caseworkers hold a tremendous amount of discretionary authority. The difficulties of access to resources are compounded by the fact that interpretation and enforcement of these policies often differ not only between states but also within states, and even between employees in the same welfare office (Rosen, 1988; Franklin, 1984). As a result of direct restrictions or more covert restrictive practices, many women simply do not participate in higher education.

"Invisibility" of Low-Income Women in Higher Education

Older, low-income women with dependent children continue to remain "invisible" to educational and social welfare policymakers. Despite revisions in both federal and state financial aid policies to extend college opportunities to disadvantaged groups, current definitions of "disadvantaged" do not specifically extend to low-income women with dependent children.[8] Many of these women's expenses, which do not appear in a "regular" student's budget, are not recognized in current financial aid accounting. Research conducted for this article showed that eleven out of twelve students who were AFDC recipients faced "extraordinary" expenses of this kind, including children's school trips, proms, and sports equipment, funerals, car repairs, and bills related to former spouses. None of these can be found as a line-item in financial aid forms. The definition of "unmet need" further reflects this. Unmet need refers to

Table 12.1   Sources of Support for 12 AFDC Recipients Attending Institutions of Higher Education

Sources of Support	Times Mentioned
Students	8
Faculty	7
Friends and family	6
Special programs for returning students	6
AFDC and ET caseworkers	5
Agencies: women's shelters, food programs	4
Churches	4
College administrators	3
Welfare rights organizations	2
Total	45

the gap between allocated financial aid and actual costs. Each student is expected to provide a contribution based on personal or parental earnings. This expectation presents an almost insurmountable obstacle for AFDC recipients who, by definition, have extremely limited assets and limited (if any) personal or parental earnings that could contribute to unmet needs.

OVERCOMING OBSTACLES

In order to initially enroll and then remain in college, AFDC recipients and other low-income women must overcome several major obstacles. Analysis of in-depth interviews with twelve AFDC recipients in college revealed that all women adopted a variety of survival strategies in order to stay in college. Indeed, many became very skillful in finding allies and resources to confront the numerous obstacles they encountered. A survey of their actions showed that they encompassed the range of strategies typically described in the literature on women and grass-roots activism—mutual support and self-help groups, consciousness raising, and protests and demonstrations; they also used strategies described in the more traditional literature on women and public policy—leadership training and coalition building, lobbying and monitoring official practices, collecting information, drafting legislation, and litigation (Gelb and Palley, 1982; Gartner, 1988). Table 12.1 summarizes the women's sources of support and Table 12.2 the types of activism they pursued.

Sources of Support

The majority of students placed an enormously high value on the mutual help and support of their peers; informal networks among students constituted critical sources of support and encouragement. Jennifer, 40

Table 12.2 Actions Taken by 12 AFDC Recipients Attending Institutions of Higher Education

Actions Taken	Times Mentioned
Talking to other women in similar situations	7
Persistence with local caseworkers	5
Information seeking at state agencies	5
Formal appeals processes[a]	3
Lobbying with welfare rights groups	2
Writing to state representatives	2
Writing petitions	1
Engaging in litigation	1
Providing testimony to Congressional hearings	1
Total	27

Notes: [a] One woman engaged in two appeals.

years old with grown children, attending a community college, commented about her peers that "the support they give, it's invaluable. I know there are a lot of women in my age group here and I don't feel out of place at all." Joan stated: "Many times, if I hadn't had that interaction, I don't know if I could have made it through. It takes the communication of those who've been through it. Maybe one person has learned in one area and you haven't, but you've learned in another area that they haven't; and by sharing this you survive and you last that little bit longer." Stephanie also spoke positively about support from "regular" as well as "nontraditional" students: "I mean when you're as crazy as you are a lot of different times, friends listen to you and other [older students] are really wonderful; and in some ways traditional students are too."

Students also sought and received support and encouragement from a variety of other sources, including faculty and other college personnel, community agencies, family, and friends. Within educational institutions the presence of understanding and helpful faculty, college administrators, and financial aid officers was critical. Mildred, 37 years old, divorced with three children, attending a women's college stated: "I think that the base of support I've really had was from the school itself and the people in the school. I almost think that if they hadn't been who they were I might have given up." Jackie, 30 years old, at a state university, divorced with two young sons, said: "The person that specializes in the women on AFDC knows the ins and outs and the ropes. I never knew I would be eligible for emergency assistance [from the Department of Public Welfare]. She was the one who said 'It's out there, go and get it.' " She also received substantial help from college financial aid offices: "They're a great help. They're amazing up there. They gave me a financial statement to take with me; and anything you could possibly figure they had there on a piece of paper, saying this is what I need to survive."

Stephanie recalled how she had been helped in a critical housing situation: "I came to talk to the lady in charge of housing and told her I couldn't stay where we were staying. I was already two months behind in the rent, and if I didn't do something quickly I was going to have to put my kids in foster care [again]. She had me in [university housing] on the third of November—before I was even accepted at the University."

Stephanie also discussed how one of her professors had helped her: "The advisor is really very flexible; and I've even found that the University's professors on the whole are more responsive to older people. There is, in essence, a feeling that the older student is back for a good reason; and 33 percent of our students are honor roll students—most of these are women—and 80 percent go on to graduate school." Joan, attending community college, also discussed the support of faculty: "I needed that personal interaction that you get from the students and the teachers that first semester. And they're handpicked. They're the type of teacher who gives you more interaction, who treats you individually, who understands that you have other responsibilities besides school." Pauline also commented on the support instructors offered: "I like the atmosphere; and it's small. And the teachers that I've had contact with so far have been helpful, really helpful. I think I would be lost in a university . . . that's one thing that scared me."

Within the local community, a number of public and private agencies—churches, food banks, women's organizations, and human service agencies—provided valuable encouragement. Although women discussed many instances where they have been discouraged by caseworkers, they also mentioned helpful caseworkers. Bertha, attending a women's college, and the mother of a four-year-old boy, commented: "My second [case]worker would say 'Ignore this, they don't even check on that, so don't worry about it, and do this instead.' She was very helpful. She made me go around a lot of rules that didn't really matter."

Dora reported: "The social worker put down that I had already done two years [of college] and only had two years left. So he lied so that I could do college [and not sign up for WIN]. So if somebody likes you that's taking your application, you've got it made." Jackie said of her ET caseworker: "She's fabulous. She's very, very helpful. She helped me get benefits from DPW that the Hearing office had not told me about. And I ended up getting a hearing and winning both of my hearings with her help."

It is clear from these women's experiences that without the mutual support of other women in similar situations, the assistance of those with discretionary authority over critical resources—who often bent the rules and even lied for them—they would not have been able to enroll and stay in college. In addition, the women who managed to stay in college exhibited a considerable amount of determination: "It became very easy for me to give up when they started deducting things and to say 'Well, I could never have done it anyway, therefore why try?' I've decided this is what I want to do and whether it's going to be hard or it isn't going to be hard, we're going to suffer four more years."

Students' Activism

Although they are taxed for time and other resources, the majority of these women engaged in some form of activism—individually or collectively—for a wide range of purposes. Eleven out of twelve women had undertaken one or more actions relating to policy issues affecting them. They shared knowledge and information; they requested clarification of policies; they protested, demanded, lobbied, appealed, and litigated (see Table 12.2).

For example, several students at the community college discussed their frustration with a local department of welfare office's transportation policy and described their efforts to confront it. Sharon, 30 years old, divorced, with a one-year-old son, discussed her own persistence: "[Students who did not get their transportation money] . . . didn't go ask for it. Or their welfare worker tried to pull a fast one on them. I just walked in and said, 'I can't deduct my Pell Grant for the mileage anymore, you pay it.' She filled out the papers. The first semester I did not collect it. . . . I could have got it, but the way she put it to me I didn't think I was eligible. Then I just went in and within two days I had checks for January and February."

She also discussed how a number of students organized petitions and meetings: "There is a lot of conflict in that area . . . everybody is interpreting it differently. We're petitioning for a bus . . . two semesters we've been working on it." Pauline, discussing the same issue, remarked: "One of the people from [the Regional Office of the Department of Public Welfare] came here, and I told him [about the problem] . . . and nothing came of it."

Some students tried several strategies to resolve their concerns. Dorothy, 34 years old, attending the women's college, has four children and lived in a rural area; she commuted thirty miles each way each day. She discussed several actions she had undertaken: "I know I did a lot of calling, and I said things to the director of Welfare about closing the [local] office down. . . . I appealed it [a cut in food stamps because of work-study income] and it's still in court. And I'm suing the Department of Public Welfare and the United States Department of Agriculture. The same day [the case] was heard was the day the Farm bill passed—with the new food stamp regulations. So I won, but I lost all in one day. I also love to go lobbying. I don't lobby, I educate." Nelly, attending the state university said: "I think it would be great if they moved the welfare grant up to poverty level. . . . I did that campaign last summer. . . . I worked for the Massachusetts Housing Coalition—lobbying, calls, writing letters, explaining to other welfare mothers to get them to do it."

Although students were able to find support from a variety of sources, they also expressed a sense of frustration at not being able to communicate with more students like themselves and at the difficulty of sustaining activism on campuses. Several also expressed a desire to communicate with students on other campuses.

Students' Networks and Organizations

As a result of the expressed desire for more support, a low-income women's group was initiated at the women's college, and its members have met regularly for three years—finally becoming an official student organization. The group has performed several different functions. Primarily, the meetings have served to help students provide support and encouragement to each other and to obtain and share information regarding financial aid, housing, child care, welfare benefits, work-study, and other resources. In this regard, students have invited personnel from the Department of Public Welfare, local welfare rights organizers, city housing administrators, and college administrators to discuss financial aid policies and the effects of changes in regulations and other concerns of low-income women. Students have also educated the college community about some of their concerns through meetings and articles in the college newspaper.

Students have also become more directly involved politically. Twice a year, during college vacations, students from this and other colleges from across the state have met to discuss mutual concerns and strategies. At one such meeting, students shared their concern about the composition of a task force assembled by the chancellor of higher education to reassess state financial aid policy. The students represented themselves as a statewide coalition and successfully pressed for a voice on the task force; of nineteen members, only two were women and none were students. As a result of the coalition's efforts, two low-income women were placed on the task force in an ex officio capacity. They have since played an important role, helping task force members to clearly understand the significance of "unmet need" for AFDC recipients and the impact of revised state financial aid policies. Other students have become involved in drafting legislation to support low-income students.

While these efforts focus on students in Massachusetts, preliminary research reveals that similar efforts are being made in other states.[9]

Although these attempts may not be regarded as constituting a "movement," there is clearly a concern developing among low-income women to obtain better access to higher education, to be heard in the policy process, and to press for improved circumstances for those who follow in their footsteps.

IMPLICATIONS FOR POLICY IMPLEMENTATION

To involve students in the policy process, we should first consider how low-income women's wishes and experiences might be reflected in current policy implementation by students, faculty, administrators, and other human service agencies.

Faculty, college administrators, program administrators, and financial aid officers within higher education can work in a variety of ways to provide supportive educational environments for low-income women. They can provide academic, administrative, financial, and counseling resources specifically targeted to low-income women's needs. Further, they can provide assistance with support services, including housing, child care, and transportation. However, in addition to providing concrete resources, it is important that colleges facilitate students' supportive networks and their representation in policymaking, both on and off campus.

Faculty can play important roles in improving academic support. They can develop curricula that incorporate—and provide a context for—the experiences of low-income women. Such curricula could be interdisciplinary, including the literature of public policy, economics, and government and material on the conditions, causes, and consequences of poverty for women and people of color. The curricula also could include both historical and contemporary accounts of organizing by low-income women, as well as autobiographical and fictional accounts of low-income women's lives.

Faculty can also support students by demonstrating an understanding of women's multiple roles and pressures, and being sensitive to these pressures as they set deadlines and exam schedules. Faculty members also can be more active; they can offer to facilitate student meetings, become advisors to student groups, and teach planning and organizing skills. Faculty can also facilitate efforts to educate the college community about the effects of public assistance/financial aid conflicts on women's opportunities. They can improve communications among faculty, administrators, and students to explore issues and identify resources for low-income women. Finally, faculty can play an important role by engaging in sorely needed research on low-income women in higher education. They could collect data on the numbers of students already enrolled, conduct follow-up studies of graduating and nongraduating students, and analyze effective programs for low-income students (See Gittell, Chapter 11).

Program administrators, financial aid officers, and others working in institutions of higher education participate in a number of professional organizations and informal networks through which they share information and discuss ways to stretch resources and assist low-income students. Some of these personnel already have developed innovative approaches to stretching financial aid dollars and could contribute considerably to the formulation of policies to encourage enrollment and improve retention rates.

It is even more critical today, given the limited success of previous efforts and the current political climate regarding welfare reform, that these groups form alliances to continue to work together for better access to higher education and to avoid the policy fragmentation and conflicts that currently exist. They can exchange information on services and resources provided to low-income women by women's resource centers at colleges and universities, lobby state agencies and legislators to include higher education as an option to job training for AFDC recipients, and establish networks to ensure that state, federal, and local policies affecting financial aid and other resources do not conflict. They also can work within educational and other institutions to encourage student organizations and mutual support networks. And they can continue to conduct research to ascertain the strengths of various specialized programs designed to support low-income women who are students and to disseminate this information.[10]

CONCLUSION

Exploratory research into the experiences of a small group of low-income women attending college shows that women find among themselves a very strong source of support and assistance. They share their strengths and knowledge of survival strategies; in addition, and in spite of their heavy commitments to their studies and their families, the majority of women engage in some form of group action to deal with the policy contradictions and conflicts that affect their lives. Many also find support and form alliances, mostly informal, with nonstudents. In some cases the ally is an understanding teacher or administrator within the educational institution; in other instances it is a caseworker who ignores rules, a legal service officer who provides women with knowledge of their rights, or a local agency that provides necessary resources. Thus, building on some important beginnings and drawing on current initiatives by groups of students, faculty, administrators, human service professionals and policymakers, stronger alliances can be developed to provide better access to higher education for low-income women.

NOTES

1. The author wishes to acknowledge the invaluable assistance provided by college administrators and program counselors who facilitated the interviews with low-income students. In addition, several students provided assistance: Abbie Satcher and Lucy Chambers helped with the interviews; Cora Jean Robinson, Diane Salls, and Carole Hunter provided interesting insights from their own life experiences and their participation in a public policy seminar. Thanks especially to the courageous and strong women who agreed to be interviewed for the study. Financial support for this study was provided by the Public Policy Program and the Office of the President of Smith College.

2. Although data are not widely available, current estimates of the proportion of AFDC recipients attending college range from a national average of 2 percent to 13 percent in Massachusetts. The national estimate is from "Women and Student Financial Aid," Policy Brief (Washington, DC: American Association of University Women, June 1985), p. 4. The Massachusetts estimate is from a draft of Alan Werner's "Work, Training and Welfare Reform in Massachusetts: The ET Choices Program," p. 19, to be included in Sharon Harlan and Ronnie Steinberg (eds.), *Job Training for Women: The Promise and Limits of Public Policies* (Temple University Press, forthcoming). In New York State alone the number of AFDC recipients in college has been estimated at 22,000–25,000 people. The New York figures are from Marilyn Gittell, speaking at the Center for Women Policy Studies' Seminar, "Occupational Segregation and Its Roots in Education." Washington, DC, May 1988. (See Gittell, Chapter 11.)

3. The twelve students who were interviewed attended three institutions of higher education in Massachusetts; four attended a state community college; four attended a private women's liberal arts college; and four attended a large public university. As initiator and facilitator of a low-income students' group, the author attended the group's meetings over a period of three years.

4. The Ada Comstock Program at Smith College and the Frances Perkins Program at Mt. Holyoke College are two such comprehensive programs in Massachusetts for older women, many of whom have transferred from community colleges.

5. For a more detailed description of these problems, see Erika Kates, "Access to Higher Education: A Way Out of Poverty for AFDC Recipients?" Unpublished paper prepared for NOW-LDEF PEER Conference, "Equal Education for Girls Is Poverty Prevention for Women," Washington, DC, March 1988.

6. Mary Moran's comprehensive survey of twelve types of financial aid showed that funds are less advantageously distributed to women when compared to men. While a slightly larger proportion of women receive aid in some form, they generally receive *less per capita and less prestigious forms of support.* (Moran, 1986).

7. Amendments to the Higher Education Act, 1986, state that "Federal student assistance used for tuition or fees *may not be counted as income* when determining

eligibility for other benefit programs such as Food Stamp Program" (emphasis added). Tuition and fees are defined to include an allowance for books, supplies, transportation, and miscellaneous expenses.

8. Both Massachusetts and federal redefinitions of "disadvantaged students" omit specific mention of low-income women and dependent children. In the reauthorization of the Higher Education Act a disadvantaged student was defined as a student, neither of whose parents had completed a baccalaureate degree or, if the student resided with one parent, if that parent did not have a degree. "The Reauthorization of the Higher Education Act: A Side-by-Side Comparison of Current Law and the Conference Agreement on S.1965." Washington, DC: National Association of Financial Aid Administrators, 1986. In Massachusetts, a state task force convened by the Regents of Higher Education to reformulate policy on financial aid was given the charge "to examine the changing demographics of higher education which include many more black and brown students whose first language is not English and more students from homes with single parents" (*Boston Globe*, March 16, 1987). Further, the needs of older low-income women were excluded from *One Third of a Nation*, a report of a 'blue ribbon' Commission on Minority Participation in Education and American Life, established by the American Council on Education and the Education Commission of the States, May 1988.

9. A group called HOME (Helping Ourselves Means Education), with a national office in Ohio, provides consultation services to groups (including low-income women who wish to enter college) that seek to become better informed about access to higher education for low-income women. The meetings are forums that "do not seek rule change but [provide] a place to learn exactly what the rules are and their potential impact. The objective is to allow more effective problem-solving within the system as it exists." Cited in a HOME newsletter, 1987.

10. These goals were developed at the National Women's Studies Association Conference, Minneapolis, June, 1988. A number of women representing a variety of women's constituencies met to form a working group after a workshop/presentation by the author and a low-income student.

REFERENCES

American Association of University Women (1985). *Women and student financial aid*. Washington, DC: AAUW.
Bane, M. J. (1986). Household composition and poverty. In S. Danziger, and D. Weinberg (eds.), *Fighting poverty: What works and what doesn't*. Cambridge, MA: Harvard University Press.
Burke-Tatum, B. (1988). Setting aside welfare myths. In M. Ackelsburg, R. Bartlett, and R. Buchele (eds.), *Women, welfare and higher education: Toward comprehensive policies*. Northampton, MA: Smith College.
Family Support Act (1988). Public Law 100–485; Title II, section 201(F), 2358.
Franklin, P. (1984). *College opportunity and public assistance programs: Ideas for resolving conflicts*. Washington, DC: College Board.

Gartner, A. (1988). Self-help. In A. Bookman, and S. Morgan (eds.), *Women and the politics of empowerment*. Philadelphia, PA: Temple University Press.

Gelb, J., and Palley, M. L. (1982). *Women and policy*. Princeton, NJ: Princeton University Press.

Gueron, J., and Nathan, R. (1985). The MDRC work/welfare project: Objectives, status, significance. *Policy Studies Review* 4:417–432.

Houseman, A. W. (1988). Citation in *The Chronicle of Higher Education*, November 13, A1.

Kates, E. (1988). Access to higher education: A way out of poverty for AFDC recipients? Unpublished paper prepared for NOW-LDEF PEER Conference. Washington, DC: March.

Kluver, J. (1985). *ET: Workfare under another name, or a stepping stone to self-sufficiency?* Cambridge, MA: American Friends Service Committee.

Moran, M. (1986). *Student financial aid and women: Equity dilemma?* ASHE-ERIC Higher Education Report, 5. Washington, DC: ASHE-ERIC.

National Association of Women Deans, Administrators and Counselors (1980). *Returning women students: A review of research and descriptive studies*. Washington, DC: NAWDAC.

National Commission on Working Women of the Wider Opportunities for Women (1987). *Work, women and poverty: A fact sheet*. Washington, DC: NCWW.

Rix, S. (ed.) (1987). *The American woman 1987–88*. New York, NY: Norton.

Rosen, D. P. (1988). Poverty, welfare and educational opportunity: Redeeming a national resource. In M. Ackelsburg, R. Bartlett, and R. Buchele (eds.), *Women, Welfare, and Higher Education: Towards Comprehensive Policies*. Northampton, MA: Smith College.

United States Department of Labor (1984). *Time of change: 1983 handbook on women workers*. Washington, DC: U.S. Department of Labor.

Werner, A. (forthcoming). Work, training and welfare reform in Massachusetts: The ET choices program. In S. Harlan, and R. Steinberg (eds.), *Job training for women: The promise and limits of public policies*. Philadelphia, PA: Temple University Press.

Wise, W. M. (1961). Student personnel work: Future trends. *Personnel and Guidance Journal* 3:705.

Zinn, D. K., and Saari, R. (1984). Turning back the clock on public welfare. *Signs* 10:355–370.

PART FIVE

Conclusion

13

Occupational Segregation and Its Roots in Education: A Policy Map

BERYL A. RADIN

To paraphrase Charles Dickens, this compilation of research and commentary indicates that the topic of occupational segregation and its roots in education is experiencing both the best of times and the worst of times. The chapters in this volume and the seminar that stimulated the collection provide a glimpse of the cacophony of approaches that circle the topic. At this point, the reader of this volume has been tossed between analyses of the education system as well as the employment scene. Diverse strategies and methods of intervening within the policy world have been advanced. And the differences between the separate epistemologies of the multiple academic disciplines represented are perhaps most striking.

For some, the complexity and formlessness that is depicted in this volume are terrifying. Unlike many other policy areas that have been debated, studied, and evaluated over many years, this topic is in an inchoate stage. It is not well defined either conceptually or through the political action of its attentive public. The policy worlds of education and of employment are difficult to grasp as individual systems, let alone as connected policy labyrinths. And when issues related to gender, class, race, and ethnicity are added to this mixture, the result for some is gridlock. For them, if every aspect of the world is connected to another, then comprehensive action for change is impossible.

But for others, the flip side of this formlessness and complexity is opportunity. The energy and concern depicted by this volume suggest that there are many paths to change in this policy area. While it may not be possible to comprehensively link the various approaches to occupational segregation and education (jobs and education, race and opportunity, education and income, formal systems and informal practices, macro-level and micro-level changes, for example), the chapters in this volume suggest that change may be possible in many areas and through multiple avenues.

This concluding chapter will help the reader sort out the issues, strategies, and methods of intervention described in the earlier pages through the depiction of a "policy map." It assumes that change will not come about when proponents of change determine the single best way to link the two systems of education and employment. Rather, it asks the reader to think about this issue as a landscape filled with many contours and obstacles. This is a world full of criss-crossing paths and roads that emerge from (and lead to) other policy locations. Like a geographical map, this "policy map" does not tell the user where to go—it simply provides a picture of the many paths that can be taken once the policy actor determines her own agenda.

STAGES OF THE POLICY PROCESS

Although there are many ways to describe and present a policy world, I have chosen a framework that depicts the overall policy process through identifiable activities and patterns. Rather than looking at policymaking as a single decision point, it looks at multiple activities through different institutional settings over time (Radin and Hawley, 1988; Jones, 1970; Anderson, 1975). It assumes a policy process that is continuous and open-ended. While each specific stage of the process has its own functional demands and institutional setting (providing new opportunities and new constraints), each new decision stage is shaped by decisions that have been made earlier.

This chapter follows six policy stages: (1) defining the policy problem; (2) getting the issue on the policy agenda; (3) formulating the substantive policy approach; (4) adopting the policy; (5) implementing the program or policy; and (6) ensuring accountability and evaluating the policy. As each stage is discussed, specific strategies for change are presented. In addition, questions of equity, race, and ethnicity are raised within each section of the discussion. Where possible, examples from the earlier chapters are given to illustrate substantive, analytic, and disciplinary variations.

1. Defining the Policy Problem

Although each of the chapters in this volume discusses an important and legitimate aspect of the educational and employment status of women, the authors of the analyses approach policy issues in very different ways.

Given this diversity, defining the policy problem may be the most difficult aspect of approaching the problem of occupational segregation and educational inequities. For some of the authors, the issue is an expression of broader societal problems. Both Edwards and Banfield link the issue to historical patterns of racism. Rendón and Nora see it tied to larger issues faced by the Hispanic community. Gittell and Kates place the issue within other patterns of stratification and class biases within U.S. society.

As the volume indicates, there is even little agreement about the substantive basis for the issue. Although the seminar's title suggests that occupational segregation is "rooted" in education, some of the contributors imply that occupational segregation and education are both branches of similar economic and social pressures. Thus the education sector—rather than being viewed as the causative sector—is also constrained by the same institutional barriers that limit employment opportunities. Educational inequities, in this view, are *symptoms* rather than *causes* of occupational segregation.

Whatever the expression of the problem, there appears to be a shared perception that occupational segregation is closely entwined with other concerns. It is linked to failures of the education system, to characteristics of the labor force and changes in the labor pool, to constraints and disincentives within the welfare system, and to limitations in the availability of social services. Whether viewed from the perspective of the single population group (for example, Latinas) or the aggregate population, it is difficult to put neat conceptual boundaries around this topic.

These approaches to the issue reflect very different assumptions about the scope and scale of change. Several of the authors are extremely pessimistic about the possibilities for change within U.S. society, pointing to past patterns of racism, classism, and sexism as evidence of the inability of the nation to respond to the diverse needs of many of its citizens. For these individuals, the policy systems that they confront are rigid and difficult to change. Yet others, while acknowledging these past patterns, find that changing demographic and economic conditions provide the opportunity to modify the constraints of the past. For example, labor market shortages and the relative accessibility of new technologies give these individuals a sense of hope. Similarly, the recent acknowledgement of the importance of higher education for groups such as low-income women on welfare is viewed positively. In a related fashion, there are some commentators who see the public sector as the only source of solutions (or at least ameliorations) of these problems. Others, however, are less sanguine about public action and look to the private sector or to informal systems as the institutional setting for change.

The difficulty of establishing a shared view of "the policy problem" is also evidenced by divergent methodological and disciplinary approaches to the issue. As an example, the chapter by Palmer and Spalter-Roth describes the many ways that an apparently simple concept such as "choice" has very different meanings when approached by lawyers, economists, historians, and sociologists and by the popular press. Some of the chapters reflect the perceptions and concerns of researchers or academicians, for whom the pathway to change begins with the documentation of "the problem" (whatever it is). They reflect concerns such as the need for new data collection, particularly data that is disaggregated, to allow policymakers to understand the specific needs of specific populations. Yet for others, data collection and research are useful only as a vehicle to produce evidence to support existing policy positions.

There are few agreed-upon strategies that are useful in framing and defining the policy problem. As this discussion indicates, this stage of the policy process requires a policy actor to approach the issue with a large dose of modesty. Self-reflective analysis will allow the individual to be clear about assumptions that are made concerning the scope of the problem, its causes and linkages, as well as the opportunities or limitations for change. Research strategies (such as those discussed in the chapters by Lott and Rendón and Nora) do have the ability to assist policy actors in documenting the extent of the problem that they perceive, particularly through demographic and macroeconomic analyses. In an area where issues are not well understood, research can play an "enlightenment" function in opening up possibilities for change (Weiss, 1990).

2. Getting the Issue on the Policy Agenda

Several of the chapters in this volume provide evidence of implicit rather than explicit strategies for putting some aspect of the issue on the agendas of policymakers. The very diversity of approaches to these problems offers the opportunity to raise questions related to occupational segregation in a number of settings, and thus to place the issue on a number of diverse policy agendas. The Sadkers, Gittell, and Banfield all indicate that issues involving education, income, gender, and race are a part of some reform efforts within the education community. But without explicit attention to diversity and equity issues, it is possible for policymakers to respond to current concerns about the "crisis" in American education in a way that simply reinforces existing distributional problems. Similarly, as Edwards indicates, national attention to science education and the availability of technology by-passes young women, particularly low-income women of color. Palmer and Spalter-Roth as well as Johnson indicate that occupational segregation issues can be raised within the venues that debate and implement job training and employment schemes. Several of the authors note that current changes within the welfare system—particularly new work and job training requirements and the new concern about availability of child care—provide a vehicle for raising, if not addressing, these issues.

The strategies that are useful in this stage of the policy process emphasize maximizing political power, organizing, and publicizing the need for change. Advocates for change in this area appear to be constrained in two ways. First, many of them do not have access to resources that allow the issue to be raised in a way that provokes the interest of policymakers (that is, individuals who are in positions of authority and influence). The issue is often perceived as one that is invisible, has a long time horizon, and is rarely a priority for its supporters. Thus it is difficult to capture the attention of policymakers who respond to highly public, immediate, and intense issues. Second, some of the advocates for change around this topic are not comfortable working inside the system and avoid the kind of interaction that is often required to raise the issue to policy consciousness. In part, this is due to the perceived burden and biases of the past: Why should advocates place their trust in individuals and institutions who have been a part of—if not the cause of—the past problems?

3. Formulating the Substantive Policy Approach

The chapters in this volume indicate that the alternative approaches to policy change vary in terms of scale of intervention, appropriate location for action, and strategy to be employed. Some of the authors focus on very specific issues—for example, Edwards' concern about the provision of computer education for children of color or Johnson's discussion of programs for women in the skilled trades. By contrast, others focus their analysis on broad social issues and patterns, such as Lott's discussion of patterns of demographic change. Still others define a middle ground, such as Banfield's discussion of cultural diversity or the Sadkers' analysis of sexism in American education.

One is struck by the variety of ways that authors have determined what they believe to be the appropriate location for action. Palmer and Spalter-Roth emphasize change that can occur within the private sector, through programs that sensitize corporations to the potential of otherwise underutilized individuals as well as through the direct provision of training and day care programs to these individuals. They focus on the role of the public sector in providing tax incentives and other forms of indirect action. The Sadkers and Banfield, by contrast, hone in on the education system and emphasize actions that can be taken by a diverse array of actors within the education sector—federal, local, and state agencies, school principals, and administrators—in areas such as the development of curriculum materials and training.

Other contributors are more eclectic in their locale for action. Rendón and Nora submit recommendations for employers, for researchers, and for policymakers. Edwards' interest in computers evokes recommendations for federal, state, and local governments as well as professional associations and computer vendors. Gittell and Johnson both emphasize the action that can be taken at the state level because of the discretion that has been given to states for the implementation of federal programs. This transfer of responsibility and authority from federal to state governments is true for programs in education, welfare, and employment, to varying degrees. Edwards, for example, notes that efforts in computer education are taking place within every state; however, not every state has indicated a sensitivity to the establishment and implementation of equity standards in the programs. Johnson's discussion provides examples of model employment programs in several states and emphasizes the ability of governors and other state officials to respond to these issues.

By contrast, Nettles and Kates suggest that neither the public sector nor the for-profit private sector are the appropriate locale; rather, social organizations and informal systems that provide personal support for individuals are the places where change and action are most effective.

The policy changes that are proposed also employ a repertoire of approaches and strategies. For some, the major thrust involves methods of changing values and norms, appreciating the skills and potential of otherwise underutilized individuals. For others, the goal is to empower the various actors who are found within the multiple policy systems, providing them access to existing resources and programs.

Most of the authors in this volume focus on the need to provide new resources to women and girls who are otherwise ignored by the system. These include funds for research, technical assistance, and the development of materials to be used and shared across the country. Several of the chapters call upon the public sector to play an active regulatory role, enforcing existing standards involving employment and educational equity and creating new requirements in areas of concern. In addition, a number of the authors emphasize the linkage between the provision of child care and the ability of women to utilize new employment and educational opportunities.

4. Adopting the Policy

Each of the alternative approaches to change in this policy area has its own set of actors who have the authority to adopt proposed changes. All of the alternatives advanced by authors within this volume require the assistance of other groups and institutions, either through their involvement in a coalition of outside advocates for change or through the agreement of actors who have the ability to provide resources or otherwise respond to the demands.

As we have seen, changes involving occupational segregation can be made in multiple policy sectors: in elementary, secondary, and higher education; in employment training and placement activities in the private sector (through corporations as well as trade unions) as well as those provided by public support; and in public social services and income transfer programs. Each policy sector has its own natural set of active interest groups and individuals whose support is often essential to the modification of existing patterns and programs.

For example, efforts to change the elementary and secondary education system not only require agreement of federal, state, and local education agencies but also are assisted by support from teachers' organizations, school administrators, educational researchers, and schools of education. Similarly, as Johnson indicates, attempts to help women enter skilled trade jobs require support from trade unions as well as existing apprenticeship and vocational education programs.

There is a common strategic thread in all of these efforts: broadening the base of support through coalition development and policy reformulation. In some cases, advocates of change may be required to seek the assistance of individuals and groups who do not support a particular policy proposal out of the same motivation or value set. While advocates for a policy must recast their issues in a language that gains acceptance by others, they are challenged to do this without losing their original constituency.

Some of the authors in this volume are not comfortable with the realities of working within the system, where compromise and incrementalism are a part of standard operating procedures. At least one chapter in this volume expresses a strong aversion to employing the tactics required to work within the system. For Kates, change takes place within informal systems of support—systems that operate in parallel to the formal avenues. She notes that women will overcome obstacles to attaining higher education through their own efforts: organizing peer support groups and finding allies operating at the margins of existing institutions who will support them.

5. Implementing the Program or Policy

This volume contains a number of recommendations that focus on "windows of opportunity" created by programs and policies that are already in place. Lott reminds us that existing data systems, while not totally adequate, provide a valuable source of information on many issues. Johnson points to the possibilities that are available through the federal Jobs Training Parnership Act, antidiscrimination laws, and other policies that are contained in U.S. Department of Labor programs and pronouncements. Edwards emphasizes the opportunity to target state-level resources available for computer purchase, curriculum development, technical assistance, and training. The Sadkers call for the redirection of funds for curriculum materials and training to uncover the "hidden curriculum" in elementary and secondary education. Nettles focuses on some of the state-level experiences available through the WIN demonstration programs, providing higher education for low-income women and women on welfare. And Gittell notes that the recent welfare reform efforts provide authority for states to permit four-year college enrollment for women on welfare.

Each of these examples emerges from a careful analysis and understanding of the ways in which existing policy systems operate. The authors who look at these systems identify areas of discretion within them and make recommendations for redirecting existing programs. In several instances, by focusing on the level where the services are actually delivered, attention is paid to the availability of resources, technical assistance, or even regulations that may be used to improve the employment or educational status of women. Focusing on the service-delivery level also allows the identification of relevant attributes of the informal systems that surround this issue, such as provision of mentoring programs, sponsorship, and other efforts that assist the individual woman to cope with personal change. Understanding the system, whether at the service-delivery level or at the macro-policy level, allows advocates for change to craft proposals in a way that appears to be less threatening and familiar to those who have been (or will be) given responsibility for policy implementation.

6. Ensuring Accountability and Evaluating the Policy

The diversity of approaches to this policy area makes it extremely difficult to determine whether particular modes of intervention are effective. For some of the authors in this volume, even marginal shifts in the existing policy landscape are an indication of "success"—an approach that assumes that change occurs at a slow incremental pace. For others, however, "success" only occurs when occupational segregation ceases to exist and change cannot take place without a total, comprehensive strategy.

As we have noted, the advocates for change do not even share a common language. Palmer and Spalter-Roth's discussion of the concept of choice provides clear evidence of the difficulty of comprehending—let alone evaluating—the various approaches that emerge from different academic disciplines and theoretical conceptual lenses. Given this propensity to identify different goals and strategies for change, it is easy for advocates to fall into a "divide and conquer" trap. In the process of establishing standards for defining success, the defender of an incremental approach to change may be roundly attacked by advocates of comprehensive change. The overall effect of this conflict may be the elimination of any change at all.

Given this sensitivity, it appears that several of the authors in this volume sidestep the question of development of standards. Instead, they call for the provision and organization of various data sources that might be used by multiple actors and advocates. While there are several different approaches to the data issue, there seems to be agreement that analyses of existing programs and populations and development of new data systems are useful. For some of the authors, particularly Lott, data provision is an important strategy for change. For others, such as Palmer and Spalter-Roth, data cannot be viewed as a free-standing product apart from those who both collect and interpret it within their own social realities.

It is interesting that there is very little in this volume that focuses on the development of oversight mechanisms to assure the monitoring of whatever programs and policies are adopted. This is in contrast to the policy discussions of the 1960s when various forms of advisory groups and participatory mechanisms were developed to serve evaluative, monitoring, and feedback roles.

CONCLUSION

This chapter has attempted to provide a way for the reader to sort through the multiple issues, approaches, strategies, and goals that are presented in this volume. It is obvious that the issue of occupational segregation and its roots in education cannot be addressed without attention to the nation's position in the world economy or to the acknowledgement that an educated, technologically skilled work force involves many actors within the education and employment policy worlds. The contributors to this volume emphasize these issues and the special problems of addressing them in a way that provides new opportunities for low-income women and women of color. Policy change comes in diverse forms and in many different settings. The chapters in this volume indicate that it is possible to raise the educational, training, and employment needs of women in both academic and policy development discussions. This book—and the recommendations that emerge from its chapters—provide a point of departure for continuing debate and policy discussion.

REFERENCES

Anderson, J. E. (1975). *Public policy making.* New York, NY: Praeger.

Jones, C. O. (1970). *An introduction to the study of public policy.* Belmont, CA: Wadsworth Publishing Company.

Radin, B. A., and Hawley, W. D. (1988). *The politics of federal reorganization.* New York, NY: Pergamon Books.

Weiss, C. H. (1990). Congressional committees as users of analysis. *Journal of Public Policy Analysis and Management* 8 (3):411–431.

Acronyms

AASA	American Association of School Administrators
AAUW	American Association of University Women
AFDC	Aid to Families with Dependent Children
BAT	Bureau of Apprenticeship and Training
BLS	Bureau of Labor Statistics
CAI	computer-aided instruction
CIBC	Council on Interracial Books for Children
COLAs	cost-of-living adjustments
ECIA	Education Consolidation and Improvement Act
EEOC	Equal Employment Opportunity Commission
ERISA	Employment Retirement Income Security Act
ESAA	Emergency School Aid Act
ESEA	Elementary and Secondary Education Act
ET	Massachusetts Employment and Training Choices Program
GPA	grade point average
JAC	Joint Apprenticeship Committees
JOBS	Job Opportunity Basic Skills
JTPA	Jobs Training Partnership Act
NAACP	National Association for the Advancement of Colored People
NAEP	National Assessment of Educational Progress
NACME	National Action Council for Minorities in Engineering
NCWW	National Commission on Working Women
NEW	Nontraditional Employment for Women
NIE	National Institute of Education
SES	socioeconomic status
SWEC	Southeast Women's Employment Coalition
WEEA	Women's Educational Equity Act
WIBT	Women in the Building Trades
WORC	Women's Opportunity in Road Construction

About the Book and Editor

Despite nearly two decades of advocacy for equal education and employment, women remain clustered in the lowest-paid, lowest-status jobs in clerical, service, and industrial work. Occupational segregation also continues within professional and technical fields. This book examines the critical link between sex stereotyping in education and occupational inequities in the work place. Contributors first assess the impact of sex and race stereotyping and discrimination on girls in school. Next they examine workplace issues—including job training, access to nontraditional jobs, and occupational segregation. A final section takes up the question of the role of education in perpetuating or alleviating women's poverty. The book concludes by offering a number of policy recommendations and strategies for change.

Leslie R. Wolfe is executive director of the Center for Women Policy Studies and is the former director of the Women's Educational Equity Act Program in the U.S. Department of Education.

About the Contributors

Beryle Banfield is program manager at the Metropolitan Center for Educational Research, Development and Training at New York University and is the former president of the Council on Interracial Books for Children.

Carol Edwards is director of Project MiCRO of the Southern Coalition for Educational Equity.

Marilyn Gittell is professor of political science and director of the Howard Samuels State Management and Policy Center at CUNY Graduate School and University Center.

Wendy Johnson is executive director of the Appalachian Community Fund and is the former executive director of the Southeast Women's Employment Coalition.

Erika Kates is director of the Project on Women and Social Change at Smith College and is a member of the faculty of the Department of Sociology at Western New England College.

Juanita Tamayo Lott is president of Tamayo Lott Associates, a policy and management consulting firm, and a consultant to the Census Bureau for the 1990 census.

Saundra Murray Nettles is research associate at the Center for Social Organization of Schools at The Johns Hopkins University.

Amaury Nora is associate professor in the Department of Adult, Higher, and Professional Education at the University of Southern California.

Phyllis Palmer is academic director of the Women's Studies Program at George Washington University.

Beryl A. Radin is professor of public administration at the Washington Public Affairs Center of the University of Southern California.

Laura I. Rendón is associate professor in the Department of Adult and Community College Education at North Carolina State University.

David Sadker is professor of education at The American University.

Myra Sadker is acting dean of the College of Education and professor of education at The American University.

Roberta Spalter-Roth is assistant professorial lecturer in the Women's Studies Program at George Washington University and is the deputy director for research at the Institute for Women's Policy Research.

Leslie R. Wolfe is executive director of the Center for Women Policy Studies and is the former director of the Women's Educational Equity Act Program in the U.S. Department of Education.

Index